Goethe

Twayne's World Authors Series

German Literature

David O'Connell, Editor
Georgia State University

TWAS 884

JOHANN WOLFGANG VON GOETHE
German Information Center and J. N. Press

Goethe

Irmgard Wagner

George Mason University

Twayne Publishers
New York

Twayne's World Authors Series No. 884

Goethe
Irmgard Wagner

Copyright © 1999 by Twayne Publishers

Twayne Publishers
1633 Broadway
New York, NY 10019

Library of Congress Cataloging-in-Publication Data

Wagner, Irmgard.
    Goethe / Irmgard Wagner.
       p. cm. — (Twayne's world authors series ; no. 884. German
  literature)
    Includes bibliographical references and index.
    ISBN 0-8057-1685-8 (alk. paper)
    1. Goethe, Johann Wolfgang von, 1749–1832. 2. Authors,
German—18th century—Biography. 3. Authors, German—19th century—
Biography. I. Title. II. Series: Twayne's world authors series ;
TWAS 884. III. Series: Twayne's world authors series. German
literature.
PT2049.W34   1999
831'.6—dc21
[B]   99-28819
                                         CIP

10 9 8 7 6 5 4 3 2 1

Printed in the United States of America

To the memory of Bernhard Blume and Henry Hatfield,
my teachers of Goethe

Contents

Preface

Since Lieselotte Dieckmann's meritorious study of Goethe in this series (1974), much has changed in the way Goethe is seen and studied. The "classics war" of the 1970s against German canonic authors, and particularly Goethe, is over. Critics have since rediscovered Goethe as precursor and anticipator of modern and even postmodern trends. His most recent biographer, Nicholas Boyle, declares him central to and a sort of focusing lens for the modern experience: "a free man responding to the social, spiritual, and intellectual demands of modernity, as they formulated themselves around him."[1] Goethe's creative life, from 30 years before to 30 years after the turn of the nineteenth century, spans a time of momentous crises and transitions. It was the age of revolution—political, economic, and spiritual—and in many ways resembled our own age of permanent revolution, in which new world orders and multimedia highways to new (cyber)spaces are around ever new corners. These similarities are why it pays to pay attention to Goethe again, to the empathetic, intelligent, and creative contemporary of his own epoch, whose life had placed in a position to engage actively in public events and intellectual developments. His works allow us to experience such transitions vicariously, to reflect on them, and to practice how to deal productively with crisis and change.

An increasingly interdisciplinary and cross-cultural orientation in academic curricula has opened Goethe to programs beyond those focused on German language and literature. The new Suhrkamp-Princeton edition of Goethe's *Collected Works* in English provides easy access, including in paperback format, and translations of superb quality. It is now possible for the general public to read Goethe for content and enjoyment without the pain or effort of foreign language translation impeding the pleasure of the text.

This study presents the works in chronological order, with two exceptions. The two *Wilhelm Meister* novels are discussed in sequence, moving the first one, *Lehrjahre (Apprenticeship)*, out of its place to follow *Hermann und Dorothea* and *Wahlverwandtschaften (Elective Affinities)*. The other exception is *Faust*, the work that occupied Goethe during his entire writing life. Here *Faust* takes up the last chapter as a summary and conclu-

sion to Goethe's lifework. The chronological arrangement is part and
parcel of my approach, which argues Goethe's contemporaneity and sees
the works as (by-)products of a life lived with and through the crises and
developments of a changing epoch. For such a perspective, life matters.
For enlightenment about this life of 200 years ago, I owe great thanks
to the work of many scholars, some of whom I had the good fortune to
know as teachers and mentors. Concerning biographical information,
including the context of the age of Goethe, I am particularly indebted to
three works: Richard Friedenthal, *Goethe: His Life and Time*,[2] Karl Otto
Conrady, *Goethe: Leben und Werk*,[3] and Nicholas Boyle, *Goethe: The Poet
and the Age.*

Life is context, not text. The works are analyzed as texts, from varying perspectives and approaches. Their reception history as canonic texts
is part of the approach to each work. In particular, the comments in the
two ongoing critical editions of Goethe's works, the *Frankfurter* and
Münchner Ausgabe, are taken into account to reflect the current reception
status. The interpretations, however, are my own. It has been my aim to
give a fresh look at each of the works discussed. In fact, the greatest
reward of the long labor in researching and writing this book was the
discovery that, despite the mountain of secondary literature, it was still
possible to provide a new perspective. There is no surer mark of quality
for a creative writer's work than this.

Given the volume of Goethe's works and the scope of this study,
selection was unavoidable. I have chosen the works that are most widely
read or that should be most widely read. As interesting as his scientific,
aesthetic, and autobiographical writings may be, Goethe is foremost and
most significantly a poet, a writer of the imagination. Thus, although
nonfictional texts are considered as part of the context of composition,
where we can locate points of origin of a poetic text, the topics of discussion are the poetic works. Among these, choices still had to be made. No
one as yet claims to have identified those works that might constitute
the essential Goethe. It is still a judgment call. I can only hope that I did
not miss too much that is essential Goethe.

Chronology

1749   Johann Wolfgang Goethe born in Frankfurt/Main 28 August.

1755   Lisbon earthquake, 1 November.

1765–1768   Studies law at Leipzig university. Meets Gellert, Gottsched, and the music publisher Breitkopf.

1768–1770   Returns home to recover from severe illness. Becomes interested in religion (pietism), esoterics, and alchemy.

1770–1771   Completes law studies at Strasbourg university. Meets Herder and Friederike Brion. Writes *Sesenheimer Lieder.*

1771–1775   Opens a private law practice in Frankfurt. Writes for the review journal *Frankfurter Gelehrte Anzeigen.* Writes Sturm und Drang poetry (the Great Hymns). Visits literary court circle at Darmstadt; meets Louise, future wife of Carl August of Saxe-Weimar.

1771   Gives the speech *Zum Schäkespears Tag.* Writes the drama *Götz von Berlichingen* (first version, unpublished).

1772   Attends Imperial Court at Wetzlar from May to September. Meets Charlotte Buff and fiancé J. C. Kestner (*Werther* background). Writes the essay *Von deutscher Baukunst* (Strasbourg cathedral).

1773   Publishes the drama *Götz von Berlichingen* (second version).

1774   Writes the novel *Die Leiden des jungen Werthers.* Writes the tragedy *Clavigo* and *Farcen* and *Hanswurstiaden.*

1775   Becomes engaged to Lili Schönemann. Undertakes first journey to Switzerland. Meets J. J. Bodmer. Writes the drama *Stella.* Begins *Egmont.* Arrives in Weimar on 7 November on invitation from Duke Carl August of Saxe-Weimar to join his court. Meets Charlotte v. Stein, C. M. Wieland, and Dowager Duchess Anna Amalia.

1776–1786   Participates in Weimar government work and provides court entertainment. Begins nature studies: geology, botany, and anatomy. Discovers intermaxillary bone (1784). Visits Harz Mountain (1777, 1783, and 1784) and the Bohemian spa Karlsbad (1785 and 1786) for the first time.

1777   Goethe's sister Cornelia (age 26) dies. Begins *Wilhelm Meisters theatralische Sendung.*

1779   Takes second Swiss journey with Duke Carl August. Writes *Briefe aus der Schweiz* and *Iphigenie auf Tauris* (first version).

1780   Begins *Torquato Tasso.*

1782   Goethe's father dies after years of senility.

1786–1788 Travels to Italy and Sicily, with longer stays in Venice, Rome, Naples, and Palermo, and studies architecture, sculpture, botany, and anatomy (September to June). Revises and completes works for first *Collected Works* edition (1787–1790): *Iphigenie auf Tauris* (1786) and *Egmont* (1787).

1788   Returns to Weimar. Begins liaison with Christiane Vulpius. Breaks with Charlotte v. Stein. Limits responsibilities in government.

1789   Son, August, born. Completes *Torquato Tasso* and *Römische Elegien* (published in 1795).

1790   Publishes *Collected Works,* vol. 7, which includes *Faust: Ein Fragment.* Travels to Venice to await Dowager Duchess Anna Amalia. Writes *Venetianische Epigramme.*

1791   Appointed director of Weimar Court Theater. Writes the comedy *Der Groß-Kophta.* Begins work on optics.

1792   Receives house on *Frauenplan* as gift from the duke. Accompanies the duke on campaign in France against the revolutionary army.

1793   Accompanies the duke on a siege of the revolutionary city Mainz. Writes the epos *Reineke Fuchs* and the comedy *Der Bürgergeneral.*

1794   Forms alliance with Schiller (Jena). Publishes in Schiller's review *Die Horen.* Writes *Unterhaltungen deutscher Ausgewanderter,* including *Märchen.*

1795 Publishes *Wilhelm Meisters Lehrjahre* (books 1–6). Writes *Xenien* with Schiller.

1796 Completes *Wilhelm Meisters Lehrjahre*.

1797 Embarks on a third journey to Switzerland. Resumes work on *Faust*. Publishes *Hermann und Dorothea* and *Balladen*.

1798 Buys farm at Oberroßla (sells in 1803).

1799 Schiller moves to Weimar.

1803 Death of Herder. Meets Mme. de Staël. Writes the tragedy *Die näturliche Tochter*.

1805 Death of Schiller. Begins publishing *Farbenlehre*.

1806 Resumes summer visits to Karlsbad. Napoleon's victory at Jena. Goethe's house invaded. Marries Christiane. Completes *Faust Part I*.

1807 Death of Dowager Duchess Anna Amalia. Begins work on *Wilhelm Meister's Journeyman Years* and *Sonnets*.

1808 Death of Goethe's mother. Summoned to meet Napoleon at Erfurt. Publishes *Faust. Der Tragödie erster Teil*. Begins writing *Die Wahlverwandtschaften*.

1809 Publishes *Die Wahlverwandtschaften*. Begins work on autobiography, *Dichtung und Wahrheit*.

1810 Publishes *Farbenlehre*.

1811 Writes *Dichtung und Wahrheit* (part 1).

1812 Meets Beethoven at Teplitz and Karlsbad (Bohemia). Writes *Dichtung und Wahrheit* (part 2).

1813 Death of Wieland. Napoleon defeated at Leipzig. Begins Chinese studies and work on *Italienische Reise*.

1814 Travels to Rhine-Main area. Meets Marianne v. Willemer. Continues Oriental studies. Writes *Dichtung und Wahrheit* (part 3). Completes first poems for *Westöstlicher Divan*.

1815 Takes a second journey to Rhine-Main area. Visits (unfinished) Cologne cathedral. Focuses on meteorological studies. Writes the bulk of *Divan* poetry.

1816   Death of wife, Christiane. Begins *Noten und Abhandlungen* for *Divan*. Writes more *Divan* poems. Publishes *Italienische Reise*, part 1. Writes the essay *Kunst und Altertum am Rhein und Main*.

1817   Resigns from Weimar Court Theater. Marriage of son, August, to Ottilie v. Pogwisch. Writes *Italienische Reise* (part 2) and *Urworte Orphisch*.

1818   Birth of first grandson, Walther Wolfgang. Resumes spa visits to Bohemia (Karlsbad).

1819   Publishes *West-östlicher Divan*.

1820   Birth of second grandson, Wolfgang Maximilian. Begins work on *Campagne in Frankreich/Belagerung von Mainz*.

1821   Takes first spa summer in Marienbad. Felix Mendelssohn (age 12) visits Goethe. Publishes *Wilhelm Meisters Wanderjahre* (first version).

1822   Publishes *Campagne in Frankreich/Belagerung von Mainz*.

1823   Marriage proposal to Ulrike v. Levetzow (age 19) at Marienbad rejected. Writes *(Marienbader) Elegie*.

1825   Resumes work on *Faust* and *Wilhelm Meisters Wanderjahre*.

1827   Death of Charlotte v. Stein. Birth of granddaughter, Alma Sedina Henriette Cornelia. Continues Chinese studies. Writes *Novelle, Chinesisch-deutsche Tages- und Jahreszeiten*. Publishes *Helena: Klassisch-romantische Phantasmagorie* and *Zwischenspiel zu Faust* (act 3 of part 2).

1828   Death of Duke Carl August. Resumes work on *Italienische Reise*.

1829   Publishes *Italienische Reise* and *Wilhelm Meisters Wanderjahre* (second version).

1830   Death of Duchess Louise. Death of Goethe's son, August, in Rome. Resumes work on *Dichtung und Wahrheit*.

1831   Completes *Dichtung und Wahrheit* (published in 1833). Completes *Faust Zweiter Teil* (published posthumously in 1832).

1832   Death of Goethe on 22 March.

Chapter One

A Life in World Historical Context, 1749–1832

It is surely no coincidence that the life of the man who invented the bildungsroman should appear from two centuries away like a bildungsroman itself: time passed in search of meaning. Indeed Goethe, who also invented the literary autobiography, lived his life as a work in progress, constructing "the pyramid of [his] existence."[1] It was anything but easy. Subjectively, Goethe experienced life as a persistent restlessness combined with a compulsion to reflect. His last letter, written five days before his death, sees this as the law of his life: "such a long active-reflective life."[2] To the outside observer, the law of Goethe's life appears to be a drivenness not knowing, but always asking, whereto.

The unsettled age in which he lived made it hard to find and follow a direction; we know it today as the age of revolution—political, social, industrial, and cultural. As a boy of 15 Goethe witnessed the pomp and circumstance of the Holy Roman Empire: the coronation of Emperor Joseph II in Goethe's hometown, the Free Imperial City of Frankfurt. In his 50s, he saw the thousand-year-old empire crumble under the footsteps of Napoleon's armies, while he, next to the humbled princes of the former realm, paid court to the new emperor at the Erfurt Convention of 1808. Less than a decade later the Napoleonic Empire, too, had disappeared.

Goethe was no unconcerned spectator. As principal councillor to the duke of Sachsen-Weimar, a neighbor and close relative of the most dangerous of German princes, Frederick II of Prussia, it was Goethe's duty to be concerned with the movements in ideas and events that would shape the fate of nations in his lifetime. His first year of governmental responsibility at Weimar was the year of the American Revolution. At age 40, just back from a two-year sabbatical in Italy and as he was trying to reorganize his life with a domestic and cultural emphasis, the French Revolution threw him into the middle of history-in-the-making. Ordered to the side of his duke at war, Goethe became a reluctant participant in the defeat of the monarchic Allies and witness to the demise of the first German republic of Mainz.

In the early nineteenth century he watched the rise of European nationalism, in Germany as a reaction against Napoleonic usurpation, in Greece against Turkish rule, and in Italy against Hapsburg domination. In his ninth decade, as he was completing his life's work on *Faust,* and having survived all of his life's companions, he saw the return of the central event of his lifetime, the French Revolution, in the 1830 revolt in Paris. This "earthquake" brought aftershocks very close to home: student riots at his Jena University.

Genius in Search of a Mission: From Rococo to Sturm und Drang

Johann Wolfgang Goethe was born on 28 August 1749 in Frankfurt on Main. His birthday would always matter to him, and he tended to correlate important actions with the date. His childhood and youth, especially as we read his own account in *Dichtung und Wahrheit (Poetry and Truth),* "that most misleading of autobiographies" (Boyle 1991, 101), would have seemed enviable to most Germans of his generation. His caring, well-educated, and wealthy father provided excellent home instruction, an extensive library, and a rich collection of artworks. His young, loving, and imaginative mother came from a well-connected and equally wealthy family. His congenial sister played enthusiastic audience to the brother's literary efforts. The extended family supported educational interests with gifts of a puppet theater and a subscription to the French theater from the grandparents, whom the grandson honored in turn with poetry practiced as a social skill. Goethe's first known poem is a New Year's wish composed by the six-year-old for his grandparents.

But there was a darker side to this picture of protectedness and privilege. Four younger siblings died between the ages of two and seven. Wolfgang was 7, 10, and 11 years old when these deaths occurred, old enough to take note and perhaps imprint the fear of death that Walter Benjamin considered Goethe's most basic feature.[3] The impact of the devastating Lisbon earthquake on the six-year-old boy is well documented (Conrady, 1:36–38). The father, despite a first-rate education, including an Italian tour and a law doctorate, never held public office or a job. Instead he transferred his ambitions onto his son, who, far too closely held under the father's gaze, would in turn model his own life to an uncanny degree after his father's few achievements and unfulfilled aspirations. And then there was the madman in the attic. A foster son of the father was insane and, as long as young Goethe lived at home, occupied the room next door on the top floor of the house.

Goethe left home at age 16 for Leipzig University, where he was an undistinguished student of law for the next three years. Leipzig was the fashionable German university at the time; its elegant urbanity earned the city the name of Little Paris. Luminaries of German literature Christian Fürchtegott Gellert and theater czar Johann Christoph Gottsched made their home there. Goethe paid the obligatory visit to both and even took a rhetoric course from Gellert. But the real attraction for Goethe was the theater. The success just then of Lessing's new comedy, *Minna von Barnhelm,* must have seemed a propitious omen to our young theater enthusiast. Twenty years earlier Lessing had been a student in Leipzig, too. And indeed Goethe's first dramatic efforts date to his Leipzig years. Among many drafts and even, to believe his letters, some completed tragedies, only an erotic pastoral, *Die Laune des Verliebten (The Lover's Spleen),* has survived. There was also a book of poetry in the fashionable rococo style, set to music by the publisher Bernhard Theodor Breitkopf, a familiar name in music circles even today.

But young Goethe's career derailed. Felled by a serious illness, he left Leipzig on his birthday, 1768, to return home for an extended recovery. It was the first of the infrequent but dramatic health crises in Goethe's long life, accompanied, as later, by a spiritual crisis. At this time Goethe divorced from Christianity. Keeping company with Frankfurt pietists, he engaged in a deep search for faith, studying hermeticism, alchemy, and the renowned *Unparteiische Kirchen- und Ketzerhistorie (History of Heretics, 1699–1715)* by the unorthodox theologian Gottfried Arnold. In an illustration of the paradoxicality that bedevils Goethe biographers, it was also during this time that he wrote his most skeptical work, a drama of cynical realism in Alexandrine verse, *Die Mitschuldigen (Partners in Guilt).*

The next year took him to Strasbourg and a decisive turn. He missed the goal set by his father, namely to complete his studies. His doctoral dissertation was rejected, and Goethe senior had to content himself with his son's passing the lesser examination for the licentiate in law. (Goethe would call himself "Doctor" anyway.) Instead, the son found new directions that would set the course for the rest of his life. He discovered the charms of nature and the folk in the Alsatian countryside. He had his first profound love experience with Friederike Brion, a pastor's daughter in the village idyll of Sesenheim. And he found the mentor who would provide him with a mission, Johann Gottfried Herder.

Herder's harsh life experiences had put him, though Goethe's senior by only five years, light-years ahead of the playful junior student of law and life. In addition to his impressive knowledge of languages, literatures, the Bible, and history, Herder had the proselytizing zeal of a missionary. Goethe, who quickly learned things that interested him, absorbed from Herder knowledge, insights, and above all inspiration to explore new models—writers and cultures ancient and modern, English and Nordic instead of the dominant French and romance models. The immediate result of the Strasbourg experience was a few radically innovative poems, the *Sesenheimer Lieder (Sesenheim Songs);* the creation of a new genre—historical drama—and a German folk hero in *Götz von Berlichingen;* and the start of a new literary movement, *Sturm und Drang.*

Back in Frankfurt after little more than a year, Goethe set up a law practice (he applied for the permit on his 22nd birthday), which he, eagerly aided by his father, conducted, however, in a rather desultory fashion. Goethe's real efforts went toward establishing himself as a writer. He struck up a friendship with Johann Heinrich Merck, editor of the review journal *Frankfurter Gelehrte Anzeigen* and leader of a literary circle at the grand ducal court of nearby Darmstadt. A speech for Shakespeare's name day (*Zum Schäkespears Tag {On Shakespeare's Day}*, October 1771) announced the ambition and direction of Goethe's literary career with unmistakable clarity. The celebration was held contemporaneously at Goethe's home in Frankfurt and in Strasbourg among the comrades of the literary revolution, who began to see Goethe as their leader. His contributions to Merck's journal (1772) had to be anonymous because of editorial policy. He chose anonymity, too, for the publication of his drama in the Shakespearean manner, *Götz von Berlichingen* (1773). Here ended anonymity. The drama was an instant sensation, the secret of authorship was divulged, and Goethe was recognized as the head of new German literature (i.e., *Sturm und Drang*).

The following year brought European fame. A brief stay in the small town of Wetzlar during the summer of 1772, still following the father's career plan of gaining legal expertise at the somnolent Imperial Court, would have been no more than a distraction in the budding writer's development. But a fresh love entanglement and another leave-taking from the impossible beloved sparked Goethe's first novel, *Die Leiden des jungen Werthers (The Sorrows of Young Werther,* 1774). Its spectacular success made Goethe a celebrity. The youthful counts Stolberg enticed him on a Wertherian voyage into romantic Switzerland in 1775. Later that year, the 18-year-old Duke Carl August of Sachsen-Weimar invited him to join his court. Leaving behind a broken engagement to Lili Schöne-mann, daughter of a prominent banker, Goethe, at the age of 26, made the most consequential decision of his life when he left home for Weimar. The four Frankfurt years had been the most productive period in Goethe's long career. Besides *Götz* and *Werther* he completed two dramas, *Clavigo* and *Stella*. Dramatic fragments on Prometheus, Muhammad, Julius Caesar, and Egmont were brought up to varying lengths. The most important of these was a substantial body of scenes for a Faust drama, destined to occupy Goethe for the rest of his life. A handful of long poems in free verse continued the expression of self learned at Strasbourg. Finally, at the opposite pole to the pathos and sentimentality of *Werther, Stella,* and *Clavigo,* we find a group of farces and Hanswurstiads: short dramatic pieces in popular verse, spanning the spectrum from the mock pathetic to the obscene. Goethe's Frankfurt production offers a picture of unlimited and chaotic potential. The move to Weimar was also an escape from such chaos, a new search for direction and, if need be, for delimiting definition.

On the Road to Weimar and Italy, 1776–1788

Life was certainly different at Weimar. Instead of the walled in city of Frankfurt, home was now an entire principality. Though on the small side and consisting of disconnected territories, it was ideally suited for the restless new arrival, offering space and opportunity to move about and explore. Goethe did not even settle down in the city. Instead, he walked back and forth between the court, a pied-à-terre in town, and his main residence in a cottage on the yonder bank of the river Ilm, which still regularly overflowed. Much of his time was spent away from Weimar, on the road and in the towns, in the woods and on the mountains of Thuringia—Eisenach and the Wartburg, Jena and the university, Apolda and its stocking industry, and Ilmenau and its silver mine, which he tried to rescue. Goethe's travels now had a purpose. Duke Carl August had made him his most influential minister, with a host of administrative responsibilities, mostly concerning the economic development of his agrarian duchy.

The purposeful roamings of the inspector-developer gave a new perspective to Goethe's experience of nature: that of the scientist and draftsman. His fascination with geology and his original approach to botany and zoology originated in this first Weimar decade. But he also wrote poetry along the way: the gemlike *Über allen Gipfeln ist Ruh (Over all the hilltops is calm)* in a hunting shelter on Kickelhahn Mountain and scenes from *Iphigenie auf Tauris (Iphigenia on Tauris)* on a trip to recruit soldiers. And he drew the natural environment he saw wherever he went. His drawing became so important for him that he came to see his calling as an artist rather than a writer, and it took the Italian experience of overwhelming artworks to disabuse him of this idea.

His other major function was that of court poet. It was what the Weimar Court of the Muses, assembled around Dowager Duchess Anna Amalia and the eminent writer Christoph Martin Wieland, expected from the literary celebrity. Goethe adapted readily to his courtly public, which could not have been more different from the young rebels of Frankfurt and Strasbourg. His break with Sturm und Drang was immediate and radical. He staged entertainments for birthdays and other occasions, organized a private theater, and wrote playlets, for some of which the dowager duchess composed incidental music (*Lila, Proserpina, Der Triumph der Empfindsamkeit {The Triumph of Sensibility}, Jery und Bätely {Jery and Bätely}*, and *Die Vögel {The Birds}*). For this venue, too, he produced two full-length dramas, both in prose: *Die Geschwister (The Siblings*, 1776) and *Iphigenie auf Tauris* (first version, 1779).

A new love attachment contributed to Goethe's metamorphosis from Sturm und Drang radical to court poet. Charlotte von Stein, seven years older and married to a high court official, was the most refined lady-in-waiting at Weimar. She tamed the young firebrand and held him captive for the next 10 years in a singularly one-sided[4] and intense relationship. Goethe in turn had to play mentor to the duke. He took the education of his prince seriously, including the supervision of ducal pleasures such as boar hunts and frolics with peasant girls, much to the dismay of intellectual Germany. In 1779 he led his princely charge on a four-month tour of Switzerland. A seven-hour mountain hike through waist-deep snow was "the toughest thing I have ever done," according to Carl August (Boyle 1991, 1:311). The duke passed the test, and Goethe considered the tutelage over. From then on the two men would remain close and trusted friends.[5]

The poetic harvest of the first Weimar decade was meager, particularly if compared with the productivity of the Frankfurt years. Between ministerial and theatrical duties, nature explorations, and educating the duke, there was little time left for creative writing. *Iphigenie* was the sole major work Goethe managed to complete. Two other works, both dealing with the problems facing poets and theater enthusiasts, were abandoned: a drama, *Torquato Tasso* (1780–1789), and a novel, *Wilhelm Meisters theatralische Sendung* (*Wilhelm Meister's Theatrical Mission,* 1776–1785). Poetry diminished to a trickle, much of it addressed to Frau von Stein or devoted to special occasions, with the poet's subjectivity receding to the vanishing point. A new objectivity began to emerge instead, in universalist poems such as "Grenzen der Menschheit" ("Limits of Human Nature") and "Das Göttliche" ("The Godlike"), in the songs of Mignon and the Harpist in *Wilhelm Meister,* and in ballads of nature magic such as "Der Erlkönig" ("The Erl-King") and "Der Fischer" ("The Fisherman"). Objectivity marks above all Goethe's first venture into autobiographical writing, *Briefe aus der Schweiz (Letters from Switzerland,* 1779). After 10 years of steadily decreasing administrative and poetic activity, at a point when his most recent biographer deemed him "intellectually and emotionally on the verge of bankruptcy," it was time to move on. "I felt I was dead," Goethe himself described the mood that had taken hold of him (Boyle 1991, 1:354, 391).

Much speculation has been expended on Goethe's repeated starts, all broken off (twice in 1775 and again on the Swiss journey in 1779), to follow the single most important dream inherited from his father: Italy. It is much easier to guess why he finally went on his Italian journey, from September 1786 to June 1788. First, it was to escape Weimar bonds. Goethe literally ran away, leaving secretly and keeping his whereabouts secret from even his closest friends, particularly Charlotte von Stein. Nobody knew, including Goethe himself, when or even whether he would return. Second, he needed to refocus away from the distractions of Weimar. He started out with a new identity, traveling incognito as "Johann Philipp Möller, merchant," and seemingly without a plan. When in Rome, he led the quiet life of an apprentice in the midst of the hardworking German artists colony, where he took lessons in drawing and sculpting. He toured Naples and Sicily as any tourist would, except for his risky climbs up to the crater's edge on Mount Vesuvius—a very much alive volcano at that time.

The Italian experience yielded not just a new direction but also opened new dimensions. The strongest impact came from classical art and architecture. Even though Goethe found the Greek and Roman monuments in ruins, he saw them reborn in the Italian, particularly Palladian, renaissance. Here was a focus to impart meaning to his own life: aesthetic and ethical norms that would withstand the changes of time

and space. If renaissance was possible in Italy, why not in Germany?
Supported in his Winckelmannian conversion by the aesthetic theories
of Karl Philipp Moritz (*Über die bildende Nachahmung des Schönen {On
Imaginative Imitation of Beauty}*, 1788), whom he befriended in Rome,
Goethe returned to Weimar with the ambition to bring about a German
renaissance. The result was German neoclassicism: *Weimarer Klassik*.
Having found stable norms in art, the fledgling scientist transferred
them to the domain of nature. Goethe postulated an archetypal plant
(he thought he had found it in the botanical garden at Palermo) and a
similarly abstract animal to achieve a universal law that would inform
the structure and evolution of all living things.

During his Italian sabbatical Goethe was engaged in a major task:
He was under contract to prepare his writings for the first edition of his
collected works. So, with his past catching up with him, he worked continuously on his texts, many of which were fragments in need of completion. At the same time, the overwhelming experience of great art jux-
taposed with his own unsatisfactory efforts at drawing and sculpting
convinced him that he was, after all, a writer and not an artist. The literary yield of the Italian sojourn was substantial, though some of it was
reaped only after the event. Goethe managed to complete, at long last,
Egmont (1787), a drama dating back to Frankfurt. He recast *Iphigenie* in
blank verse form (1787). He thoroughly reworked *Tasso* and sent off the
final manuscript on the day before his 40th birthday (1789). He revised
and substantially expanded *Werther*. Only *Faust* resisted completion; he
could only add two scenes. Finally, the only new work inspired by Italy
was composed entirely in the post-Italian phase: his first cycle of poetry,
the *Römische Elegien* (*Roman Elegies,* 1788–1790; published in 1795).

Underlying the renewed productivity and the reorientation in
thought was southern Italy's Mediterranean culture. Goethe was an
extremely visual person who experienced the clear sky and sea and the
bright light and colors on landscapes and buildings with the intensity of
an artist's eye. Upon returning to Weimar he lamented: "When the
barometer is low and the landscape has no colors, how can one live?"[6] As
different as the atmosphere was the lifestyle. Goethe found Italy relaxed,
open, sensuous—in short, natural—and proceeded to share its pleasures, including a sexual relationship. (Scholarly consensus deems this
his first physical love relationship.) It was this facet of the Italian experience that finally broke the transcendental spell of Weimar and Charlotte
von Stein. Emancipated, Goethe returned to Weimar but not to Charlotte. Instead, he began a sexual relationship with an uneducated young

girl, Christiane Vulpius, with whom he spent the rest of her life, eventually in marriage. Weimar was shocked; Goethe had drawn a demarcation line: Weimar would never again own him as it had before his Italian escape.

Strategies of Earthquake Survival: Revolution and Classicism

The year 1789 was a milestone in Goethe's life. He had finished work on his first *Works* edition, his first son had been born, and he had set up as a substantial householder. His collection of minerals and artifacts would soon make his big house on the Frauenplan resemble a museum. It was his attempt to create order in the face of the disorder wrought by historical events that threatened to interfere with his agreeably redrawn job description. He was put in charge of the arts and sciences in the dukedom as well as of public construction, an ideal stage on which to promote the German renaissance. Major building projects included a new theater, the ducal palace, and, as always, roads. The first project that Goethe executed was a quasi-Italian refuge for the duke, a Roman villa in the Weimar park setting.

Still, Goethe remained the duke's closest friend and foremost foreign policy adviser. And foreign policy was in turmoil, as the major German powers repositioned themselves in reaction to the French Revolution and Napoleon, with the smaller princes jockeying among them for cover. The duke had taken service as an officer in the Prussian army, and Goethe had to accompany him on maneuvers: on the failed French campaign of 1792 and on the successful siege of the Mainz Republic a few months later. Both experiences would become part of Goethe's autobiographical oeuvre (*Campagne in Frankreich/Belagerung von Mainz {Campaign in France/Siege of Mainz}*, 1822). With French armies surging back and forth across the Rhine, and Napoleon redrawing the map of Germany, the existence of Carl August's dukedom was endangered more than once. War rudely intruded into Goethe's privacy when pillaging soldiers invaded his treasured home after Napoleon's victory at Jena (1806). It was this event that finally led Goethe to marry his long-time companion, Christiane, and legitimize his son.

Goethe sought refuge from such turbulence in his efforts at cultural reform. Under his direction the Weimar theater became the foremost stage in Germany. Birthplace of German classicism with first performances of Goethe's and Schiller's dramas, the Weimar theater could claim the name of German National Theater, a title it kept even during the era of the German Democratic Republic, when the concept of a German nation had officially disappeared from east of the Elbe River. As minister in charge of higher education, Goethe established the first arts and crafts academy in Germany. Here his artist friends from Italy drew on the duke's generous patronage to reform popular taste in the classicist direction. This Weimar tradition eventually led to the foundation of the Bauhaus during the time of the Weimar Republic, which owes its name to Goethe's activities there.

But mainly higher education meant the Jena University. Through his interest in science Goethe had long been involved in university matters. Now Jena University was his responsibility. The task turned out to be more difficult than anticipated. Goethe's project for classical education and political stability ran counter to the zeitgeist among German youth and intellectuals. Where Goethe wanted cultural reform, his students and professors wanted cultural revolution. Revolution prevailed and resulted in the romantic movement and the patriotic fervor aroused during the Napoleonic occupation.

By the turn of the century Jena had become the most important German university. Goethe was the magnet that attracted innovative spirits from all over the piecemeal German states; some of them he himself hired as professors. It was from the Jena amalgam of Herder (in Weimar), Schiller, Fichte, Hegel, Schelling, the Schlegel and the Humboldt brothers, Tieck, Wackenroder, Novalis, Kleist, and Hölderlin that Kantian aesthetics and ethics, idealist philosophy, and romanticism began to revolutionize European thought. Intellectual revolution spilled over into political reality when Jena students marched in the vanguard of the patriotic movement. From their 1817 Wartburg Festival, the antiabsolutist fervor spread all over the German lands. This event on Weimar soil led in turn to nationwide repression, which forced intellectuals (e.g., Marx and Heine) into exile in droves and eventually brought on the revolution of 1848.

On a personal level, in the role of German renaissance poet that Goethe had assigned himself, life after Italy was a severe disappointment: His emancipated behavior estranged him from Weimar friends, his *Works* edition was a commercial failure, and the revolutionary turmoil with the forced military excursions wrought havoc in his domestic life. He cut short a second trip to Italy, stopping in Venice and pouring his bile into the *Venetianische Epigramme* (*Venetian Epigrams*, 1790), a collection of poetry close in form yet far in mood from the joyful recreation of Italian pleasures in the *Römische Elegien*. Other baleful works dealt with the revolution itself. Three hastily written prose dramas (*Der Groß-Cophta {The Grand Cophta},* 1791; *Der Bürgergeneral {The Citizen General},* 1793; and *Die Aufgeregten* [*The Agitated,* fragment], 1793) were followed by the acerbic *Reineke Fuchs (Reynard the Fox,* 1793), a mock-heroic epos in Homeric meter adapted from folk literature that tells the fable of the rogue outfoxing a depraved animal kingdom.

Beginning in 1794, the 10-year alliance with Friedrich Schiller, whom Goethe had appointed professor of history at Jena University, would prove to be a blessing for Goethe and German literature but could not totally undo the post-Italian crisis. Goethe seemed to have lost faith in his mission: "He considers his poetic career over and overeats dreadfully."[7] A severe illness in 1800–1801 once again brought him close to death. Schiller proved an enthusiastic collaborator in the creation of German classicism, but public resonance was lacking. Schiller's literary review *Die Horen,* to which Goethe contributed eagerly, was short-lived, as was Goethe's own review, *Die Propyläen.* The partners vented their spleen over the opposition in polemical epigrams (*Xenien,* 1797), which stand out for their aggression and arrogance. Another failure was Goethe's carefully planned Italian tour of 1797, which he broke off after four months of slow travel through southern Germany and Switzerland.

More important than failures and polemics was the constructive aspect of the collaboration. In the 10 years until his death in 1805, Schiller became the driving force of Goethe's poetic production, pushing him to complete the long-dormant *Meister* novel (1796) and *Faust Part I* (1806) and to compensate for the naughty *Xenien* by a stream of narrative poems in the "ballad year," 1798. Together they reflected on literary theory (Goethe later edited their *Correspondence*) and, to balance Schiller's production of dramas, Goethe focused on narrative. His model of a modern novel, *Wilhelm Meisters Lehrjahre,* was followed by a short epos on a contemporary topic in classical form, *Hermann und Dorothea* (1797). Still Goethe was not altogether willing to cede the place as Germany's premier dramatist to his younger colleague. In complete secrecy he worked on a grand project to rival Schiller's monumental trilogy, *Wallenstein,* of 1799. His own trilogy, *Die natürliche Tochter (The Natural Daughter),* was to be his definitive statement on the French Revolution. But he wrote only the first of three planned five-act dramas, and when he staged it at his own theater in 1803, it was a resounding flop. Goethe never wrote another drama in conventional form. The Revolution, it seemed, was beyond the poet's grasp.

Goethe's continuing work in science was another way of opposing revolutionary turbulence. Stability could be found in the laws of natural structure and evolution, as Goethe showed in a meticulous essay, *Die Metamorphose der Pflanzen* (*The Metamorphosis of Plants,* 1790). In Goethe's obstinate crusade of 20 years (1790–1810) to unseat Newtonian optics we might see a displacement of pent-up aggression from the forbidden historicopolitical into the intellectual realm. Particularly after Schiller's death in 1805, the work on Goethe's *Farbenlehre* (*Theory of Color*) became an obsession. In the dispirited decade following the death of his closest colleague, Goethe set up several large projects that would last him for the remainder of his own life, however long that might be: *Faust Part II;* a sequel to *Wilhelm Meister,* which spun off an overgrown episode, *Die Wahlverwandtschaften* (*Elective Affinities*) in 1809; and, after 1808, his autobiography, *Dichtung und Wahrheit.* Goethe had relied heavily on Schiller in an effort to navigate the turbulence at the turn of the century. It would take a new impulse to awaken him once more for an extended period of creative activity that would enable him to conclude, in the remaining decade and a half of his life, the great projects he had set before himself.

The Weimar Sage: Resource Management and World Literature

The end of Napoleon's reign supplied that impulse. To evade the turmoil of French occupation and the wars of liberation, Goethe had sought refuge in the backwaters of Bohemian spas for years. Because everyone in Europe who could afford it did likewise, Goethe continuously met new people there who inevitably expanded his interests. One of them was Beethoven. Even though Goethe was a staunch conservative in music and preferred Mozart, his reaction to piano performances showed how his mind had been opened to Beethoven's new form of art. Goethe was looking in another new direction. Beginning in 1812 he had turned to the Oriental studies recently prominent in England. He began a subtle play of identification with the medieval Persian poet Hafis, which led to a surge of creative inspiration in his second poetic cycle, *West-östlicher Divan* (*The Divan of West and East,* 1814–1819). When peace finally came with Napoleon's demise in 1815, Goethe joined in the collective sigh of relief. Newly productive in his west-easterly verse, Goethe the poet had proved that he could survive the man of power, whom he had been able to comprehend only by demonizing him.

The fall of Napoleon's empire was an eye-opener of yet another sort. It changed Goethe's perspective on the fall of the Roman Empire. Now he looked past the erstwhile ideal of classical antiquity toward the post-classical Byzantine and early Christian era as another source of Western art. In the great essay that marks this new departure, *Kunst und Altertum am Rhein und Main (Art and Antiquity in the Rhine and Main Region,* 1816), the sole illustration, discussed in depth, is an iconic painting from that period. Prodded by the art collector brothers Boisserée, Goethe consented to help save the religious artworks of the Rhine area from postwar ravages. His travels to explore this new field of interest brought about the final piece of experience needed to renew creativity: the encounter with Marianne von Willemer. Former actress, dancer, and then carefully educated companion of a Frankfurt merchant, Marianne was Goethe's congenial partner. Some of the poems of the collection she inspired, the *West-östlicher Divan,* are her compositions, which Goethe included without revealing the different authorship. It was a new kind of authorship for Goethe as well. The poet took on the role of educator. His *Noten und Abhandlungen (Notes and Essays)* published in the *Divan* volume aimed to expand Germany's horizon beyond the narrowly national and potentially nationalistic, where Goethe saw the romantic school heading, into the domain of world literature.

The expanding intellectual horizon had to compensate for the progressive shrinking of Goethe's real, geographical horizon. A travel accident stopped him on his third journey toward the Rhine-Main region and Marianne: The man who did not believe in coincidence turned back and forthwith limited his travels to spa excursions. After a final erotic temblor in 1823, when the unrequited love for young Ulrike von Levetzow at just such a spa gave us his last great poem, the *Marienbader Elegie (Marienbad Elegy),* he stayed entirely within the familiar surroundings of Weimar. But his interest in the foreign remained undiminished, and he knew how to nourish it otherwise.

Visitors flocked to the Weimar sage who, no matter how controversial his conservatism in a politically restless age, was becoming a world legend, a role that Goethe had no trouble living up to with appropriate pomp and circumstance in his impressive residence. His voluminous correspondence with friends such as explorer Alexander von Humboldt provided a worldwide information network. A steady diet of reading—a pocketbook-size volume per day—kept him abreast of foreign literary and cultural developments. The Italian *L'Eco* and the French *Le Globe, Le Temps,* and *La Revue Française* were among his favorite journals. Byron,

Carlyle, Calderón, and Manzoni fascinated him, and he spread their fame through essays and book reviews. American news found his unflagging interest. The hero of his *Meister* novels eventually immigrates to America; in Bohemian spa development he saw American-style conquest of the wilderness[8]; he was convinced a Panama canal had to be built and the United States would own it[9]; and in 1828 he coedited the travel diary of Prince Bernhard, Duke Carl August's younger son, who had toured the New World in 1825. In the last years of his life Goethe traveled a yet farther distance when he took up the study of Chinese culture and wrote a last cycle of poems after the Chinese model, *Chinesisch-deutsche Jahres- und Tageszeiten* (*Sino-German Seasons and Hours*, 1827).

He remained involved in the development of science and technology. From 1815 his own activities expanded into the new field of meteorology, and he had several weather stations built around the duchy. At Jena University he reorganized the libraries and produced the first comprehensive catalog. To his extensive collections at home he added a model of the first railroad. He published his own newsletters, one on culture and two on science (*Über Kunst und Altertum {On Art and Antiquity}*, 1816–1824; *Zur Morphologie {On Morphology}* and *Zur Naturwissenschaft überhaupt, besonders zur Morphologie {On Natural Science in General, Particularly on Morphology}*, 1817–1824). In fact, the Goethe residence resembled a publishing house; every aspect of the great man's productive life was turned into books, with the aid of (mostly unpaid) secretaries, assistants, and conversation and correspondence partners.

The output of the Goethe establishment was considerable. As the aides labored to prepare letters and autobiographical material for publication (*Dichtung und Wahrheit*, 1811–1814; *Italienische Reise {Italian Journey}*, 1816–1817; *Campagne in Frankreich {Campaign in France}* and *Belagerung von Mainz {Siege of Mainz}*, 1822; *Der zweite römische Aufenthalt {Second Roman Sojourn}*, 1829; and *Die Schweizer Reise im Jahre 1797 {Swiss Journey in 1797}*, 1833), Goethe kept expanding *Wilhelm Meisters Wanderjahre* (*Wilhelm Meister's Journeyman Years;* first version in 1821, final version in 1829), mainly by inserting a number of short fictions. But he published one such shorter piece separately under the simple yet provocative title *Novelle* (1827), just to show that he was ready to compete in this newly fashionable genre, which had been launched by the rising generation of romantic writers.

In addition to the *Divan* cycle there was still poetry, now from the perspective of wise old age, that yet responded with imaginative urgency to philosophical issues (*Urworte Orphisch {Primal Words Orphic}*,

1817), to a deeply personal experience of passion (*Trilogie der Leidenschaft {Trilogy of Passion}*, 1823), and to nature and time (*Chinesisch-deutsche Jahres- und Tageszeiten,* 1827). And, finally, starting in 1825, Goethe returned to his most daunting project, *Faust,* which had lain dormant since Schiller's death. He completed the work in August 1831. Then, on his 82nd birthday, his last, he could consider his life's work done. His only son, unfortunate August, had died a year earlier; his grandchildren were well provided for by the grandfather's carefully planned income from his *Works.* Goethe sealed up his final achievement, *Faust Part II,* the eagerly awaited sequel to his most famous work, for posthumous publication. He celebrated his birthday in the company of his grandchildren with a last visit to his favorite mountain, the Kickelhahn near Ilmenau. Six months later he died from complications following a cold, on 22 March 1832.

Chapter Two

Sturm und Drang Poetry: The Great Subjectivity

That literary history dates the beginning of modern German poetry from Goethe's *Sesenheimer Lieder* appears amazing for such a small body of texts. Of the 11 short poems assembled under that name, most are held to be of negligible significance; only two make the difference: *Willkommen und Abschied (Welcome and Farewell)* and *Mailied (May Song)*. Literary scholarship has tried to define ever anew what precisely makes these two poems so extraordinary, so paradigmatic for whatever it is that constitutes modern German poetry. All agree that they are love poems and that they were occasioned by the brief but emotionally intense encounter with Friederike Brion in the idyllic Alsatian country setting at the Sesenheim parsonage.

All also agree that the poems are miles away from the love or nature poetry practiced by Goethe's predecessors in that genre, Klopstock and Hölty, or by the rococo crafters of occasional verse, including Goethe himself at Leipzig. But there agreement stops. Instead, critics have made the two poems serve to represent their particular views of the essence of Goethean, or the new kind of, poetry. Here began poetry as immediate expression of experience *(Erlebnislyrik);* as preromanticism endowing nature with spirit; as glorification of the self; as youthful enthusiasm sweeping aside age-old conventions; as redefinition of love, nature, and the divine; as declaration of artistic autonomy; and as revolution of traditional metric forms by means of radical dynamic force.

There is no question but that a self is at the center of the two poems, but the self is not the center unless we mean by center a place where the world—nature and the beloved—is being processed as in a focus: perceived, reflected, refracted, transformed. Goethe knew what was happening, if not consciously at the moment of composition then soon thereafter. In the introduction to a collection of essays published at the height of his Sturm und Drang fame *(Aus Goethes Brieftasche {From Goethe's Portfolio}),* he used the focusing lens as central metaphor to explain artistic production: "Every form, no matter how deeply felt, is to some extent untrue; but form is once and for all the glass through which we gather into a fiery spark for the human heart the holy rays of extensive nature."[1] Goethe knew that he needed a metaphor because the artistic process could not be explained rationally; the word *magic* for the artist's experience recurs in the first essay of the collection ("Nach Falconet und über Falconet" ["After Falconet and about Falconet"]) with leitmotivic insistence. One such passage about the "power of this magic" seems a fair summary of the *events* of the threshold poem, *Willkommen und Abschied:* "Every human has felt in his life the power of this magic which seizes the artist everywhere and animates the world around him. Who has never been overcome by shivers when entering a sacred forest? Whom has the embracing night not shaken with uncanny terror? Who has never seen the whole world golden in the presence of his girl? Who has not felt heaven and earth flowing together in most blissful harmonies when holding her arm?" (*HA,* 12:24).

At the beginning of the era that discovered the subject, Goethe's Sesenheim poetry is self-reflexive literature. The text is about those mental and emotional events that produce it, the lyric. Yet it is not a matter of introspection; instead, we observe a self testing the limits of selfhood, exploring the potential for expansion of the subject. The poems are experiments in crossing the border between self and world, discovery trips carefully controlled through strictly observed metric form and artfully structured—even constructed—language.

In the process of interpenetration, both the self and the world undergo a profound change, for which Goethe at this stage found only the word *magic.* The self, by taking in the world, by individualizing it through experience, becomes an individuality with an ever-expanding horizon of apperception. Through such expansion of consciousness, the self is remade into a great subjectivity or, in the language of the time, a genie. In the mutuality of the process, the self's consciousness of the world is changed to the point where, for example, love may be transformed from the individual erotic emotion into a trope for God. As his fictive *Brief des Pastors zu *** an den neuen Pastor zu **** (*Letter from the Pastor at *** to the New Pastor at ***,* 1772) sets forth, Goethe has abolished God in the understanding of Christian dogma. The spiritualization of love by poetic magic offers a substitute religious experience (*HA,* 12:234).

Four key elements of the Strasbourg experience, each of them climactic—a high—brought about the magic of poetic consciousness for Goethe. One was, of course, the ecstasy of love of which the poems speak most particularly. Another was the exaltation of self-esteem when Goethe found himself chosen as a sounding board by Great Man Herder for his extraordinary ideas on language, literature, culture, history, and creativity. Self-esteem soared when Goethe realized that he not only could think on Herder's level but also could use Herder's ideas to dare compete with the greatest modern poet, Shakespeare. It was this experience that boiled over in Goethe's Shakespeare panegyric (*Zum Schäkespears Tag*) shortly after he left Strasbourg and that inspired the creation of the radically innovative drama *Götz von Berlichingen*. A third high was an experience that outweighed grumpy and sick Herder's grating acknowledgment: Goethe became the charismatic collector of enthusiastic disciples who would constitute the Sturm und Drang movement, with Goethe as their uncontested leader. J. M. R. Lenz, the most gifted among them, illustrates this followership to an extreme degree; he even tried to adopt Goethe's abandoned beloved, Friederike.

The fourth key element was the literal experience of height, an entirely fortuitous event and yet as signally tied to Strasbourg as the great cathedral that is its landmark. Goethe, who among other physical shortcomings of his youth suffered from fear of heights, used the cathedral tower to cure himself. But the repeated ascent and view from the platform affected him in unforeseen ways. In his essay *Von deutscher Baukunst* (*On Gothic Architecture*, 1772), we find the evidence of this epiphany. He narrates his shock of first sight, which with one stroke wiped his head free of ingrained prejudice about disreputable gothic art. The shock of seeing the Strasbourg cathedral as art founded for this novice an aesthetic of the sublime.

Goethe describes a quasi-religious experience, the mystical union of earthly and divine pleasure, inaccessible to rational cognition and explanation: "I was able to savor and enjoy, but by no means understand and explain. They say it is thus with the joys of heaven, and how often I returned to savor such heavenly-earthly joys."[2] In the oft-repeated enjoyment of the artwork, the artist's spirit reveals himself to communicate the secret of his art: "There revealed itself to me . . . the genius of the great master. 'Why are you amazed?' he whispered." Finally, the artist as "giant spirit" is apotheosized in religious metaphoric as "Saint Erwin," as "God's anointed prophet," even as divine creator himself, "who can look down on such a creation and speak, godlike: It is good!" (*Works*, 3:6–8).

Goethe's familiarity with unorthodox religious thought and language from his post-Leipzig recovery days in Frankfurt is well attested, particularly from his reading of Arnold's *Unparteiische Kirchen- und Ketzerhistorie*. It is to the mystical unity of the physical and spiritual realms that Goethe now associates the magic of the poetic process. The most famous passage in the cathedral essay enunciates a crossing of borders between mind and nature, human and divine, organic and inorganic: trees and artworks. The great cathedral that dominates the surrounding countryside—"like a towering, widespreading tree of God. With its thousands of branches and millions of twigs and as many leaves as sand by the sea, it shall proclaim to the land the glory of the Lord, its master" (*Works*, 3:5)—revealed to the budding poet the essence of the artwork and of the creative process that could make it happen.

The Threshold Poems

Willkommen und Abschied

At first glance *Willkommen und Abschied* appears rather conventional.[3] The traditional eight line strophe of four iambic meters with alternating male–female rhyme calls up devotional poetry, as in Protestant hymns, or narrative poetry, as in folk ballads. The narrative structure, too, is transparent enough. The poem of four strophes falls neatly into two halves, the first describing a ride through the night, the second half, subdivided into two halves again, evoking arrival and departure: the welcome and farewell of the title. If the second half (third and fourth strophes) appears weaker than the first, as many critics have found, our first impression confirms it. The forward drive of the night ride is arrested and, with the third strophe, passes into a vacillating motion of stop and go, up and down. Both of the later strophes end in a rococo hangover, which disrupts the innovative intensity and dynamism established in the first half of the poem. The closing couplets of strophes 3 and 4 strike a reader looking for the new poetry as retrograde to the intellectualism of the preceding, Anacreontic era. Goethe uses the abstraction "Zärtlichkeit" (23), the rationalizing point of hope versus reward (24), and the clever punning in the active–passive play on love and happiness (31–32). And, finally, he includes that standard item of rococo furniture, the gods used as expletive: "Götter!" (32).

A closer look reveals surprising depths. The poem describes a threshold experience, the crossing over coded in the two title words, *Willkommen und Abschied* (*welcome* and *farewell*). Although duality is implicit in border crossings, the ideational and emotional structure of the poem is not dual, not one of opposition. Instead the structure resembles a roller coaster of rapid and violent motions, reversals, and extreme polarities that finally remain suspended in ambiguity. Ambiguity is not, any more than duality, however, the last word of the poem. Rather, the goal is ambivalence: to assert the validity of dual, traditionally opposed values. If mystical experience, for Goethe, meant pleasure without cognition, his poem stakes out the higher claim to both enjoyment and cognition. Both participate in the poetic magic, in the experience of creativity, that this poem performs and narrates.

The poem opens in an eruption with no hint of either cause or goal. A high-intensity physical affect, heart palpitation, is vented physically, in bodily transference from racing heart to racing horse (1). Both move-ment and affect continue over the length of the first two strophes until they reach their ultimate point in the melting of the heart: "mein ganzes Herz zerfloß in Glut" (16). The path to this alchemical-mystical dissolu-tion of the heart constitutes the magic of poetic process: It is the many ways of seeing the invisible, of perceiving darkness and night. The poet's relation to the gathering night develops slowly and ambiguously, with the first step intimating the comforting embrace of cradle and curtains in a lullaby setting (3–4). The next step, with the oak as giant (5–6), suggests the bush-or-bear delusion familiar to Goethe, avid reader of Shakespeare, and creates a suspension between benign and malign. Next, the paradox of darkness seeing with a hundred eyes makes night an antagonist and competitor that easily conquers the two-eyed human observer.

The vision of and by the moon (9–10) shifts us back to the benign image of cradle and lullaby. On pillows of clouds peering out sleepily from a veil of haze, this moon is darkness's drowsy baby. But at the same time the moon image emphasizes distance that can be bridged only by the visual sense. Close, by contrast, is the night air, which reaches the closer and closest senses of hearing and touch. Goethe would have learned from Herder to distinguish between sensual experiences.[4] As night now closes in, despite the far-off vision of the moon, vision is dis-placed by the physical senses. Wind *sounding like* birds' wings is felt and heard, producing for the first time an explicitly negative emotion: "schauerlich" (12).

In a parallel development, analogic image making ("wie ein getürmter Riese," 6) is displaced by the magic of metonymic transfor-mation. Winds are sensed and responded to as (birds') wings, with the logical link—birds—not spoken. The last four lines of the night ride

(13–16) present a summary of the path to poetic magic, to artistic creation: night has proven monstrously, a thousandfold creative. And only
now, after the event, a purpose appears. The hero had ridden out to
meet a challenge, to face the creative provocation of darkness with his
own "more thousandfold" creativity (14). As a result his mind and heart
(15–16) have grown into the immeasurably potent dimension of the
mystical-magical poetic self.

The second part of the poem breaks the spell with what appears to be
the previously unstated goal of the quest: seeing the beloved (17). In a
counterpoint move the magic meltdown now is channeled ("zerfloß," 16
→ "floß," 18); the flow is defined as gentle joy (17) and redirected in the
loving gaze toward the self, who in turn redirects his totality, the feeling
soul and the living body ("Ganz . . . Herz / jeder Atemzug," 19–20),
toward the beloved. The limiting movement of this strophe superim-
poses the beloved's "sweet gaze" (18) onto the hundred eyes of darkness,
the "rosenfarbes Frühlingswetter" (21), conjured up from rococo inven-
tory onto all of the preceding night experience. Here poetic magic
breaks down in the Anacreontic mentalizing of "Zärtlichkeit" (23). Yet
ambiguity returns under cover of certainty in the concluding line: "Ich
hofft' es, ich verdient' es nicht!" (24). This seemingly resolute judgment
harbors its own opposite meaning, because *nicht,* the last—negating—
word of the love scene, can be taken to apply to both verbs or merely to
the last verb. If the latter, then hope for a loving encounter was
rewarded even though the reward was not deserved. If the former, however, then a loving encounter was not hoped for. This line does not even
exclude a subversive reading of the love poem: that the encounter in
some way went against the night rider's hope. After all, we have
observed that seeing the beloved halted the poetic self's limitless expansion.

How to end the magic experience is the question now. The last strophe has to perform the comedown from the heights of—poetic or
erotic—ecstasy. Helplessness and a feeling of loss pervade until the
abrupt change of the final couplet. Another crossing must be achieved,
this time in reverse. The return course is marked by halts, reversals, and
changes of diction every two lines. The first word announces that rupture is necessary—"Der Abschied" (25)—but the refusal to take action
shines forth in the erasure of verbs during the first half of the strophe.
Exclamations, ejaculations, and eruptions attempt to hang on to ecstasy
through the avoidance of action on the part of the self. Until the separation is effected in the fifth line by an action of the other ("Du gingst"),

there is only one verb, and it is a predicate of the other ("sprach dein Herz," 26).

Yet within the moment of ecstasy a significant evolution still takes place. The ambiguity of (non)hope at the close of the third strophe unfolds into an ambivalence that connotes *unio mystica* in the lovers' kiss (27–28). Here thine and mine, self and other interpenetrate in a subtly graded progression. From kisses, clearly "thine," issues love, still implicitly assigned to the thou (27), but, then, to whom should "Wonne" and "Schmerz" (28) be ascribed? After all, I can only feel my own pleasure and pain. Thus, although a first reading may attribute pleasure and pain, like "your" love and kisses, to the other, we must come to understand these feelings as truly shared by the two-in-one of love's union. The paradoxical pleasure-equals-pain formula, designating the coincidence of opposites, encodes the parallel between love's and the mystic's experiences.

Precisely from the closest, physically most intensely sensed moment of the kiss must the wrenching separation proceed; each must cross the border back into his or her self again. So, after four lines of near-verbless ejaculations, verbs take over in profusion to enact the separation. The three verbal signifiers in the first enactment verse (29) ring the changes of this performance in their monosyllabic vowel chord: *gingst, stund, sah.* It should be noted that to achieve this vocalic harmony Goethe had to take recourse to an anachronistic form; the old-fashioned *stund* had long been replaced in common usage by *stand.* But Goethe needed the *u* sound, and he had to avoid preempting the *a* sound of finality, the dominant in this farewell chord. For it is indeed the vowel of the verb *sah* that now strikes and maintains in its repetition (29, 30) the dominant key for the moment of leave-taking, of separation and distancing.

The distancing that follows maximum closeness in the kiss is tracked by the far-reaching visual sense: *sah.* Communication between the lovers had taken place outside of language, through the gaze—from the "sweet gaze" of greeting (18) to the explicit "From your gaze spoke your heart" (26). Now "downcast eyes" (29) cut off the communicating gaze. As the other walks away ("du gingst") the lover's gaze is left behind: "sah dir nach" (30). Yet once more the gaze returns, this time to express mourning: mourning "mit nassem Blick" (30) the loss of the magical moment. But the tears of mourning do not exhaust Goethe's meaning here—why state the obvious?—the moist gaze means that now vision is blurred. The vision that was an epiphany is fading in correlation with the disappearance of the beloved in the distance, with the vanishing of love into the past. Presence fades into absence; the magic is over. When the final couplet closes off the vision in a rococo mood of pun and games, mixing active and passive voice in loving and being loved with a double dose of the ambiguous signifier "Glück" and the obligatory appeal to the gods, we are almost glad to be back to normal again. For all its air of frivolity deplored by critics, the conclusion to this threshold poem is eminently functional: it translates ecstasy back into normalcy.

Maifest (Mailied)

Maifest, the original title Goethe gave to the poem known generally today as *Mailied*, points in a highly significant direction. The word is a synonym for *Frühlingsfeier* (spring celebration), the title of Klopstock's most famous poem. The aspiring poet in Strasbourg had to compete not only with Shakespeare the dramatist but even more crucially with Klopstock, the originator of the modern German poetic idiom. For German poets of Goethe's generation, Klopstock was the founding father whose sons had no choice but to wrestle with their anxiety of influence lest they be destroyed by the influence as Young Werther was.[5]

Mailied is considered the most successful of the Sesenheim poems. There is no trace of *Willkommen und Abschied*'s somewhat cumbersome form, with its obtrusive binary structure, the repeated two-part division of the four long strophes with their long, regularly rhymed lines. On first hearing there seems to be hardly any formal structure in *Mailied*. Rhyme occurs only in every other line and is minimal in itself: all-male rhyme means that only one syllable is involved. Ultrabrief lines of two iambs skim lightly along to create an approximation of speech rhythm; by far the majority of unrhymed lines, in fact, are run-on lines. The short, four-line strophes, too, show frequent enjambment.

The cumulative effect of this minimalism is to hide whatever formal architecture there is and to create a cataract of words sweeping the listener along, giving no pause for reflection or distance. Maximum reader involvement is the poem's most immediately evident achievement; it is the dynamism identified by critical consensus as the truly innovative feature of *Mailied*. Such irresistible drive was the goal in the first half of *Willkommen und Abschied*, too. But there, because of the obvious formal architecture, the goal was reached only partially and with visible effort: the effort of a rhetoric of the sublime.

The rushing-on dynamic in *Mailied* is further aided by an unusual accumulation of appellations; with their "O-plus-one" pattern they function as minimal sentences: "O Erd, O Sonne." The absence of verbs here, those carriers of temporal structure in a text, contributes to the unstoppable movement across time and approaches a feeling of timelessness. The forward drive is aided, too, by minimal logical articulation. *Wie,* that vaguest of conjunctions, dominates the syntactical structure. Otherwise, simple enumeration suffices, rarely linked by an equally bland *und.* The effect is that we stop looking for syntax and lose track of logic, thought, and reflection.

When we finally encounter the sole instance of syntax that demands reflection, in the long sentence beginning with "So," which ties the last three strophes into one unit of meaning, we keep on rushing toward the end.[6] We no longer expect demands on our reflection, so we do not want to ask how the *wie* in the final line is meant: "wie du mich liebst." The meaning of this line is still hotly debated, as witnessed by the two most recent editions of Goethe's collected works. Does it show alienation and instrumentalization of the beloved, as the commentator of the Munich Edition (1985) thinks? Or should we follow the commentator of the Frankfurt Edition (1987), who embraces a Neoplatonic perspective? Or might we simply relate the last line to *ewig* in the preceding line, asserting the infinity and thus totality of love?

In this poem of deceptive simplicity let us examine the development of meaning to answer the question. The dynamic flow hides two competing structures of meaning. On the one hand, there is a basically triadic sentence structure. Three statements unfold one event or phenomenon each, resulting in five triads of lines: 1–4, 5–10, 14–20, 22–24, and 25–30. A triadic architecture might likewise be seen in three segments of three strophes, where the first segment opens with the human response to nature's spring phenomena, the middle three strophes present love's work in the cosmic and individual dimensions, and the final triad focuses on the creative effects of individual love.[7]

But a case can also be made for an apparently asymmetrical division into five and four strophes, the first five speaking about love in nature and the following four about individual love. A closer look reveals a subtly symmetrical structure, with the axis formed by the central fifth strophe. This strophe makes the most consequential statement on the cosmic function of love. In clearly religious language ("Du segnest," 17), love here represents divine power, creative and nurturing. Here, too, we find poetic language itself becoming creative as it produces the striking neologism "im Blütendampfe" (19). Goethe's Sturm und Drang poetry stands out for his bold new word creations; here is the first instance of literally creative power claimed by the new poet.

The axis strophe of maximum power in the signified—love's divine essence—is staged by the preceding fourth strophe with maximum signifier power. The unique sonority of modulation through full-sounding vowels and consonants (o ↔ ö; liquid-stop combinations repeated as a leitmotif in Lieb–Liebe modulate through "golden" "Morgenwolken") creates on the semantic side the most picturesque view offered by the poem: "golden schön / . . . Morgenwolken auf jenen Höhn" (14–16). The beautiful picture visualizes the words "so schön"; the music of sound creates the beauty of vision. Thus prepared, the central fifth strophe radiates meaning in both directions, forward and back. Retroactively, it explains what is really happening in strophes 2 and 3, in the three factual statements organized around the predicate "Es dringen" (5). We are to see love's generative power in all creatures, in all expressions of life: blossoming plants, singing birds, human emotions.

From the axis forward, the cosmic power called love radiates into the life of individuals. It inspires creativity in the speaking self through the multiple conduits of life's force: the loving beloved, the lark's song, the floral aura ("Morgenblumen / Den Himmelsduft," 27–28), the self's own life energy ("warmem Blut," 30). At the same time, the interweaving synergy that constitutes this poetic text inspires creativity ("du . . . gibst," 31–34) and bliss in the beloved loving other.

The ending also illuminates the beginning. The first-person pronoun *Mir* appears at the very outset (2) to set up the interactive process between a self and the totality of the world. The pronoun's emphatic position in the metrical scheme has caused objection to the poem as the height of self-aggrandizement and self-centeredness, placing the subject in sole and equivalent correlation with nature ("Mir die Natur"). The poem in its entirety, however, clarifies the function of the self as focus for the reflections and transformations that take place in the world through the mediation of a self, which is itself not a solipsistic subject but exists in the creative processes described in the poem as part of a reciprocal relation with an other.

Willkommen und Abschied reflects the effort to overcome duality between self and nature, self and a beloved other in a momentary experience of two-in-one. *Mailied* represents a relationship of reciprocity among self, nature, and the beloved, a reciprocity that in turn aims toward the mystical experience of one-in-all and all-in-one. And unlike the two threshold moments of ecstasy achieved in the earlier poem, this poem renders the mystical now, the timeless moment of eternal consciousness as durative ecstasy, as a potentially never-ending ("ewig," 35) emotion that lasts exactly as long as creative activity can maintain and renew itself.

The Great Hymns

Literary history calls the five long poems in free verse that date to Goethe's Frankfurt years (1772 to 1774) the Great Hymns: *Wandrers Sturmlied (Wanderer's Storm-Song), Mahomets Gesang (Song of Mahomet), Prometheus, Ganymed (Ganymedes)*, and *An Schwager Kronos (To Coachman Chronos)*. Like the *Sesenheimer Lieder,* they have become paradigmatic in the development of German literature. They founded the genre of *weltanschauungs* lyric that inspired poets from Goethe's younger contemporaries Friedrich Hölderlin (1770–1843) and Novalis (1772–1801) to Rainer Maria Rilke (1875–1926) in his *Duino Elegies.* In Goethe's own development the Hymns mark a clear break with the Sesenheim lyrics. Ignoring the formal conventions of meter, rhyme, and strophic structure observed in the earlier poems, the new poetry presents itself as radically emancipated. The poet chooses and changes meter, rhythm, and length of lines and strophes at will, and there is, of course, no trace of rhyme, that most visible mark of formally bound language.

The difference is no less pronounced thematically. Love and happiness, the foci of yore, are gone. There is no twosomeness here; the sole focus is the self. This is poetry of self with a vengeance, whether in first-person perspective (*Wandrers Sturmlied* and *An Schwager Kronos*) or in the guise of a mythological figure (Muhammad, Prometheus, or Ganymedes). Where the earlier poetry sought ways to break out of the self, to overcome selfhood through union with a thou or a mystical nature, the Hymns explore the manifold aspects of self. Yet again this is not introspective poetry. Rather, we see the poet on a quest: questioning, challenging, searching, and trying on versions of a new self that has jettisoned the anchorings of tradition to find himself in unknown waters. Goethe's letters of these years are obsessed with the imagery of seafaring, overwhelmingly emphasizing the dangerous aspects (i.e., the shipwreck).

Two of the five Hymns (*Mahomets Gesang* and *Prometheus*) formed part of a host of mostly dramatic projects about great heroes of myth and history: Julius Caesar, Faust, Egmont, Luther, Muhammad, Prometheus, and Jesus Christ. These figures and their projected life stories served the poet for experimental identification. They were models or imagoes in the tentative construction of self, in answering the question: Whom do I want to become? They had the function of personal myths: to explain myself to myself. Goethe's creative responses to these myths, in the Hymns and in the two dramas that he eventually finished (*Egmont* and *Faust*), became poetic explorations of a rich subjectivity. Such exploration in turn involved imaginary experimentation with a variety of life projects, with different views of life, and with the consequences entailed for the individual at the center of each text. And thus another question evolved: What might happen to me when I become that?

Wandrers Sturmlied

Two crucial issues of the Frankfurt years are addressed with particular urgency in the Hymns: the question of genius, that buzzword of the age, and human autonomy as central issue in the history of Enlightenment and secularization. *Wandrers Sturmlied* (1772), the first, the longest, and by common agreement the most difficult of the Hymns, confronts the question of genius directly.[8] The first line, "Wen du nicht verlässest, Genius," recurs in liturgical invocation to open the next three strophes with hypotheses on existence under the wings of genius, but the poem does not offer a conclusion. What we find is a statement of the existential problem of the artist, which would long occupy Goethe, most prominently in the drama *Torquato Tasso* (1789). The old Goethe no longer understood his youthful poem; in his autobiography he referred to it as "half-nonsense." Literary criticism followed his judgment until quite recently, when Goethe's *Wandrers Sturmlied* was discovered as anticipation of modernist poetry.

The poem is about the anxiety of genius, akin to what we know from Harold Bloom as anxiety of influence.[9] For Goethe, there was the additional complication of trying to establish himself as a poet of genius but against the accepted definition of genius, against tradition, and against the literary and cultural establishment of his time and place. In eighteenth-century Germany that establishment was Francocentric to a quasi-colonial degree. Acting on Herder's revolutionary ideas of regionalism, plurality, and diversity, Goethe embraced new models: "German" architecture and folk poetry,[10] Shakespeare, Old Testament poetry, and the ancient Greek poet Pindar. In his enthusiastic address *Zum Schäkespears Tag* (autumn 1771) Goethe had invented for the genius Shakespeare the figure of the wanderer. Still borne aloft by the heady days of Strasbourg, Shakespeare's fiery follower was confident in his quest to emulate this "greatest wanderer . . . [because] we carry in ourselves the seed of merits which we can understand and appreciate" (*HA*, 12:224).

Wandrers Sturmlied of half a year later discovers the trials and tribulations involved in the literary quest. It is the song of a wanderer in distress, as Goethe remarked to a friend a few years later.[11] The distress is precisely the problem of not knowing how to deal with genius or how to walk alone on the road that is supposed to lead to mastery. This anxiety found expression in Goethe's 1772 review of a book on aesthetic theory. After demolishing with youthful arrogance the theorist's traditional views, Goethe concludes by rejecting theory altogether on the grounds that it does not help the artist. What the artist needs is a "real master" who would share his own experiences on his way to mastery: "his efforts, the difficulties that impeded him most, the powers that helped him overcome, . . . the spirit that inspired him momentarily and illuminated him on his entire road" (*HA*, 12:20).

The poem represents the challenge to the traditional aesthetic by a genius of the new age, whereby *genius* means both the wandering poet (Goethe) and the new, as yet uncertain understanding of poetic production. Genius's great antagonist appears in the figure of Apollo, who as sun god and master of the Muses stands for traditional art in the spirit of Enlightenment and Francocentric high culture. His reign in the outer world of beauty and fame ("Was der Welt / Phöb Apoll ist," 57–58) is to be overcome by the inner fire ("Glut," 55) of true poets such as Pindar and his present acolyte, the wanderer. Our quester rejects other options from classical Greek culture that the eighteenth century had adopted as models: Anacreon for rococo poetry (84–90) and Theocritus for the idyll (92–100). Seeking a patron power strong enough to withstand Apollo's might, the poet appeals to the sun's antagonist: the rain god, "Jupiter Pluvius." He therefore must endure his divinity's rain, snow, hail, sleet, and storm (71–83).

Goethe is well aware of the fundamental difficulty of translating the Pindaric enthusiasm represented in the glory of Olympic victories (101–10) from Pindar's very different culture to the modern age. Herder had cautioned against such attempts,[12] so here Goethe is challenging his own theorist and mentor, too. As a solution, *Wandrers Sturmlied* offers the modern poet from northern and rainy climes, instead of Pindar's clouds of auratic dust around Olympic chariots (106), mud. Mud, dignified as "the son of [much invoked] water and earth" (51), is simultaneously obstacle to be overcome by means of genius ("Wirst ihn heben übern Schlammpfad / Mit den Feuerflügeln," 11), original matter for a new creation ("Deukalions Flutschlamm," 15), and, finally, in the humorous tail end of the stormy journey, plain real mud that the wanderer must wade through (116).

In Goethe's first Pindaric poem the medium is the message and the content is implicit in the form as the meaning of genius is explored through a language of genius. Pindar as patron saint of "free speech" in poetry was a productive misunderstanding of the period. Scholarship had not yet recognized the formal laws of Pindar's odes, and so Pindar had come to mean poetic speech shaped by and immediately expressing the enthusiastic soul, inspired genius. Pindaric language was considered free from the strictures of meter, strophe, and rhyme; it could take liberties with grammar and even language itself in creating new words. Goethe's poem exuberantly bathes in such emancipation. For example, the one-word line "Wärmumhüllen" (25) represents the contraction of an abbreviated prepositional object (*mit Wärme*) with its verb (*umhüllen*).

Rejecting regular form meant choosing meter and rhythm to express content most adequately. *Wandrers Sturmlied* proceeds in a basic trochaic rhythm of strong forward strides, but there are variations in synchrony with significant divergences in substance. Two longer exceptions to the rhythmic base stand out. In the seventh strophe (39–51), where iambic rhythm predominates, a counterfigure to the chilled but determined wanderer appears: "the small dark fiery farmer" hurrying home to his hearth and wine, the genius ersatz of the decadent age ("Vater Bromius [Dionysus] / . . . / Jahrhunderts Genius," 52–54). The second exception to the basic rhythm occurs in the final segment of the last strophe (110–16). Trochees collapse and dissolve into small bits of varying metrical shapes in ultrabrief lines as the poet runs out of breath and gives up in his competition with Pindar. He ends up imitating the despised little peasant of strophe 7, in his much reduced hope not of flying, as on the wings of genius, but of wading through mud to his tiny home.

Form, we see, is anything but arbitrary; it is a matter of "inner form," a major concept in German literary history modeled on the unity of formal and semantic structure first practiced here. *Wandrers Sturmlied* reveals a triadic structure (as do Pindar's odes). Part 1 (1–38) links the first four strophes by their first-line refrain: "Wen du nicht verlässest, Genius." These subtitles announce the transports of genius that carry the poet into an imaginary utopia, signaled by the grammatical markers of future and hypothesis: *wirst* and *wird*. The last two strophes of the first part (28–38) translate utopian timelessness into virtual reality. Poetic imagination aided by the Muses ("ihr Musen, / Ihr Charitinnen,"

28–29) can change future into present tense. The second strophe's utopian comparison of the poet with the god of art, Apollo ("leicht, groß," 16), now is asserted by a new, conclusive refrain, "göttergleich" (33, 38): the poet of genius is the peer of gods. Yet the wandering poet's distressing physical reality remains present throughout. Rain and cold supply the dominant themes—water, earth, warmth—of the imaginary dimension, most pointedly in the second strophe, as the poet's real "Schlammpfad" (11) metamorphoses into the fertile *Ur*-mud of the mythical Great Flood: "Deukalions Flutschlamm" (15).

The three strophes of the middle part (39–70) create a countermovement to the acceleration of the first segment. These antistrophes (again following the Pindaric model) introduce counterfigures, counterthemes, and counterrhythms. Iambic meter intrudes at the outset (39), together with the counterfigure of the little peasant. In the following strophe of uniformly short lines (52–58), trochees are back but painfully foreshortened. Together with the repetition in the awkward rhyming pattern of lines 52 through 54 (*Bromius–Genius–Genius*), the result is monotony, idling in place, a stalling of the forward drive. The last strophe of the middle segment (59–70) attempts to break out of the blockage by varying and thereby lengthening the lines, but to no avail: the foreshortened trochees persist by a 9:3 ratio. The poet-wanderer remains fixated on the phantasmic figure of "Phöb Apoll" (58, 63), the sun god who is obviously not there in this storm-drenched quest. Progress threatens to come to a halt. The wanderer's gaze, like the imagined (i.e., absent) sun god's, is arrested ("verweilen") by a tree ("Zeder"), paradigm of rootedness. The last word of the stalling middle segment, "harrt" (70), finally seals the stopped motion.

The blockage can only be dissolved with a deliberate new start-up. In part 3 (71–116) the poet finally ("zuletzt," 71) returns to the original impetus of his song and reasserts his own patron saint of genius, Jupiter Pluvius (75, 83), against that of tradition, Apollo. Long, trochaic lines begin to flow again with the thrice-repeated initial invocation of the rain god, "Dich," until, in the most self-reflexive line of this poem, the text speaks what it is doing (flowing): "Dich, dich strömt mein Lied" (76). Now the poet can reject out of hand ("Nicht," 84, 92) the pleasant images of cozily happy and facile conventional poetry ("Castalischer Quell / . . . ein Nebenbach," 77–78) in a parody of conventionally mellifluous language: "bienensingenden / Honiglallenden" (97–98).

After having thus set the stage with negative counterimages, Goethe can spring on us the true hero of *his* poetry. In a radical rhythmic rupture, now really ignoring meter, with stress following stress, ignoring syntactical structure in an effort to make words express directly the glowing excitement of Pindar's dithyrambs ("Glüht deine Seel Gefahren, Pindar, / Mut.—Glühte—," 109–10), the poem launches into an onomatopoeic rendition of a chariot race. All the more astonishing, then, is the conclusion of this Pindaric strophe, and of the challenging poem as a whole (111–16), with a whimper. The poor modern poet ("Armes Herz"), in truly impoverished, repetitive language ("Dort . . . Dort . . . Dort"), is humbled to struggle with his last breath toward a very modest goal: through the mud to his hut on the hill.

Prometheus

The figure of Prometheus as creative artist had become a topos in eighteenth-century culture, ever since Shaftesbury in his *Soliloquy* or *Advice to an Author* (1710) had used it to promote a new concept of originality in art. In this view, the poet as Prometheus, a Titan who according to Greek myth had created the human race, was an original maker. As nondivine creator, this figure would inevitably come into conflict with the divine creator of the Bible, in whom the eighteenth century still officially believed. This implication of the Promethean topos, however, remained latent until Goethe's Hymn seized on it as its main theme.[13] In his prose manifestos on the new art (*Von deutscher Baukunst* and *Zum Schäkespears Tag*) Goethe had used the conventional meaning of the metaphor for his favorite master artists. He bestowed the "Prometheus medal of honor" on both the architect of the Strasbourg cathedral and the British poet. His poem *Prometheus* decisively reinterprets the Greek myth in a way that applies it not merely to the artist but to man generally as rebel against divine authority.

The poem presents other difficulties than those of *Wandrers Sturmlied*. Apparently easy to understand, it yet contains a multiplicity of meanings and continues to generate a broad range of interpretations. Rebellion against authority—divine, legal, state, familial, and so forth—invokes power relations and holds a continuing fascination for the modern mentality. Three major levels of meaning are addressed here. At one level, *Prometheus* reworks the *Sturmlied*'s theme of genius. In contrast with the earlier poem's defensive stance on the basis of a beginner's doubts and insecurities, here speaks the self-assurance of a man of genius.

In the intervening year and a half, Goethe had published his drama *Götz von Berlichingen* and reaped overwhelming praise. More than accolades, the competition with his Promethean model, Shakespeare, had brought an unprecedented burst of inspiration. In the most intense period of gestation of his entire literary career, Goethe was working on a half-dozen dramatic plans. Like the Prometheus of his drama he was living an intoxicated life amid the figures of his imagination. Bringing to life his creations by means of his own spirit, not by divine inspiration (God's in the biblical Genesis, Athena's in the Prometheus myth), he was realizing in his work the image he had drawn of Shakespeare in his speech: "Competing with Prometheus he imitated his humans in every feature . . . and then he brought them to life with the breath of *his* spirit" (*HA*, 12:227).

In the last of the Frankfurt Hymns, *An Schwager Kronos* (dateline: "In the stagecoach, on 10 October 1774"), Goethe would repeat the Promethean gesture of self-confidence to confirm the conviction that the path taken with such trepidation in the *Sturmlied* had, after all, been right for him.[14] Recalling that first Hymn in first-person perspective, theme, and Pindaric style, the later poem, written after the incredible success of *Werther*, unabashedly places the poet-speaker by the side of the greats of antiquity. At his approach they will rise from their seats because "ein Fürst kommt" ("a prince is coming," 39).[15] Surreptitiously, the poet has now become the equal even of Apollo, focus of dread and awe in the earlier poem. There the poet feared and craved the god's "Fürstenblick"; here he is a "Fürst" himself.

At a second level *Prometheus* is about individual religious development. Based on Goethe's own path from heretical idiosyncrasy and pietist devotion to rejection of the Christian concept of God, Prometheus is a proto-Nietzschean anti-Christ figure (Boyle 1991, 1:164). For Goethe's contemporaries this iconoclastic meaning took center stage. In the hotly debated religious controversies of the time, an unauthorized publication of the poem in 1785 had the power to put Goethe, the prime minister as heretic, on an embarrassingly hot seat: "on the stake," as Goethe complained in a letter.[16] It is the long middle section of the poem (13–42), the emotionally most agitated and rhetorically most prominent part, that speaks to the theme of an individual's religious crisis. But the text assigns that crisis to the past. Past pain no longer hurts but functions now as memory to confirm the experience of pain overcome, of need outgrown and unmasked as delusion.

The past as delusion is foregrounded in the development from lost and duped child (22–24, 35–36) to the man shaped and steeled ("geschmiedet") by life experience (43–45). The crisis in fact is staged as an illusionary scenario, tagged with the biggest, showiest words, which in truth, however, mean nothing. In a radical change from Goethe's past joy of creating neologisms for high-valued meanings in the Sesenheim lyrics and still in the *Sturmlied*, here the big words are marks of inflation, of worthlessness: empty words. Accumulated in the strophe that introduces the crisis of faith, "Opfersteuern und Gebets-hauch" (16–17) stand for the essential poverty of so-called divine majesty. Prayer and sacrifice are inflationary currency; hope, the main-stay of faith, deflates like the empty balloon of folly in the full-sounding sequence of the vowel *o* of the strophe's closing line: "Hoffnungsvolle Toren" (21). Concluding the retrospective, youthful dreams and illusions are totaled up and marked down in a purposefully egregious million-dollar word that spans two lines, the biggest word creation of Goethe's fertile Sturm und Drang inspiration: "Knabenmorgen- / Blütenträume" (50–51).

A third level of meaning, finally, involves the second crucial issue Goethe was wrestling with in his Frankfurt years: human autonomy as collective and individual consequence of secularization in the age of Enlightenment. The premier philosopher of German Enlightenment, Immanuel Kant, defined *enlightenment* as deliberate exit from depen-dence with freely willed assumption of responsibility.[17] For the collec-tive, enlightenment meant the delimitation of a human sphere of responsibility and the exclusion of God from that sphere. Late-eighteenth-century constitutions of secular governments in the United States and revolutionary France put the collective meaning of human autonomy into practice. For the individual, enlightenment meant that humans could no longer derive their concept of self from the idea of transcendence as a divinely inspired soul. Instead, the human must dis-cover himself or herself as subjectivity, who can say *I* and who, as sub-ject, is the origin for his or her own self and the creator of his or her own world. The philosophy of German idealism, with F. G. Fichte as preemi-nent proponent, would supply the theory to go with the requisite self-constitution of the human subject.

The first and the last strophes of *Prometheus* engage this topic. The assertion of subjective autonomy in the strongest and most explicit terms is the point of departure and arrival of the poem. In addition, the maintenance of the autonomous position supplies the underlying struc-ture of the middle section as the sovereign self looks back on its struggle to overcome past dependence. For it is precisely here, in the center of the poem and of the self-assured reminiscences in a stream of rhetorical questions, that the key statement is placed: "Hast du's nicht alles *selbst* vollendet, / Heilig glühend Herz?" (33–34; emphasis mine). The self (*selbst*) as subjectivity (*Herz*) is the sole agent and has in fact created itself. Here, as in *Wandrers Sturmlied, glühen, Glut* encodes creativity, and it is through its self-creation that the heart has now become sacred ("heilig," 34), displacing the deity.

In the first and last strophes the territory of the sovereign subject is demarcated against divine power. The first lines unmask divine power as impotent rage, excluded from the safe domain that the subject has created solely by his own power. The last strophe finally includes humans ("Menschen," 52) in the Titanic revolt. Promethean autonomy is to serve as model for human autonomy, for humans are created—quoting the Bible subversively—in his image. Language in the two framing strophes implements the claim of the subjective dimension, marking it off with strong contrasts against the transcendent realm. Where the field of the divine in the middle section of the poem boasts the splendid vocabulary of illusion, the field of the self is denoted with small, seemingly modest but immensely powerful words. Here Goethe uses "Pindaric" freestyle to turn banal little words into powerful speech by means of rhythm, placement, length of lines, elliptical syntax, repetition, and alliterative instead of rhyming patterns.

The first strophe stakes out the realm of the subject by means of the initial *m*. Indo-European languages share this marker for the subject function (English: *me, my, mine*; French: *me, moi, mon*; the Spanish, Italian, and Russian languages follow a similar convention), and Goethe harnesses the phenomenon in lines 6–12 by insistent repetition of *mein, mir,* and *mich*. Significantly, to set the pattern with unmistakable clarity, he uses a shortcut so that the first line in this sequence can start out with a triple-*m* alliteration: "Mußt mir meine." Flouting the cardinal law of German syntax, which assigns the verb to the second position, Goethe erases the grammatical subject, *du* (Zeus), from first place and thus suppresses the divine antagonist. The erasure gives precedence to the actual subject of the statement, the speaker who here states his claim to sovereignty. This subject is multiply represented in the *m* words before eventually the pronoun *du* is allowed to enter in line 9.

Goethe takes a similar grammatical liberty in the middle of the poem. Eliding the verb (*soll*), he directly confronts the challenger, Prometheus, with his antagonist in the most provocative gesture of the poem: "Ich dich ehren?" (38). The missing verb compels a considerable lengthening of the word *Ich* and sets it off by a pause from the following *dich*. The *Ich* has been thrown into high profile, completely overshadowing the *dich* in the unstressed position. The final strophe raises the *Ich* to absolute prominence as the poem's last word. The closing line stands out not because of grammatical irregularity but because of its utter brevity: "Wie ich." The entire last strophe proceeds in the calm rhythm of ordinary speech, which reflects the relaxed posture of the winner in an uneven contest. Prometheus, we now discover, never had to stand up to his opponent; he won sitting down ("Hier sitz' ich"). His definitive victory is won not by what he says but by what he does: sculpting his creatures, who will perpetuate his victory over other-dominated transcendence and who will eternalize him, the self as locus of origins. It is this, the installation of the self as absolute subject, that the two words of the last line enact. "Wie ich" asserts that all selves from now on will be sovereign, self-creating subjects.

Chapter Three

Discovery of History and Ideas in Drama

Götz von Berlichingen

In Strasbourg Goethe had learned from Herder that Shakespeare wrote histories. Herder's own essay on Shakespeare (1774) emphatically embraces this perspective. It was the synthesis of history and literature in the realm of ideas that recommended the Elizabethan dramatist to Herder, when he was working out his innovative philosophicocultural approach to history. In Herder's organicist scheme of cultural flowering and decay, Shakespeare, the greatest English poet at the apex of English might, proved a crucial point. Furthermore, in Herder's multicultural theory of literature Shakespeare was relevant even for foreigners—Germans—because his dramas were staged on a cosmic scene, within the frame of universal ideas. Their meaning was accessible to everyone. Thus Shakespeare could serve as a model to eighteenth-century German dramatists eager to shake free from French cultural supremacy.

To an era enchanted by Rousseau's call back to nature, Shakespearean drama recommended itself by its characters. Unlike in French classicist drama, Shakespeare's figures were not abstractions designed to illustrate some moral thesis. They were *Menschen, Natur:* fully realized human beings. Goethe's Shakespeare speech emphasizes this aspect: "But I cry: Nature! Nature! nothing is so like Nature as Shakespeare's figures." But, he hastens to add, they are not just your ordinary average people; *nature* here does not mean banal realism. Indeed they are overdrawn figures, nature enhanced to *"colossal scale"* (Goethe's emphasis): suitable models for the Sturm und Drang ideal of the oversized personality, the *Kerl.*[1]

From Herder's chronotopical perspective, where time and place (*Zeitgeist* and *Lokalgeist*) are constitutive factors in culture and art, Shakespeare was far superior to the banal daylight settings of French classicist drama in some nondescript antechamber or boudoir. Herder's essay vividly depicts Shakespeare's rich, deep, intense atmosphere. Created through the special effects of dark, gloom, storm, heath, spooky castles, cemeteries, ominous birds, and supernatural phenomena such as witches and ghosts, this mood was designed to achieve maximum audience involvement, for the age subscribed to an aesthetic of affective impact. Literature, drama particularly, could and should change minds and souls and influence the shape of culture and the fate of nations. Shakespearean drama, it was believed, had helped make England great, whereas effete French classicist theater was the first step on the road to France's decline. If Herder's and even more so Goethe's Shakespeare essays sound derisory on the subject of French high culture, it was part of the campaign for a German national literature, for which emancipation from French dominance was a prerequisite.

The experience of Strasbourg, capital of the Alsatian frontier region, with its deliberate cultivation of German tradition and scorn for official French superstructure, helped awaken the fledgling dramatist's national consciousness. It was at Strasbourg, too, and under Herder's guidance that Goethe first developed an interest in German history. Latin tomes on legal history were part of his law studies. But he also studied the *Patriotic Fantasy* of a minor provincial official at Osnabrück, Justus Möser, on the beauties of the medieval legal system of *Faustrecht*, the right of the strongest. Möser's glorification of this law of the jungle fit right in with the young intellectuals' ideal of the powerful individual. When Goethe, back in Frankfurt, chanced upon the idiosyncratic autobiography of a German knight, who seemed the perfect embodiment of fist-law lifestyle, the spark flew that ignited his revolutionary drama, *Götz von Berlichingen*.

Yet *Götz* is more than a dramatized life story, as the title of the first version would indicate: *Geschichte Gottfriedens von Berlichingen mit der eisernen Hand, dramatisiert (History of Gottfried von Berlichingen with the Iron Hand).* It is the first historical drama in the modern sense of the term, for history itself is the true topic. Indeed the drama is about understanding the idea of history; it considers the question of the interaction of the individual with collective changes over time. It was a question Goethe found in Shakespeare, too, albeit under a more general cloak. At issue in Shakespearean drama he saw "the secret point (that no philosopher has yet seen or defined) where our individuality, our claim to free will, collides with the necessary course of the whole" (*HA,* 12:226).

Goethe's definition of history revises Herder's theological reading of Shakespeare from a secular perspective. For Herder, Shakespeare's drama represented a theodicy, an assertion of divine order within which the individual had a preassigned place; it showed "what we are in the hand of the creator of the world—ignorant, blind tools . . . dark little symbols of the outline of a divine theodicy."[2] For Goethe's historical drama, there is no preordained hierarchy of ideas; rather, there is a contest between the individual and the whole that must remain inconclusive, because we do not know the ultimate purpose of human existence. More astounding yet, there is in Goethe's view no absolute good or evil in history: "what we call evil is only the other side of good, each is a necessary part of the other's existence and of the whole" (HA, 12:227). His own drama gives glorious play to evil in the fascinating figure of Adelheid, the first femme fatale in German literature.

Götz von Berlichingen represents history as both a momentous whole and a highly particular event. The hero is at home in Franconia, Goethe's own home region. The region enters the play with its dialect and with its cities and towns, as the action moves between Würzburg, Bamberg, Nuremberg, Heilbronn, and the villages and castles engraved on regional consciousness through the events of the peasant war. (Even an upwardly mobile lawyer from Frankfurt appears, singing the praises of the new, "Roman," law.) But the moment that came with Goethe's hero was a key moment in German national history, too, and Goethe's text involves that horizon of the whole. Götz's time was an era of crisis and transition. It brought the Reformation and the permanent division of Germany into Protestant and Catholic parts. Social and economic divisions exploded with the first violent class conflicts in the peasant wars and the knights' revolt. The empire began to break apart into a loosely constituted league of principalities, fiefdoms, and free imperial cities, which still made up the Germany of Goethe's time. Goethe placed his drama at a point of origin of his own historical consciousness. And indeed the passionate engagement of the poet in his text bears out the author's quest for roots, for origins. In a letter to a paternal Strasbourg friend he revealed that in his drama he aimed for a deeper knowledge of "our ancestors, whom we know unfortunately only from their tombstones."[3]

More than presenting the past, Goethe's drama stages history as a theater of ideas in which hot topics of Goethe's own time are confronted and contested. Under this aspect Götz von Berlichingen is a powerful cultural critique, and the enthusiastic reception by Goethe's contemporaries is due in large measure to this feature. There was, first of all, the longing for vitality and heroism of an age that saw itself as weakened by overrefined rococo civilization. There was the dream of freedom before the era of revolutions could begin to develop definitions of freedom. There were questions of law and justice, of good and bad government, of religious versus secular claims, of class barriers and conflicts, of the will to power, and of generational and gender rights and responsibilities. Beyond transacting contemporary issues in historical guise, Goethe succeeded in bringing the dead ancestors to life. This achievement accounts for the play's enduring popularity in Germanophone countries. A drama, Goethe knew, could not just be a reproduction of history; it had to be a new, original creation inspired by the individuality of the poet. The Shakespeare speech decreed that the new Prometheus must "bring to life [his creatures] by breathing *his* spirit into them" (*Works*, 3:165; Goethe's emphasis). So Goethe treated his historical sources with creative liberty. The real Herr von Berlichingen died at the ripe old age of 82, his honor restored after several campaigns for the emperor from peasant war days and survived by seven sons and three daughters. (His descendants today manage the annual Götz festival at Jagsthausen.) Goethe's hero dies a premature death in prison, his only son becoming a monk. Symbolizing the end of an era and of an ideal, his life and his line end at the same time as the life of the "old Emperor." Here Goethe takes more poetic license: Emperor Maximilian died at age 60, before the peasant wars and more than 40 years before Berlichingen.

In addition to changing his sources, Goethe inserted into the historical lives of his characters his own poignantly personal experiences and fantasies. He invented the figures of Weislingen and the fatal Adelheid and around them created a subplot in the private sphere: a story of trust and betrayal, lust and temptation, desire and revenge. It was this invention that worked poetic magic on the *Götz* material, the magic we saw at work in Goethe's poetry of the time. The poetic imagination could charge up the dry historical data with the passion of lived experience and could transform a thoroughly pedestrian and not too truthful robber knight into a character of heroic stature and depth of soul that has made Götz a figure of identification for generations of Germans.

Finally, in *Götz von Berlichingen* history is not a tragedy. This is where Goethe's drama differs most notably from his model, Shakespeare, and where Herder's organicist vision asserts itself. Goethe called his second, published version of *Götz* a "Schauspiel": simply "drama." History is a natural process of growth and decay, and the end is implicit in the beginning; collective existence is in this respect no different from individual life. The dramatist's function is to describe, with empathy, the more or less satisfactory participation of individuals in the historical process into which they are placed by birth and circumstance. The real interest of the drama lies in playing out this participation of individuals: spectacular or middling, with variations of grace and beauty, wisdom and folly, blindness and insight. And the ending, steeped in melancholy with the death of the hero, yet assures us that life will go on, even if Götz's family and the empire do not. The analogy between the dying Götz and the falling leaves of autumn contains the knowledge that new leaves will grow in spring. When Götz's friends look out into the future, their words play on the knowledge that a later period in history— Goethe's own—will revive Götz's ideals precisely in this, Goethe's drama.

The first impression of this drama in the Shakespearean style is of chaos, or at least of anarchy: 23 named characters, plus 10 other individuals, plus another 10 groups (such as peasants, citizens, and gypsies) throng in a total of 56 scenes, some only a few lines long. Yet the profusion of actions and personnel is not arbitrary. The drama is structured so that its architecture represents the essential idea of the text: one historical era's supercession by another in a violent struggle. This central idea is the organizing principle of the dramatic action, of the scenic representation, and of the constellation of characters, as two different worlds and their conflicting values are embodied and acted out. Amazingly in light of the value-laden perspective, the two worlds receive almost equal time on stage. Yet they are not neatly separated into acts, nor is there a regular pattern of alternation. Instead the "good" world of Götz on the one hand and the "bad" world of the antagonist Weislingen on the other are confronted, interacting and interweaving within each of the five acts. As a result, the threat of conflict remains ever present; an atmosphere of foreboding sustains high tension and audience involvement.

Act 1 is evenly split between the two worlds, drawing the starting line for the contest: the first half introduces Götz's world, and the second half introduces Weislingen's world. In the second act, long Weislingen scenes alternate with short Götz scenes. The central third act focuses on Götz. His world dominates the scene, but his world becomes a conquest of the forces ranged around the antagonist Weislingen. Twenty-two scenes of embattled Götz crowd this act, followed by a mere five scenes in act 4. Of these scenes, Götz's world, defeated and deprived, gets four scenes whereas victorious Weislingen is allowed only one. The moment of retardation at this point in the drama is realized in relaxation, in moral and philosophical reflection, and in weighing options for future action.

The hyperactive act 5 is in extreme contrast to the slow fourth act. The two worlds explode into new dimensions. The conflict expands to draw new worlds into the fray, including warring peasants, gypsy outsiders, and a secret system of justice. Although Götz and Weislingen are about equally involved in these new worlds, with Götz having a slight dominance, they cede their place of prominence to what was previously hidden from their and our view. Infra- and superstructures emerge: the underbelly worlds of peasants, gypsies, and underground justice and the metaphysical realm represented in saintly Maria, Götz's sister and Weislingen's rejected bride, the one figure who can link the worlds and values of the two antagonists.

The extraordinary fifth act stages the end of the world. Acts 1 through 4 play out, on the basis of opposition between individuals, the conflict between two value systems and the supercession of two historical eras. Now forces beyond individuals, values, and history take over, forces that Goethe would later call "demonic," out of human control (HA, 10:177). In Goethe's view, demonic force could be defeated only by other demonic forces. In the fifth act, the peasant war unleashes unimaginable atrocity on both sides. It is this force that will destroy Götz. Weislingen falls victim to another demonic force: Adelheid's magic, the power of unfettered sexuality now exploding in a chain reaction of killings. The original version of the drama positively indulged in the Adelheid effect; the author himself, Goethe explained later, had been drawn into her demonic force field (HA, 9:571).

The apocalyptic vision of act 5 shows the world turned upside down ("if the world were turned around," Young Georg had quipped in act 4),[4] when the previously hidden is revealed. Lust of annihilation drives the peasant leaders and the leader of the opposing aristocrats, Weislingen. Unfettered sexual desire contaminates and kills Weislingen's servant Franz, Weislingen, and eventually Adelheid herself. The underbelly of the body politic shows up in the despised world of the gypsies and in the criminal court, which convenes at night in an underground location. For the final act is above all about judgment, just as the end of the world includes a Last Judgment. The final act includes five judgment scenes, plus constant questions of guilt, conscience, retribution, and vengeance. Quest of justice had been the original cause of the peasant war, but the just cause overturned into sheer vengeance.

In the first judgment scene (5.4), Götz's decision to lead the peasants is condemned by his own wife, Elisabeth. With Götz's man Lerse arguing for the defense, Elisabeth makes the case against Götz: he has broken his solemn promise, and he will never be able to forgive himself. Nor will his judges of peers forgive him, for the knight has betrayed his and their class. On the level of history, Götz's betrayal signifies the end of the feudal order. When knighthood, the foundation of this order, makes common cause with peasantry, knighthood abolishes its own world.

The second judgment scene (5.10) brings closure to the Weislingen plot in self-condemnation. Having been seduced to murder his master, servant Franz sentences himself and commits suicide. Weislingen sees divine retribution for his destructive life in his painful death by poison. Maria appears to her unfaithful fiancé as an avenging angel. The first in the long Goethean line of female redeemers, with such successors as Iphigenie and Faust's Gretchen, Maria nevertheless cannot offer Weislingen forgiveness, only forgetting. His crime is unforgivable, even before God: "Forget everything. May God forget everything you have done, as I forget everything you have done" (*Works*, 7:79).

The most spectacular judgment scene of all, which spawned a rich progeny in gothic dramas and novels, occurs when the secret court sentences Adelheid to death and dispatches the executioner. Whereas Weislingen found at least partial redemption, Adelheid is condemned absolutely. This court formalizes the need for redress in a world out of joint. The emphasis on ritual suggests that something still functions in the general dissolution, that basic values have remained. The anonymity of the masked court conveys impartiality, in contrast with the subjective motivations of the protagonists Adelheid, Weislingen, and Götz, with their finally destructive desires for power, ambition, and personal honor, respectively.

The last judgment, in the two concluding scenes, is passed on Götz, and it remains inconclusive. Formally sentenced to death, he is now pardoned by the arbitrary will of his archenemy, Weislingen, for the sake of his sister Maria. But Götz, in contrast with his self-righteous assurance after the trial at Heilbronn (4.5), judges himself severely. He has lost everything, including his good name. Although he still assigns blame elsewhere, to "them" ("They have crippled me more and more"), he yet acknowledges the judgment of God in his fate ("whomever God strikes down"). Twinned to the end to his antagonist, Weislingen, who also saw the hand of God in his downfall, Götz dies immediately after hearing of Weislingen's death, even with the same words: "my strength is sinking toward the grave." The close of the drama ultimately appeals to the judgment of posterity. We, the readers of Goethe's piece of special pleading, are called on, even threatened, to reverse the judgment of Götz's own time: "Woe to the century that spurned you! . . . Woe to coming generations that fail to understand you!" (*Works*, 7:80–82).

Egmont

Götz was written down in a flash of genius during six weeks in 1771, as Goethe proudly remembers in *Dichtung und Wahrheit*. *Egmont*, the other historical drama undertaken during the Frankfurt years, took far longer—12 years—as the author no less proudly wrote from Rome on its completion in 1787. No 12 years brought more decisive changes for Goethe. The writing of *Egmont* accompanied these changes in a way that would make the drama a crucial text for the reading of the author's life when he came to reflect on it from the vantage point of the autobiographer. *Dichtung und Wahrheit* closes with young Goethe departing for Weimar under the sign of *Egmont*. As he ventures forth into the unknown, he quotes the most famous passage of the drama he is just then writing, appropriating his hero's view of self and world in the metaphor of Time's chariot.[5]

The difference between *Götz* and *Egmont* measures the distance Goethe had traveled from carefree Sturm und Drang rebelliousness to the conflicts and compromises involved in government responsibility. The first drama, with its ancestor cult and nostalgic celebration of fist-law ideals, looks backward; the hero represents an era whose time had run out. Egmont, by contrast, the figure and the drama, explores an idea whose time was just dawning: freedom both as self-realization of the individual and as liberty in the political sense.

Where *Götz* in its search for origins narrowed the focus on Goethe's home province, the horizon of *Egmont* spans all of Western Europe, from the Netherlands to Germany, France, Italy, and Spain. Both dramas represent adjoining slices of the past: Götz's good old emperor (Maximilian I) was the father of Egmont's good old emperor (Charles V). But where *Götz* evokes the bygone time for its own sake, *Egmont* presents the past as a model for viewing the present and for looking out into the future, a lesson to be drawn from history. The drama ends with a vision of the goddess of freedom holding out the promise of liberation from Spanish repression for the United Provinces of the Netherlands, a struggle that took more than half a century to succeed. While Goethe was writing the bulk of his drama, from 1775 to 1782, the war of independence of the

Netherlands was being replayed, in fast-forward speed, by the American Revolution.

For *Egmont* is indeed theater of ideas as it explores and pits against each other in dramatic conflict the hottest ideas of the age, the ideas that were moving and making history. The late eighteenth century invented individualism and liberty as consequences of Enlightenment philosophy's call for personal autonomy. No one in Germany was more in tune with this project than the Sturm und Drang rebels. The restless young lawyer from the sleepy Imperial City of Frankfurt, acknowledged leader of the movement, could not help but get fired up by the rebellious ex-Europeans overseas. Immediately after the challenge laid down by the Continental Congress and passionately debated in the British Parliament (keeping in mind the speed at which news traveled in those days), Goethe announced his hatching of the *Egmont* plot: "I am getting everything prepared in order to begin, with the entry of the sun into aries, a new production, which shall have a tone all its own."[6]

It is no accident that of all the dramas of Goethe, whose genius he admired, Beethoven, the master of idea music, chose *Egmont* for his composition of incidental music and an overture. At the time of Beethoven's composition in 1809–1810, Austrians could well identify with the Flemish in Goethe's play. For the second time Vienna found itself invaded and occupied by Napoleon's armies, under miserable conditions. Beethoven's *Egmont* music, breathing the passion of freedom into Goethe's text, has been credited for the continuous success of this drama on stage all during the nineteenth century, much in contrast with the theatrical neglect of Goethe's other dramas.

Nor was the explosive force of ideas in *Egmont* lost on Goethe's contemporaries on the eve of the French Revolution. The Weimar friends reacted with acute discomfort; their objections to Klärchen's free morals covered deeper concerns. The duke, above all, was not happy with this result of the "untrammeled freedom of life and soul" his protégé was enjoying in Italy.[7] The position of a minister at an absolutist court, no matter how enlightened, was incompatible with the ideas expressed in *Egmont*. Goethe himself had realized this earlier, during the last phase of writing at Weimar: "If I had to write it today I would write it differently, and perhaps not at all."[8] With that, he stopped work on the drama, consigning it to the heap of fragments from his days in Frankfurt. *Egmont* needed the untrammeled freedom of the Italian sabbatical.

The drama takes a two-pronged approach to the representation of the power of ideas in history. One is to select a suitable episode from the past and shape it into a paradigmatic event, prefiguring significant aspects of the present. The other approach is to create a charismatic hero as carrier of the history-making idea: to invent a historical myth. The Sturm und Drang believer in the power of genius found it easy to imagine a charismatic hero. He had assembled a whole cast of such characters who had made history and around whom he was planning major works: Muhammad, Christ, Julius Caesar, and Egmont.

To the student of history just emancipated from Christianity, it was obvious that a most effective power in history was martyrdom. Three of the four heroes he selected had been killed for their cause. The author of *Götz von Berlichingen,* who had meanwhile witnessed the astounding success of his flawed hero, knew all about mythmaking. In *Götz,* the construction of a legend was a matter of ancestor worship, of paying respect to past glory. In *Egmont,* the creation of a hero myth drives and organizes the drama, determining structure, character constellation, and the main events insofar as they are not preset by history. Not that Goethe hesitated to change history for the benefit of his mythical hero. He needed one outstanding figure, and so he simply deleted Count Hoorn, who shared Egmont's fate. And for the role his hero had to play he could not use the historical Egmont: middle-aged, portly, and balding, a married man with a dozen children. He needed a figure in splendid isolation, unattached and undefined. Such a figure could assume the meaning conveyed on him by the people, who needed him as a symbol of their ideal selves, embodying their hopes and dreams. So the drama constructs a mythic hero, a knight in shining armor.

The perspective of the paradigmatic event came with Goethe's position at Weimar. Moving in the circle of power politics and gaining a close-up view of major players, he could think himself for a while at least an active participant in the making of history. In early Weimar days the duke's closest adviser proudly writes in terms of his drama-in-progress: "We [the duke and I] had lots of good talk about past and future. Makes me feel like Margrete von Parma: I, too, foresee a lot that I can't change."[9] A little later *Egmont* served to stylize the games the German princes played during the Bavarian succession conflict of 1778, with Goethe and his duke in attendance at Berlin: "I seem to be getting ever closer to the essence of drama, now that it concerns me more and more closely how the mighty play with men and the gods with the mighty."[10]

The hero is not the only auratic figure; the duke of Alba, his antagonist, also is. Goethe's epoch had made exemplary tyrants of Alba and his master, King Phillip of Spain. Lovers of liberty—philosophers, Protestants, and future revolutionaries—were expected to abhor them. Witness Schiller's *Don Carlos* (1785–1787) and the historical work that earned him a professorship at Jena, *Geschichte des Abfalls der vereinigten Niederlande von der Spanischen Regierung* (*The Secession of the United Netherlands from the Spanish Crown*, 1788). Schiller's first work in the historical genre had been the translation of an essay on Phillip of Spain by the later French Revolutionary delegate Louis Sébastien Mercier. For Mercier, Phillip's reign is the incarnation of evil government. Repelled by his "superstitious and terrible despotism [and] cruel character," the author aims to "spread far and wide the revulsion which has seized me." Against such tyranny the revolt of the Netherlands is hailed as a paradigmatic "revolution which compelled the astonishment of Europe."[11]

Concerning form, too, *Egmont* has come a long way from *Götz,* from drama as realistic presenting of the past to drama as a play of symbols, as symbolic action. Despite the blank verse adopted for *Iphigenie* and *Tasso,* the other dramas of the Weimar–Italian period, Goethe left *Egmont* in prose, but it is no longer the realistic, dialect-flavored prose of *Götz.* In *Egmont,* language is formalized, equalized. All characters speak alike: foreigners and native Dutch, simple soldiers, burghers, and high nobility. Gone, too, is the seemingly arbitrary structure. The five acts are built from few large scenic units. A pattern of recurring scenes with significant changes plays variations on a theme. Every act except the third begins with a scene of citizens. The first three acts conclude with a scene of Egmont's lover Klärchen, who after complete absence from act 4 opens and closes the fifth act in a metamorphic progression toward transcendence. The dramatic architecture is suggestive of musical composition. Considering Klärchen's songs, Egmont's prison monologues, and the triumphant conclusion, Schiller was not so far off when he saw this drama pass into opera (Wagener, 86). *Egmont* is Goethe's *Eroica.*

A historical myth needs two constituent components. One is a figure suitable as carrier of an idea; the other is a situation of exceptional urgency to provoke the elevation of an average individual to heroic stature. The dramatic process of *Egmont* explores these two facets: One is the construction of Egmont as carrier of the idea of freedom, which in turn forges the people's identity as future carriers of revolution. For the second component, the drama investigates the kind of power that might generate a spirit of resistance, revolution, and freedom.

The nature of power is explored from several perspectives. We observe different levels of government in practice: the distant center in Spain and its projections on-site through various agents: the regent

Margarete von Parma, the provincial governor Egmont, and the military executor Alba. Extensive dialogue on matters political undergirds practice with theory to demonstrate the mechanism of centralized, totalitarian government. The deteriorating relation of rulers and ruled is evident in the citizen scenes. Because the eventual result is revolution, the workings of the governing apparatus are slanted in such a way as to intimate their ultimately self-destructive quality. Actions, reactions, and reflections on the nature of power meet in the figure of Egmont. Participant, critic, and victim, he yet finally defeats the power that kills him.

The first act builds up the charismatic hero from three different perspectives. In the community ritual of the first scene, citizens and soldiers unite to profess themselves Egmont's constituency. He embodies their ideal selves and their civic desire for religious tolerance. Explicit myth-making occurs in a soldier's battle narrative with Egmont the heroic figure of national identity, when "we amphibious Dutch" slaughtered "the Welsh [equals French] dogs" (*Works,* 7:86). Music shares in mythmaking as the scene concludes with a chant in four-part harmony of civic ideals, culminating in "Freedom!" (*Works,* 7:89). The second scene, set in the regent's palace, views Egmont from the angle of threatened power. Against the regent's fear of conspiracy, revolt, and retribution from the distant power center, Egmont's provocative behavior stands out as an enigma that teases interpretation. With her effort to understand Egmont, Margarete adds an aura of mystery to the emerging hero myth. The third scene, at Klärchen's modest bourgeois home, opens with Klärchen's soldiers song, in which Egmont figures, if unnamed, as ideal ego. Continuing the mystification of Egmont, Klärchen's central question is how "the great Egmont," whom all the Provinces idolize, can be at the same time "simply a man, a friend, and a lover?" (*Works,* 7:96–97). Finally, a real image of Egmont is introduced when Klärchen describes a woodcut of the battle of Gravelingen. The naive imagination in this piece of folk art represents a hero imago: Egmont is as big as the city tower and the British ships.

The two long scenes of the second act expose the drama's twin focus: the prerevolutionary situation and the hero myth. Scene 1 presents the genesis of an abortive revolution. Ideas abound on civil rights, rule of law, equal treatment of citizens, constitution, and freedom of thought and religion, but these ideas are contested among the people whom they should unite. Instead of the four-part harmony in act 1 we hear a cacophony of voices clamoring for "privileges and freedom!" (*Works,* 7:103). Uninformed, uncommitted, divided by self and group interests, the people are easily swayed by the demagogue Vansen. And the situation is not yet pressing enough. Only Jetter, the proverbially timid tailor, feels the oppression in nightmares and forbidden thoughts inspired by the cruel and unusual punishments executed for public intimidation. The right ideas have not yet found the right representative. Egmont proves himself the right leader, but he still stands for the wrong idea of submitting to force. A decent citizen, he argues, always has as much freedom as he needs (*Works,* 7:103). Egmont's words are enough to put down the riot, but they fall far short of an answer to the urgent issues raised in this scene.

The second scene, staging self-portrayal, completes the image of Egmont outlined by others in act 1: the hero assumes their image of him. Prodded by his anxious secretary, Egmont defines an ethos of individualism. Goethe has given his hero memorable metaphors for his self-definition: the sleepwalker on the roof, the warrior storming a mountain peak, the dizzying charioteer of time. Such images, with their indomitable courage, zest for life, self-confidence, and drive for maximum fulfillment of individual potential, impress us, Goethe's modern readers, who were raised on the individualist ideology. From other perspectives—the "pedestrian" Secretary's (*Works,* 7:108) and chess player Oranien's—such a view appears foolhardy, reckless, and lacking foresight. The confrontation with Oranien drives home the difference between politician and hero. Oranien, as one citizen remarked in the opening scene, would be a safe place to hide, but no one wants to be like this calculating realist. By contrast, Egmont is what everyone wants to be like: a hero fantasy, emblem of our ideal selves.

The third act continues the dual themes of the political and the personal but in a different register, contrasting power and love. The first scene presents a scathing critique of power from one of the power holders, as the regent Margaret of Parma reads the hidden truth in a letter from her brother, King Phillip, that announces the arrival of Alba. Imperialist despotism, in her reading, is a system of government that dehumanizes everyone it touches. Power sharers like herself are instrumentalized, mere tools to be thrown out when used up. The governed people are viewed as cannibals, animals, or monsters to be tamed or exterminated. Perfect servants are bestialized: Alba types thrive because they can gratify their sadistic lust by having citizens "racked, burnt, hanged, drawn and quartered" (*Works,* 7:115). A spooky atmosphere haunts this scene as the regent imagines the past and the future, with herself a "ghost" of lost power. Egmont's antagonist, the "hollow-eyed

Toledan" (*Works,* 7:115), is built up to make a stark contrast with the beloved lover Egmont of the next scene.

For this scene (3.2) stages the epiphany of the hero. Here, in opposition to the haunting absences in the circle of power, reigns the irreducible presence of love. Egmont appears to Klärchen in heroic splendor—dazzling court dress, Golden Fleece emblem of highest honor —yet the effect is not distancing but the intimacy of love. The two women represent the contrast between power and love: the regent, captive of power, against Klärchen, liberated through love. Klärchen's opening song sets this theme. And the scene closes with a restatement of the theme when Egmont contrasts his two selves: one captive of his public role in the sphere of power, the other free in the love of Klärchen.

The fourth act moves relentlessly toward darkness and death. The figure of Alba grows into a countermyth, so that the confrontation with Egmont takes shape as a mythic struggle between good and evil. The citizens in scene 1 initiate the mythification of Alba, whom they depict as huge cat and poisonous spider, and his soldiers as a satanic machinery of irresistible force. The second scene, in Alba's palace, shows the perfect machinery of military enforcement in action. Blind obedience and total secrecy hold the supreme commander in awe-inspiring distance. When he finally steps on stage, he appears as an auratic figure with a dark halo. The confrontation with this Alba compels Egmont to define himself as his antagonist and to become, finally, the representative of the right ideas, the hero image that the Dutch people need to sustain their revolt.

The Alba–Egmont debate on political theory works on ideas that Goethe's era saw in the Netherlands' rebellion: power relations and types of government, the people as permanently infantile or coming of age, and individual freedom and responsibility or historical necessity. The highlight falls on freedom, as Alba challenges Egmont to define it: "Freedom? a fine word, if only one could understand it! What kind of freedom do they want?" (*Works,* 7:132). The citizens' scenes already answered that question. Even if the people may not know what freedom means in the abstract, they know what it is not: everything that Alba's rule has imposed on them.

Now that the Egmont myth has been defined, act 5 installs it as a moving force in history. An emotionally intense performance of the hero's death creates a martyr, and a vision anticipates the history to be driven by the myth. The opening scene presents a people emasculated by fear, their cowardice shamed by a woman, Klärchen, whom they in turn have to declare crazy to preserve their conviction of their helplessness. Yet the scene plays on two myths to intimate that all is not lost. Both the biblical story of Peter's denial ("Don't mention that name. It's deadly," *Works,* 7:136) and the historical myth of Joan of Arc (Klärchen as "floating banner . . . leading warriors," *Works,* 7:137) promise future redemption of the people from their abjection. Klärchen's suicide is not cast in terms of lost love but as a choice of liberty or death ("Egmont's freedom or death!" *Works,* 7:136). Yet although her death prefigures Egmont's, doubling the death of the hero, death for Klärchen means the end of hope, the end of time; for her, "the world comes to a sudden stop" (*Works,* 7:143) with the death of Egmont.

Egmont, by contrast, moves beyond hopelessness to a view of the future that envisages freedom and thus imparts meaning to his death. The victim turns into sacrifice. Ferdinand, Alba's son, is crucial to achieve this turn. Earlier, in his first monologue, Egmont was a private individual deprived of freedom, in prison. He reacted with fear of death and with the illusory hope of being freed by the people. Ferdinand's proclaiming Egmont his lodestar changes all that. The son of the despot lifts Egmont out of his private grief by reminding him of his public role. Ferdinand's rejecting his father and instead choosing Egmont's distant image as model demonstrates the power of myth. This victory of the symbol "Egmont" over "Alba" enables the victory vision at the end of the drama. On a conscious level Egmont has no hope that his death might liberate his people: "I fear it won't be so" (*Works,* 7:149). Only on a subconscious level, in a dream or vision, can he imagine such an outcome. The magnificent spectacle of virtual reality, complete with supernatural lighting and music, of the goddess of freedom crowning the hero, who, drawn into his own vision, marches to death as into battle at the head of his nation, has become the defining mark of this Goethean drama. Condemned by Schiller as a *salto mortale* into opera, it yet was undoubtedly the spark that inspired Beethoven's music.

Chapter Four

Problematic Subjectivity:
Die Leiden des jungen Werthers

The most extraordinary thing about Goethe's first effort in fiction, *Die Leiden des jungen Werthers*,[1] might well be its reception. When *Werther* burst on the scene in 1774 it became the first German work to break into world literature. Translated a year later into French, the culturally dominant language, and in 1779 into English, the dominant language of the novel, *Werther* made his author a European celebrity overnight. The impact of the work, a very short novel by eighteenth-century standards, was not limited to literature. How many suicides could in fact be chalked up to the Werther effect will have to remain in doubt, despite a rash of contemporary attributions. But there can be no doubt that *Werther* became a cult book among the young, who donned the Werther costume—yellow trousers and blue coat—and indulged in the pleasures of sentiment. Another first in the annals of German literature was the controversy the book stirred up immediately, creating strange bedfellows among its attackers. Religious orthodoxy united with pietism and with the traditional opponent of both, Enlightenment ideology, in the war against *Werther* to produce a flood of instant secondary literature, including moralistic parodies.

The title holds one of the keys to the *Werther* success story. Featuring a young man, "*Young* Werther," written by a young man, this is a book of the young. *Young* might be said to stand in for Werther's first name. Everyone in the book goes by first names—Lotte, Albert, Wilhelm—but Werther has no given name, except perhaps Young. The young who are the subject of this novel are in their 20s, in the transition period from adolescence to adulthood, when the most critical decisions have to be made about one's life. It is here that the course must be set for career, love and family relations, and sexual, social, and political orientation, here that future happiness or unhappiness is determined. Here, an individual's *life* is at stake. Young Werther's brief story engages all of these generational issues, with high emotional intensity and with a challenging degree of intellectual sophistication.

A second key lies in the innovative form. Although the epistolary novel had long been a popular genre, Werther's monologic letters created a new position for the reader. I, the reader, not the fictional correspondent, Wilhelm, who never enters the text on his own, am the true addressee. I become the confidant of this fascinating person at risk: a nonconformist with provocative ideas about all aspects of life, who walks his talk right up to the edge, and who steps across the edge in a freely willed suicide. We can compare the intended reader's position to that of the fascinated viewer in today's mediate intimacy of soul-baring television talk shows. And, as with the talk shows, I, the spectator/reader, am free of responsibility or guilt for the character's fate. For Goethe/Werther goes to great lengths to prevent any possibility of intervention from the recipient of the letters. Because we are also kept uninformed about Wilhelm's reactions to his friend's vicissitudes, we remain free to simply enjoy Young Werther's sufferings.

The emphasis on the pleasure of the text, the seduction performed by the text on the reader through vicarious suffering, becomes most visible in the suicide topic. The touchy subject is raised quite early, when Werther and Albert debate the pros and cons of suicide along rational lines of argument, leaving the reader free to agree or disagree with either side. This argument was not what worried the critics who warned against the suicide propaganda of *Werther.* The real danger came toward the end, in the extended suicide note, the long farewell letter of 21–22 December addressed not to Wilhelm but to the impossible beloved, Lotte, who has finally revealed herself as Werther's loving soul mate. We, the readers, trained to be Werther's distant addressees, now find ourselves in the lover's, Lotte's, close position. We are still free of the obligation to act, because *we* (with Lotte) will receive this letter only after it is too late, but we cannot escape the obligation to participate emotionally in the final experience of someone we love. Werther's glorification of his will to die, and still more his romancing his death in an idyll of graveyard grass undulating in the setting sun (74), far outweighs the harsh impact of the editor's curt report of botched suicide and shamed burial (*Works,* 11:86–87).

The captivating power of *Werther* goes beyond the emotional effect of a friend at risk of suicide. Goethe has endowed his hero with the kind of interesting mind whose thoughts we would most love to share: a mind that focuses and experientially tests for us the burning issues of his day. It is above all this philosophical aspect of Goethe's first novel that continues to hold scholarly interest. In the frame of intellectual history

Werther marks the difficult threshold between Enlightenment and its crisis, variously known as critical philosophy (Kant and the consequences),
romanticism, the age of revolution, or modern subjectivity.

The central question posed in *Werther* is the problem of secularization: What happens if other values—the feeling self, nature, love—are
substituted for religion and endowed with religion's claim to absolute
status? It is with his choice of substitutes that Goethe's novel ushers in
romanticism. Derived from the Sturm und Drang ethos of genius,
Werther is a giant of feeling who upsets Enlightenment's golden mean
between reason and sentiment. For Werther, feeling is living, and subjective emotions *(heart)* constitute the self; reason, precisely because it is
shared with others, counts for nothing. Nature's pretended immediacy
to the self leads to the romantic phenomenon of *pathetic fallacy,* as the
contrastive letters of 10 May and 18 August reveal. In Werther's love,
the organizing concept of the novel, we can trace the origins of "romantic" love. Other features commonly associated with romanticism include
the new ideal of the child. In provocative opposition to the Enlightenment ideal of autonomous man, authentic man in Werther's book is the
child. Kant's clarion call for "egress from self-imposed child status" in
his 1784 essay "Was ist Aufklärung?" ("What Is Enlightenment?") is
also a rebuttal of *Werther.* Finally, embedded in Werther's impossible love
as in all his approaches to life, we find that ubiquitous characteristic of
romantic humanity, *Sehnsucht,* the never-ending, objectless longing that,
from Hegel to Lacan and beyond, has placed desire at the center of
human nature.

If we add to these hallmarks of romantic man Werther's passivity
("Leiden") over action of the Faustian type, the emphasis on imagination
over reason as defining the life of the spirit, and the temptation offered
by violence and madness, we then realize that Goethe's novel is a quest
for human nature, for the human condition. With leitmotivic insistence,
Werther keeps asking: What is man? The loss of religious certitude and
the rejection of Enlightenment assurances have put in question man's
place in the cosmic and spiritual world order. Goethe's *Werther* is a radical critique of the eighteenth-century way of viewing the world but does
not yet have the answers to its radical questions. That is why Werther's
life evolves into failure from all angles and why living is finally impossible for him: he has to commit suicide. Werther is a figure of essential
lack, the lack experienced by the transitional generation—post-
Enlightenment and preromanticism—of Goethe's young manhood. We
have since learned that it is a lack relived in any period of transition, the

destabilizing effect of the no-longer–not-yet, of the ever more frequent passage from the relative security of a cultural home to a new cultural situation brought about by historical change.

Inevitably, given its threshold position between the feudal eighteenth and the bourgeois nineteenth centuries, *Werther* offers an early critique of bourgeois culture that resonates still today. Yet here Goethe's hero remains caught in ambivalence. Not a revolutionary, Werther consents to and benefits from, yet on the other hand chafes against, the rules and conventions of his society, including class barriers, marriage and family bonds, sexual mores, rules of the workplace, career path to and definition of success, and bourgeois morality in toto—in short, the entire web of responsible adult behavior. There is more than a fleeting resemblance to the rebels without a cause of later times who have become myths in their own right: turned-off, tuned-out symbols of protest for successive generations, such as the Beatniks, James Dean, the flower children and hippies, and a more recent suicide victim from the alternative culture, grunge musician Kurt Cobain.

In the aesthetic of the novel, *Werther* broke new ground. Particularly in its original version this brief "Büchlein"—in the dedicatory word of the editor—flouted the prolix mode of the contemporary novel. The innovative monologic structure nevertheless offers a variety of text types. The editor's comments and reports contrast most strongly with Werther's letters, but the letters themselves vary considerably in their generic character. Werther calls attention to this variance with his remark that one of the earliest letters (17 May) is "quite factual" (i.e., narrative), in contrast with his more habitual outpourings of inner life (i.e., lyrical). The lyrical letters in turn vary among meditation, reflection, effusion of feeling, and imagining. But there is also the sarcastic polemic or satire, the brief vignette or flash of a single thought. Most innovative are the dream and memory texts, which point to the novel's deep structure at the symbolic and unconscious level.

If Werther strikes us as irrational, it is obviously because he is conceived of as an anti-Enlightenment figure. More interestingly, though, he appears irrational because crucial events of his story take place on "the other scene" of the unconscious, as we have come to know that aspect of human existence withdrawn from the light of reason and the freedom of will. Goethe has planted large signposts pointing to this other scene with a plethora of symbolic events, characters, seasons, times, and so forth. There is almost nothing in *Werther* that is not symbolic, that does not also signify on another than the surface level of the narrative—from the telling name of his elective village, *Wahlheim,* to the felled walnut trees and the flood in the beloved valley; the changing cult books from Homer and Klopstock to Ossian; from harvesting fruit with Lotte to passing Albert's pistols through her hands as a gift of death, but, in association with Last Supper symbolism, of communion beyond death.

Breaking new ground, with *Werther* Goethe created a new and immensely fertile genre: autobiographical fiction. Overemphasizing the autobiographical has been a tendency of *Werther* criticism from the outset. Goethe's own Lotte in the love triangle at Wetzlar and his self-dramatizing letters of the post-Wetzlar period have tempted critics to construct from the published Werther letters a figure of the author in the image of his sentimental, romantic, would-be passionate reader, who loved to flirt with existential tragedy. To counteract the autobiographical temptation it is useful to remember young Jerusalem, Werther's real-life model, whose character and story provided far more than the suicide account.[2] In Werther, then, agglomerating self with other, Goethe composed a wholly new person, a self from self critical distance: a self not myself (Boyle 1991, 1:166–67). There is perhaps no surer sign of Goethe's mastery than that his creation, Werther, should carry such an overpowering imprint of authenticity that the figure and his texts have been so consistently misread as authentic.

In the context of Goethe's writing, *Werther* is contemporary with the Great Hymns, reflecting and refracting their themes, predominantly in a contrastive mode. Even the Hymn most closely related to *Werther, Ganymed (Works,* 1:30–31), with its ecstatic nature immediacy, works out a contrast. Ganymedes achieves mystical union with nature, whereas Werther's enthusiasm is debunked as pathetic fallacy. Within the productive chaos of the Frankfurt years, *Werther* highlights the dangers of selfhood, of the ideology of genius so ardently espoused by the Sturm und Drang avant-garde. Presented as exciting challenge in the Hymns, the risk involved in radical subjectivity is taken to the limit in *Werther.* Here a self founders and is wrecked on his own terms, on the very principles of subjectivity. In *Werther,* too, the mythology of self in the Hymns, in which the subject projects himself onto great figures of the past, is displaced by a real-life setting. The struggle for selfhood must be carried out by a representative, average individual in the here and now: in late-eighteenth-century, small-town, provincial Germany, Goethe's Germany. And precisely from this relentless realism derives the devastating impact of the novel's judgment on selfhood.

Goethe, however, has built one exemption into his shattering verdict on radical subjectivity: Werther is not an artist. For this reason, too, the novel is the story of Werther's "Leiden": sufferings, passion (or Passion) in passivity, reactive not active. It is not enough for survival to be a genius of feeling, it takes a productive genius, a creator—such as Prometheus, Muhammad, or the wanderer of the Hymns. Werther, as he keeps telling us in so many words, fails in his efforts to create. He can draw a nice picture, but he cannot put forth on paper what really goes on in his soul. Goethe has placed Werther's insufficient talent in the area of his own secondary artistic endeavor, painting. His experience had taught him clearly enough that to survive he had to translate feelings into creations, into texts.

The division in books 1 and 2, with the dividing line when Werther leaves Lotte supposedly forever, signals a correspondence between the two halves of Werther's story. The second half is a rerun of the first in an intensified mode, which finally takes Werther's life to its logical consequence: catastrophe and self-annihilation. (To get the point of this consequence, we need to read *suicide* in *Werther*'s original language: it is *Selbstmord*, or *self-murder*, a word that reverberates with associations missing from *suicide*.) The material of book 1 develops in three stages, taking Werther from solitude (4–30 May) through blissful twosomeness with Lotte (16 June–26 July) into the conflict-laden triangle with Albert (30 July–10 September).

Werther's letters of May, in springtime and solitude, offer an ample self-portrait: his moods, his views of life, the world, nature, and society, and his attitudes and behavior toward others. Key concepts and experiences of this exposition seem to announce a psychological novel that dissects the sickness unto death of a manic-depressive man (see, for symptoms, 13 May). The bulk of the text, however, depicts the illusionary hermitage of someone who reenacts a mythic past inspired by Homer and the Old Testament and who constructs a greater self through the powers of imagination, including the attempt to appropriate a simple peasant's authentic passion. The height of self-deception, and at the same time its ultimate failure, is reached in the letter of 10 May, with its ecstatic celebration of nature. The reader is enchanted with the authentic sound of Werther's enthusiasm, too charmed to notice the disillusioning frame Goethe has supplied. This letter is the confession of a would-be artist who finds himself suffocated by overpowering impressions because he cannot translate them into artistic expression: "But it

will destroy me, I shall perish under the splendor of these visions!"
(*Works*, 11:6).

Another letter, toward the end of Werther's solitude (22 May), tran-
scends the quotidian in an existential moment to ask the thematic question after the human condition. Out of the blue right after a chatty letter ("nothing but a report") about sundry meaningless acquaintances,
Werther tells us "that the life of man is only a dream" (*Works*, 11:20).
He develops this thought in a brief essay of imaginative power and per-
suasive skill that makes us wish Werther had, like Goethe, picked writing instead of painting as his field of artistic endeavor. The upshot of the
meditation is profound skepticism—is Werther really as unaware of his
self-delusion as we are led to believe?—and the first anticipation of the
end: man is always free to quit "this prison" of his deplorable condition.

Overall, Werther's letters in the solitary phase propose a set of opposites to the real-life conditions of an urban, middle-class, educated
young man who is bored with love, family, friends, work, and cultural
and intellectual life—in short, with social intercourse with members of
his class. Werther anticipates by a century the ennui of the late-
nineteenth-century dandy. He regales us with some pithy put-downs of
bourgeois philistinism and workaholism (26 May) and offers in opposition a string of pleasant idylls. We see the hero enthroned as benign
patriarch who eradicates class differences with servant girls at the well
(12 and 15 May); holding court in the village square and playing the
absent father's role with mom and kids (26 and 27 May); and immediately preceding the account of his own star-struck encounter with Lotte,
vicariously relishing the true—because natural—erotic desire of a peasant lad (30 May).

Yet Goethe has posted warning signs for us not to be taken in by
Werther's escapist fantasies. From the outset we are told that Werther is
running away from erotic complications at home. He makes no secret of
his self-pity and his self-pampering, though tinged with irony in the
diminutive form of that signifier for subjectivity, "heart": "I treat my little heart ["Herzchen"] like a sick child, and gratify its every fancy" (13
May). Immediately after the would-be artist's hopes in his communion
with nature are dashed (10 May), Werther introduces the first narrative
of his idyll at the well with a significant reference to deception. Deceived
either by spirits ("deceiving spirits") or by his own imagination ("fancy
in my own heart"), he felt in "paradise" (12 May). The most distinctive
mark of escapism and anachronism, of the pretense of living a Homeric

life in the age of coffee (which Goethe detested), occurs in the midst of the village idyll of 26 May under the motto "enjoying my coffee and my Homer."

The existential letter of 22 May states a program for the blissful yet illusionist love episode. With Lotte, Werther will live his dream, the dream, as the letter maintains, that is no different from life. Because he, not being an artist, cannot represent his dream—he can apprehend his inner life "more in intimation and dark desire than in representation and living force"—he must perform it in reality. Lacking creative power, he needs a model to live his dream: Homer and the *Vicar of Wakefield* for idyllic contentment, Klopstock for depth of emotion, and, dominant much later but already emerging from Werther's inner world, Ossian for uncontrollable passion.

Among the illusionists in pursuit of happiness, Werther selects for his model the children, who demand instant gratification of their gluttonous desires: "These are certainly happy creatures" (*Works,* 11:10). Werther's watchword for playing child is *carpe diem:* do not think of tomorrow and above all forget that you are *playing* at covetous child. When opportunity presents an object for Young Werther's desire, at a ball complete with thunder and lightning (Goethe's French has taught him the meaning of *coup de foudre*), he falls for Lotte and for love head over heels. In the letters of 16 and 19 June, Goethe gives us a model falling-in-love narrative. His artful tale, which represents inner processes through outer events, makes the inner events seem natural and thus inevitable. Emotion occurs and intensifies in synchrony with the dynamic of motion. The first movement reveals two kindred minds through dialogue in a carriage ride, the second movement brings bodies in touch and harmony during the dance, and the third movement climaxes and releases the mind–body tension in the violent thunderstorm. The reference to "Klopstock!" at this moment ought to remind the entranced reader that these two figures are also acting on another scene: they are performing literary models.

Writing the story and reliving the scenes in memory, Werther succeeds in completely inserting himself into his dreamworld: he invents himself as a hero in a love story. When he starts his narrative on 16 June he is not yet sure about the meaning of the encounter with Lotte: "I have—I don't know." He ends with a willing suspension of reality, in the enthusiastic voice of a reckless dreamer who no longer cares about real time and the real world: "And since that time sun, moon, and stars may pursue their course: I know not whether it is day or night; the whole world about me has ceased to be" (19 June). To protect his illusionist happiness, Werther will go in for rationalization. Because he is playing child he confers the highest value on the child as the true model of humanity (29 June, 6 and 8 July). By the same token, he devalues work and career in words that have sounded utterly reasonable to generations of young readers skeptical of adult definitions of success (20 July). Because desire for Lotte must remain ungratified, Werther, reflecting on the enigma of desire in his Homeric safe place among "his" peas and cabbages, decides that it—*Sehnsucht* (longing)—is by definition unsatisfiable (21 June).

But reality insists on asserting itself over the idyll of wish fulfillment. The mind game of literary–erotic rapture is threatened as the physical side of desire emerges with increasing urgency. The tale of the melancholic fiancé at the vicarage serves as a forewarning (1 July). Here Werther meets and berates his own future self, afflicted with uncontrolled passion, which is for the first time likened to physical illness. Mounting desire (10 July) gets a brief reality check with Albert's name (13 July) but reaches a climax that threatens to overwhelm willpower. Only the "magic power of music" can, for the moment, restore balance, but the turbulence of passion has become life threatening. Often, we hear, Werther is in a mood of utter gloom, ready to blow his brains out (16 July). Love for Lotte has become life threatening in other respects, too. Werther has lost the will and the ability to act; he passes his days passively in waiting for Lotte; he recognizes the persistent temptation to be with her for the danger that it is, but he cannot resist. The paralysis that has seized him appears in a significant sign: he has lost whatever artistic skill he possessed (24 July).

Life with Lotte concludes with a brief memory text that encapsulates in stark clarity the terminal nature of Werther's condition. The grandmother's fairy tale of the magnetic mountain forebodes disintegration and annihilation of self (26 July). It is the last of three death notices in the second segment of Werther's letters. Their explicit violence stands in strong contrast with the "sweet feeling" of liberty by suicide found in the philosophical musings of the earlier period (22 May).

In the third segment of book 1, from Albert's arrival to Werther's departure, death becomes an obsession. Paralysis of the will is the most immediate signal. Werther's instant reaction to Albert's arrival is to leave (30 July), but it takes him more than a month to do so. Even though he sees his untenable situation clearly, he cannot make the decision he knows is necessary. Torn by conflicting desires, he rejects the idea of free choice (either–or) as rationalistic idealization and instead offers the explanatory model of illness, of a material disability (8 August). This model, "sickness unto death," dominates his thinking from then on. The self-declared sufferer from the disease of indecision reacts with aggression. He lashes out at Lotte ("die Weiber"—denigrating word for *women*—want to hold onto their admirers; 30 July), at their ludicrous triangle (30 July and 10 August), but most savagely at himself. He finally needs physical hurt and self-laceration for relief (30 August). The disease reaches into Werther's very core to overturn his two strongest passions, for nature and for Lotte, from positive into negative forces. The letter of 18 August, which laments how nature now affects him as a monstrous power of destruction, is one of the lyrical high points of the novel. There is surprisingly little text on his feelings for Lotte, which indicates how Werther tries to suppress conscious desire. Desire, however, slips by the controls into disturbing dreams (21 August) and enigmatic symbols: throwing flowers in the river (10 August) and harvesting fruit (28 August, his and Goethe's birthday). The effort of repression finally explodes into violence against himself (30 August) and forces the decision to leave Lotte ("I must get away," repeatedly, 3 September).

The obsession with death structures the two high points of this text segment: the debate on suicide (12 August) and the leave-taking scene (10 September). It is Werther who brings up the issue of suicide for debate. Against the judgmental argument of lawyer Albert, he takes two deliberately provocative and contradictory stances: one of empathy with the sufferer from incurable passion, and the other of applause for the heroism of suicide. An altogether different mood suffuses the leave-taking episode. The topic of death reigns supreme, with obsession turning into attraction, as love and death fuse in "romantic" symbiosis. In this setting, "as romantic as any" (*Works,* 11:39) designed to evoke death, in the moonlight that always makes her think of death, Lotte takes over the text. Rising from near silence as Werther had tried to suppress his love and her voice, she now does all the talking, and she talks only of death. It is death in the guise of her beloved dead mother, whose figure and function Lotte now assumes. For Werther, from now on death and the beloved will beckon as one, for Lotte has become his signifier of death. With the promise of a transcendent "We shall meet again" (*Works,* 11:41), his gaze follows her white-clad figure as it vanishes down the ever-narrowing path between the dark rows of trees.

The replay in book 2 begins with Werther's escape attempt and return to Lotte (20 October–18 June), followed by another episode of togetherness until Werther's letters run out (29 July– 6 December) and the editor takes over to report the final catastrophe. The first segment, life away from Lotte, supplies what was missing from book 1: how Werther came to run away from his place in society. Here we find a scathing critique of bourgeois existence: of work in a hierarchically constricted bureaucracy and of the class friction between ambitious commoners and threatened aristocrats. But Werther's problem is special. The hero of subjectivity refuses to adjust to the rules and conventions of work and society, yet wants to be accepted and respected by the very people he so thoroughly despises. It is this ambivalence that leads to failure and flight. A true nonconformist would not care what others said about his social faux pas. Werther reacts with extraordinary verbal violence. He gnashes his teeth (a first of many such gestures of suppressed aggression), needs to see blood, and fantasizes about stabbing the rejecting others or himself (15 and 16 March).

The death theme, hidden beneath the surface bustle of urban life, emerges in a moment of solitude with the memory of Lotte. The only letter addressed to her besides the long suicide note speaks in a haunting image of spiritual death. Life is not a dream but a puppet show in which we are all played by some alien force. We have self-consciousness merely to realize that life is a puppet show and our fellow humans, like ourselves, are dead souls (20 January). When Werther leaves this show, quitting work and society once more to cast himself adrift, he drifts ineluctably back to Lotte because there is no other "end" to his life (16 June, the anniversary of his first account of meeting Lotte).

The detour via his birthplace (5 and 9 May) symbolically enacts a return to origins. Werther's "pilgrimage" is a "sacred" ritual to undo birth, to return "through the gate where my mother carried me out." Reliving his life backward, in the rewind mode, Werther recalls *Sehnsucht*, the drive that motivated him to seek afar, and reverts it to *Heimweh*, the longing for home. Shrinking his horizon from the infinity of the world that enticed his Homeric idol Ulysses, now all he desires is the bit of earth needed for a grave: "Man needs but little earth for his happiness, and still less for his final rest" (*Works*, 11:52). With the symbolic birthplace narrative, which takes place on the scene of the unconscious, Goethe reveals that it was the death drive that placed the hometown on Werther's itinerary toward his final destination: Lotte and death.

The pall of spiritual death spreads from the world of work and society to enwrap Werther's entire existence after the return to Lotte. Werther becomes a figure of lack living in a void. He loses himself, and the world around him, turning increasingly symbolic, is characterized by loss and deprivation. The beautiful walnut trees at the vicarage have been cut down. The inhabitants of his former paradise, Wahlheim, have suffered grievous losses: the mother's youngest child is dead, the passionate peasant lad has been expelled. Loss of self is signaled when Werther skips his birthday, marked so touchingly a year earlier by the love of the same people who now ignore it. The brief letters around the missing birthday brood over the inexplicable change that has come over him. They speak of an endangered self that seems to be disintegrating. Werther likens himself to the ghostly father of a lost son (21 August). His favorite suit was worn out and had to be replaced, but somehow it does not seem to suit him now (6 September). Self-loss is broadened to encompass the human condition, as Werther reflects on his spiritual void and the essential nothingness of man. His last support slips when the frustrations of his relation with Lotte drive him to consider the irrelevance of one human to another and thus the pointlessness of love (19–27 October).

For the first time religion emerges as a topic. In Werther's paradoxical attitude, his idiosyncratic interpretation of Christian doctrine on the one hand and his outright rejection of religion on the other (15 and 30 November), we can see the historical process of secularization at work but not yet worked out. Werther's attempt to replace religion with spiritualization of nature has failed spectacularly, as revealed in the desperate letter of 3 November, significantly beginning with the appeal "God knows!" His inner life is "dried up like a leaked-out bucket"; God, identified with creative nature, has withdrawn. Love, Werther's other substitute for religion, fails likewise. His hope to renew his deadened soul in returning to Lotte is disappointed (4 September). Love, it turns out, has lost its spiritual power, its sublimating side. As in the narrative of the peasant lad who finally grabbed his beloved by force, Werther's many letters on the subject depict the torment of frustrated desire, the physical hunger that demands to be satisfied (most explicitly in the bird scene of 12 September). Werther, it seems, has played the role of covetous child too well; he has fallen for his own game and turned the illusionist's fantasies into real objects of desire.

Insanity and death are the only ways out. The temptation of madness is explored in the wrenching mirror narrative of the flower seeker (30 November), who was truly happy only when he was raving mad, "when he was unaware of his condition." Werther ponders liberation of the self from itself through insanity but chooses the other option, death. The theme of violence and death is subliminally present all through the second segment, from the wish "to kill the dog who cut down the trees" and the forbidden thoughts of Albert's dying (15 and 21 September) to the elaborate death fantasy of Ossian, who has now displaced Homer (12 October). Death moves ever closer to associate with Lotte. Her friendly behavior is a cup of poison (21 November); her music provokes his death wish (4 December). In the last letter before his voice gives out, her image invades and pursues him awake or asleep; as "ocean and abyss" she is waiting for him to find the strength to "lose himself in the infinity" of death (6 December).

The last letters to Wilhelm, inserted in the editor's narrative, present fantasies of death and desire with a new explicitness: desire for death in the lyrical drama of storm ravages in the place of the erstwhile love idyll (12 December) and erotic desire fulfilled in the extravagant bliss of a dream (14 December). The long suicide letter to Lotte, despite its seductive tone of jubilant emotion and triumphant heroism, yet does not trivialize death. One of its segments expresses the existential fear of death, the realization that death cannot be understood, either by reason or through the empathy of love, but must be experienced to be known. It is at this point that the letter most decisively abandons its basic design of seduction by means of the love–death symbiosis. In his death, even though he wills himself to perceive it as mediated through Lotte—because of her, through her, and for her sake—Werther is alone.

The function of the editor, who takes over the conclusion of Werther's story, and particularly the question of his objectivity still intrigue critics. More important to the success of Goethe's story is his strategy of opening up the increasingly claustrophobic path of the univocal epistolary narrative leading to either insanity or death. Thus, although the editor takes Werther's position he speaks with a different voice and from a wider perspective. When he *reports* Werther's monologues—how does he know what Werther said when he was alone?—we read credible interpretations of Werther's behavior, but we do not hear Werther, as a comparison with the few brief *authentic* letters shows. Why else insert these letters if not to mark the difference in style, in voice. In comparison with the editor's normal voice speaking in the everyday idiom, we realize the radical individuality, the eccentricity of the character Werther. Conversely, this contrast enables the momentous impact on the reader of the editor's final, clipped report of Werther's death and burial. Finally, the editor, who purports to have collected testimony from all concerned, can give us a representation of Lotte that makes her a complex figure in her own right, beyond the imago of love, desire, and death that appears in Werther's letters.

Finally, we wonder what to make of the strange Ossian insert, filling page after page at a moment when we are utterly tense in waiting for the end; after all, Werther has already written the first installment of his suicide letter. On one level this is a replay of "Klopstock!" in the thunderstorm at the dance, that other episode of maximum intimacy under the spell of literature. Going beyond the earlier event, the reading of Ossian presents yet another death narrative—besides Werther's anticipating letter and the editor's final account—in a third voice, the multiply mediated voice of literature. We hear the lament of mourning over love and death in a different culture, translated by Werther, who can thus, in disguise, confess his love to the beloved. And we witness the immediate, intense response of the listener. Lotte, who suggested the reading, also first breaks down in tears because she *knows* through listening to Werther that she does love him and that he will die. Reading reveals truth, and in this function the scene serves as a model for our reading of this, Goethe's rendition of Werther's texts. The point of seduction through suicide—the *Werther* project—is not imitation of the act but initiation into truthful communication through literature.

Chapter Five

The Productive Paradox of Weimar and Italy

Iphigenie auf Tauris

Like *Werther, Iphigenie auf Tauris,* the first of Goethe's classical plays, was written in two phases, with a number of revisions in between: the original, prose version at Weimar in early 1779 and the final version in blank verse during the first months in Italy. *Iphigenie* shares with *Werther,* too, the lightning speed of original composition: six weeks exactly. This is all the more amazing because Goethe kept literature in the background to focus on his work in government during this period. Literary production was limited to slow progress on *Egmont* and a second novel, *Wilhelm Meisters theatralische Sendung* (after 1777). In addition, he wrote playlets for court entertainment and occasional verse, with rare moments of major poetry: *Erlkönig (The Erl-King), An den Mond ('To the Moon), Grenzen der Menschheit, Das Göttliche,* and the songs in the *Meister* novel (*Works,* 1:62–87). Documentary evidence is unambiguous on Goethe's serious commitment to his responsibilities in government and toward the welfare of the duke during the first five years at Weimar. The event that triggered *Iphigenie* came from the very center of these responsibilities.

In July 1778 Friedrich II of Prussia went to war with Austria over the Bavarian succession. In the previous spring Carl August, accompanied by Goethe, had participated in Berlin power politics aimed at avoiding this outcome. Although Weimar managed to stay on the sidelines, Prussia was demanding the right to recruit soldiers on Weimar territory. Goethe, recently appointed head of the War Commission, composed his longest piece of administrative writing, a decision paper for the duke on the Prussian demand. Five days later, on 14 February 1779, he began writing *Iphigenie* (Conrady, 1:379f). During the tense weeks of awaiting Prussian reaction to Carl August's delay tactics, often on the road recruiting soldiers himself, Goethe completed his drama.

The Iphigenie myth, dramatized by all three Greek tragedians, had risen to prominence in French culture and was therefore familiar to educated German society. During Carl August's educational tour to Paris in 1774 C. W. Gluck, Europe's foremost composer, had staged his first Iphigenie opera there, *Iphigénie en Aulide*. The sequel, *Iphigénie en Tauride*, saw its first performance in Paris less than two months after Goethe's play was staged at Weimar. Starting from Racine's drama of 1674, the eighteenth century had used the Iphigenie story of human sacrifice to elaborate the Enlightenment principle of the individual's natural right to life. Divine command of blood sacrifice in the myth served as metaphor to contest, for instance, the state's claim on the lives of its citizens in warfare. Other issues negotiated in *Iphigenie* versions included the critique of absolutism, in which unlimited power encourages arbitrary rule and outright despotism, as demonstrated by the Greek ruler Agamemnon and the barbarian king Thoas. A critique of religion and the Church was intended by showing the havoc wrought by gods, oracles, and priests.

The Iphigenie myth highlighted other Enlightenment values as well. In French versions, idealized male friendship gets extravagant play. Goethe's drama maintains proper decorum between Orestes and Pylades while yet reflecting the deep and unusual friendship of Goethe and his duke. Lacking a professional theater, Weimar relied on amateur players from the court. Both Goethe's actors and his audience in this Greek family drama were his "court family," himself included. He played Orest, and the role of Pylades was intended for the duke, who, after a first performance by his younger brother, Prince Constantin, indeed took on the role his friend, poet, and privy councillor had written for him. Finally, of absorbing attraction because of Goethe's personal situation was the opportunity to explore the many faces of love. The bewildering nature of his attachment to Charlotte von Stein, sketched in the poem *Warum gabst du uns die tiefen Blicke?* (*Why did you give us such deep gaze?* 1776) (*Works*, 1:60), found expression in the complex sibling relationship of Iphigenie and Orest.

Goethe's *Iphigenie* drama experienced a checkered reception history. Promoted in the nineteenth century to the status of school classic and idolized as a summit of classical ethos and style, the drama became a lightning rod for attacks in the battle over the classics of the 1970s. In the progressive view of that time, *Iphigenie* had to be rejected as escapist and "affirmative" literature.[1] If a classic can be defined as offering unlimited space for meaning and thus infinitely generating new interpretations, then on historical evidence *Iphigenie* is indeed a quintessential classic, because it has been read so many different ways. Here it will be read as a political play, more precisely a play about the fundamentals of politics. Following Immanuel Kant we might name *Iphigenie*'s theme transcendental politics—that is, an inquiry into the conditions of the possibility of politics, where politics means the laws that structure civic life, particularly power relations among individuals and among groups—ethnic, racial, ideological, class, and gender.

The questions to be asked in such an inquiry would be—first and foremost—is there a right and a wrong kind of politics, or does anything go? Is politics simply a matter of competing ideologies? How can we know which is the right kind of politics? Who could represent this right politics? What kind of individual would have enough credibility? How could that individual convince others in order to enable common action and thus bring about change for the better—progress? *Iphigenie auf Tauris* attempts to answer these questions through the thoughts, crises, and actions of its characters.

The point of departure in this inquiry is the question of truth. Truth is, next to humanity *(Menschlichkeit),* the most crucial concept in *Iphigenie.* If there is to be a right or wrong in politics, certain values must have absolute status, truth value. Goethe's drama depicts the secularization dilemma of his age. If religion no longer guarantees truth, if the will of the gods can be seriously contested between Iphigenie and Thoas and between Orestes and Pylades, if oracles are misleading, what then validates opinion or belief as truth? The need for truth informs the drama's major actions. In a first, symbolic action that signifies trust, Iphigenie reveals her fearfully guarded family secret: her atrocious ancestors. In the central third act, truth erupts spectacularly in an ultrashort line that breaks the even scansion of classical verse and breaks with the *Iphigenie* tradition of accidental recognition, when Orest reveals his identity: "Let there be truth!"[2] In the fourth act truth is the fulcrum of action as Iphigenie suffers a crisis of faith and identity: "Save me, and save your image in my soul!" (4.5.1717). And it is truth on which, in act 5, she finally stakes everything in her challenge to the gods: her and her brother's lives, the future of her family and country, her identity, and her faith: "If you are truthful, as men say you are, / Then show it now: stand by me, that through me / Truth may be glorified!" (5.3.1917–19).

Iphigenie subsumes the principles for which she claims truth status under the concept of humanity or, in eighteenth-century terms, natural human rights. Goethe's dramatic inquiry into the possibility of a right politics occurred at the same moment when some American settlers were engaged in their pioneering experiment of a new politics based on certain truths held to be self-evident. The first among these, they declared, was the human right to life. For the political reality of Weimar, where compulsory recruitment of soldiers was routine, such a claim was far from self-evident.

From the first act to the last Goethe's Iphigenie drama revolves around the killing of a sacrificial victim: as threat and fear, memory and nightmare. It is Iphigenie's defining experience, and she makes it the test case for the validation of truth. It is this issue that lifts her above private cares and sorrows. Whereas her first prayer (1.1) had asked for her own release from Tauris, her second prayer at the end of act 1 concerns others. In a passage of powerful poetry (1.4.537–60) marked by a change of meter, Iphigenie states a universal good that belongs to humankind as a whole. Mortals are part of the gods' immortal world, created in order to enjoy "for a little" the beauty of life. The placement of the term of life, "a little longer," at the very end of a long syntactic breath that arcs over four lines, represents in poetic terms the *long term* for human life that Iphigenie's prayer advocates.

Iphigenie's credibility as representative of the value of human life, given her experience, should be self-evident to King Thoas. He, however, blinded through the passion and outrage of an absolutist ruler in the face of resistance, needs to be reminded that she is a survivor of the inhuman practice of blood sacrifice, which he now forces her to perform: the victim is to become the killer ("You know this, know me, yet you would compel me!" 5.3.1854). Iphigenie's repeated remembrance of her death experience (six times) serves to imprint the monstrosity of sacrificial killing, to convince the audience of the correctness of the right to life.

Iphigenie is the representative, too, of the second self-evident truth in the American view: the right to liberty. Critics in the nineteenth century noted with annoyance that the otherwise ideal heroine sometimes sounded like a suffragette when she complained about women's unhappy lot in all aspects of life. In an amazing step for late-eighteenth-century Germany, Goethe makes the case for liberty by arguing gender politics. It took nearly another century to catch up with Goethe's advance, when the mythologist J. J. Bachofen (1861) theorized that the Iphigenie myth represented the defeat of archaic matriarchy by the progressive forces of patriarchy.[3] Who better to speak for women's oppression than Iphigenie, daughter victimized for male ambition in the guise of honor, patriotism, and obedience to divine command?

Iphigenie voices the complaints and accusations of woman as victim: as subordinate daughter and wife, as object of male aggression, and as mourner of the war dead. To intensify Iphigenie's feminist message of victimization, Goethe added Thoas's marriage demand to the traditional fable. However, to win victory for her politics of "humanity," Iphigenie will have to abandon her role as victim and instead claim the human right of liberty. She does so in act 5 with an amazing amendment to the Declaration of the American founding *fathers*: "I was born no less free than any man" (5.3.1858). Having seized freedom of action and thus, because she is Thoas's social peer, equality with the male ruler, she can now propose a new, feminine ethos as the right politics. Heroism no longer means the male right of putting lives at stake in the pursuit of violence; heroism is woman's equal right of risking lives for the principle of nonviolence ("Are men alone entitled / To do heroic deeds?" 5.3.1892–93). The drama's conclusion grants her victory by affirming one of humankind's most persistent dreams, "of Eternal Peace," as in Kant's philosophical inquiry of the same period.[4]

"Pursuit of happiness," that encapsulation of Enlightenment anthropology, finds its place in *Iphigenie,* too, albeit in a startling redefinition. Gone is the facile optimism of the Enlightenment formula. Pursuit of happiness, the drama tells us, requires a new human. You cannot turn from misery — from unhappiness of the serious *Werther* kind — to happiness unless you first undergo radical change. Here Christian tradition enters Goethe's myth reworking. German Protestantism, especially in its pietist variant, requires a *umgeschaffenes Herz* (transformed, new-created heart) as precondition for the achievement of spiritual rightness. In secular formations this tradition has marked moments of crisis throughout modern German history. New Man was the goal of expressionist writers after World War I, just as belief in New Socialist Man inspired the founders of East Germany after 1945. For Goethe, the necessity of rebirth and metamorphosis became arguably the most essential belief to sustain his life and work.

In *Iphigenie,* rebirth occurs in both central characters: as long-term development in Iphigenie and with the suddenness of a miracle in Orestes. We witness Iphigenie's transformation in four distinct steps, the last being the emergence of her new identity as free woman empowered to act for the right politics. To arrive at that stage, however, she first had to go through the traumatic experience of her own dying and rescue on the altar of Aulis, as she keeps remembering all through the play. Her life on Tauris since then, in the second phase, was for her "a second death" (1.1.53) or, to use a favorite analogy of Goethe's, the living death of the chrysalis wrapped in a cocoon of silence and isolation. In the third step, a surge of emotion on finding her brother bursts the cocoon and brings her back to life in a flood of imagery of flowing waters and ripe fruit (3.1.1094–99, 1196–1200).

In the most spectacular event of the drama, Orestes is cured: "Pylades: Your brother—he is healed!" (4.4.1536). Paralyzed in a state of pathological unhappiness, condemned to misery seemingly forever, obsessed by his and his family's past of ineradicable guilt, and deprived of willpower and of the freedom to choose his own actions because of a curse describe Orest through the third act. When he reappears in act 5, he is a new man. To prove Orest's transformation, Goethe, in a crucial change of the myth, devised his reinterpretation of the oracle. Previously Orest had followed Apollo's words in blind obedience—blind, that is, to the moral implications of the god's command. Against the urging of his own heart he had killed his mother. The new Orest reads the oracle in a way that allows him to avoid sin against the dictates of *humanity*. The ancient Greek tradition of rape and pillage will be discontinued; the Scythians' sacred statue is safe.

Goethe's experience since *Werther* times had convinced him that knowing the truth was possible for what he called "pure persons," *pure* as in pure glass through which the outside world might pass to the inside without distortion. In his study of the real world since moving to Weimar—social, political, and above all natural—Goethe had trained to rid himself of problematic Wertherian subjectivity. Nature, source of pathetic fallacy for Werther, had become for Goethe the great teacher of objectivity. A better term for what Goethe had in mind would be *insight* of the sort to be found in mystic and Zen thinkers, indicating a balance, a rightness of relation between the individual and the whole of existence. It is no accident that Goethe wrote the last two acts of *Iphigenie* not among the crises of government but in his "nature study," the Thuringian Forest.[5] Orest, purged through cathartic rebirth, has gained such insight.

But how does it happen, that miraculously sudden rebirth? This is the most unsettled question in *Iphigenie* scholarship. Only a sketchy answer can be suggested here, and it introduces a final major theme of the drama: love.[6] In yet another effort to unlearn *Werther, Iphigenie* performs a reconfiguration of love. Negotiating between the classical Greek concepts of love, the drama reformulates the energy and passion of eros (sexual attraction) to become agape (charity) and philia (friendship). Self-centered desire must be redirected toward other-centered, disinterested goodwill. Here, clearly, is the major influx of Christianity into the drama. In his turn away from orthodoxy, Goethe had declared love the defining substance of any Christian faith.[7] "Saint" Iphigenie (5.6.2119–27) represents this love and mediates love's reconfiguration in Orest and Thoas.[8]

From his family history Orest knows love only as evil lust, most traumatically his mother's lust for Aigisthos, which became the source of his own misery. Possessed by horror of love, which is evident in his reaction to Iphigenie's joy of sisterly love, he must relearn in his hallucination the meaning of love. What he sees in his unconscious state, and accepts by asking to be accepted into his loving family, is a revision of history, in which family love has conquered family revenge. For Thoas to do the right thing, it is not enough to renounce his desire to possess Iphigenie, to simply let her go: "Well, take your leave!" (5.6.2151). He, too, must be persuaded by mediator Iphigenie to reconfigure sexual desire as loving kindness, extended not only toward family and friends but toward strangers as well. This is what Iphigenie's future of hospitality proposes, where any stranger will be welcome and where, as the German word Gastfreundschaft (hospitality) signifies, the stranger is a friend. Thoas signals the new inclusiveness with his final "Fare well!" The German plural form, "Lebt wohl!," makes clear that this is addressed not only to beloved Iphigenie, who alone had been pleading with him, but also to the Greek strangers, her brother and Pylades.[9]

Love as essential medium of communication and persuasion and thus prerequisite for agreement and joint action adds a European ingredient to the Enlightenment vision of right politics in Goethe's Iphigenie. Life, liberty, and the pursuit of happiness as rights of the individual are here supplemented by concern for the other and for community: by fraternité, which would figure as one of the three key goals of the French Revolution. Brother/sisterhood between individuals—Orestes and Iphigenie and Pylades, Thoas and Iphigenie—expands in the conclusion to the universal brotherhood of humankind. How utopian this reading is depends on one's reading of history since the eighteenth century, from Beethoven's similarly utopian Ninth Symphony to the Beatles, the flower children, and the politics of candle-bearing nonviolence. Goethe's drama is, at least, not naive. Nothing in Thoas's reticence guarantees fulfillment of Iphigenie's dream of the future. In Orest's vision Tantalus remains excluded. As T. W. Adorno was the first to see, myth, the unspiritualizable aspect of nature, which includes human bodies and their desires, remains a powerful substratum in *Iphigenie auf Tauris*.[10]

Torquato Tasso

Tradition insists on grouping together Goethe's second classical drama, *Torquato Tasso*, with his first, *Iphigenie auf Tauris*. Strikingly similar in form, the two dramas are yet so different that one could speak of *Tasso* as the antithesis to *Iphigenie* in thematic respects. According to the old Goethe, his play about the Renaissance poet Tasso was a return of *Werther* in a higher dimension. In a comment reported by one of the first readers, Herder's wife, Caroline, Goethe saw the "essential meaning" of his new drama as "the disproportion between talent and life," which is to say that the artist is necessarily out of sync with real life.[11] The artist, we remember, was specifically exempted from the Wertherian disaster. In *Tasso*, a poet is the central figure of a problem play; *Torquato Tasso* is the first work in Western literature with an artist as hero.

For a first antithesis to *Iphigenie*, in *Tasso* truth is not a given waiting to be discovered. Instead of truth we find incessantly shifting views and values, different interpretations, ambiguity, and ambivalence everywhere. A concerned reader and artist, Richard Wagner noted as early as 1859 that in the conflicts of this play there was no right or wrong: the author was taking both sides (Grawe, 201). It is no wonder that this paradox has bedeviled *Tasso* scholarship from the outset. Reading *Tasso* is not easy, as a young Englishman once complained to old Goethe, who sternly replied that anyone with a good education and the right social background could read it (Grawe, 93). But Goethe is famous for not rereading his earlier works.

Some light falls into the *Tasso* paradox from the life of the author. During the major work phase on the drama (summer 1788 through August 1789), after returning from Italy and while he was in the first transports of his happy sexual relationship with Christiane Vulpius, Goethe also wrote the lighthearted erotic poems of his *Römische Elegien*. Where the unhappy poet Tasso is tormented by an impossible love and the harmful effects of his vocation, the poet-narrator of the *Römische Elegien* learns how to enjoy making love and making poetry together. Goethe was evidently of two minds about the fate of poets and the nature of poetry, a fact that precludes his identification with Tasso and instead indicates a perspective of double vision. It is the dual perspective that still puzzled Wagner but that had long been explored by the romantic writers: irony. It helps to keep the ironic perspective in mind while reading *Tasso.*

This poetic drama is an early instance of self-reflexive literature. *Torquato Tasso* asks about its own conditions of production: What is poetry? Where does it come from? How does it affect its practitioner, the poet, and his emotional, social, and cultural world? The answer, in a nutshell, is ambiguous. Poetry is a zero sum game, as stated by Tasso's duke in a much-quoted line: "All that the poet loses, the man will gain."[12] This statement subtextually calls forth its reverse: "All that the man loses, the poet will gain." What the poet gains out of the losses of life is the aesthetic product, pain transformed into the pleasure of the poetic word, or, in the poet's own summary, "When in their anguish other men fall silent / A god gave me the power to tell my pain" (5.5.3424–25). This is how the play ends, and Goethe, in an exceptional mode of composition, wrote the drama toward this end, from acts 5 and 4 backward.

A first conclusion follows from the duke's statement on loss and gain: that poetry is the parasite of life. Goethe chose for his model a great poet who after bouts of insanity perished sick in body and mind. Statesman Antonio, in his cruel impersonations, demonstrates Tasso's pathological lifestyle, from dietary excesses to paranoia, blaming it on the runaway poetic imagination. And Tasso himself, in the image of the silkworm using up his life substance to create his "cocoon . . . coffin" (5.4.3075–79), agrees: the poet produces his own death. On the other hand, the ladies in the first two acts present portrait after portrait of the poet as superman, an ideal human above the baser needs of life, who through his poetry lifts others into that same higher dimension of spirit over matter. In the end, however we may interpret the final imagery of rocks, waves, and shipwreck, the poet has wrecked his life. The life that he loved and the two people he needed most are gone forever.

A second point is that poetry's place in society and culture is contested. Tasso's work is awarded highest value for building a community. "Das Vaterland" ("Our country," 1.2.289) is waiting for his just completed epos on *Jerusalem Liberated* to create the Italian nation, to inspire and unite Christianity in a holy mission. A second Virgil, Tasso will be crowned in Rome as he is now being crowned by the court of Ferrara. But throughout we also hear that the poet is a pawn in the power game among the Italian princes and the pope, that poetry is worth only as much as its image value. Tasso's patron and master takes his manuscript away and leaves the useless—because sick—poet behind. In the fifth act

Tasso imagines the purpose of his journey to Rome to meet his col-
leagues but veers off suddenly into a different trajectory to describe
instead a flight into exile, where an unknown vagrant in disheveled hair
and beggar's costume has displaced the poet laureate (5.4.3133–52).
Lastly and most important, poetry is not truth. The literature of tradition created by Tasso's revered models, Homer and Virgil, of whom he
feels so profoundly unworthy, was based on myth, just like Goethe's
Iphigenie. Myth is a canon of collectively agreed-upon tales endowed
with truth value precisely because of this consensus. Modern literature,
on the other hand, as Antonio keeps reminding us, is based on individual invention, on a particular poet's subjective imaginings. Goethe, in
his Sturm und Drang era, had seen in individual creativity the glory of
humanity, the Promethean genius. His *Tasso* presents the other side of
the coin: poetry without the possibility of validation is sheer relativity.
The conflicting golden age interpretations by Tasso and the Princess in
act 2 make it obvious. In one of the pastiches with which this drama
abounds, Goethe's Tasso quotes from the pastoral *Aminta,* a work by the
historical Tasso. The Princess, to disqualify Tasso's (Goethe's and the
historical one's) definition of the golden age as a poet's flattery
(2.1.997–98), proffers an opposing quotation from a work by the historical Tasso's rival Guarini (Grawe, 30–32). If two poets have such different visions, how can either one be true?

The undecidability of poetry invades the text of the drama, which is,
after all, poetry. The words and actions of the characters that surround
Tasso routinely permit at least two interpretations, and Tasso just as
routinely picks the wrong one. (But is there a right one?) The words
kennen (know, recognize) and *verkennen* (mistake, misinterpret) function
as leitmotifs. It is as if cognition merely served to bring forth its negative: miscognition. Tasso's image of the galley slaves in act 5 makes the
point at the height of his own confusion: We do not really want to
know the others or be known by them; we prefer to construct our own
images of others, just as we want them to accept our image of ourselves
(5.5.3330–41).

In act 3, that anomalous central act from which the hero is absent,
undecidability parades as glaring untruth, as lie and betrayal. Leonore
Sanvitale asks for her friend's trust ("true confiding," 3.2.1849), the better to abuse this trust. She manipulates both Antonio and Tasso for her
own advantage, all the while confiding to the audience in her shameless
monologues. Antonio obeys the Duke's orders to capture Tasso's trust by
representing himself as a friend and father figure with—height of

irony—"sincere . . . words" (2.5.1629), irrespective of how he really feels. If Tasso gets entangled in this web of half-truths and untruths, it is not wholly due to his poetic imagination, as Leonore wants us to believe in her comment on the link between poetry and untruth (4.2.2461). The only one who does not participate in the game of deception is the Princess. She even professes belief in truth as a principle of action, but her faith is weak and she stays out of the rescue effort for Tasso. The contrast with *Iphigenie* is clear when she laments that the divine voice of truth is barely audible, and if we do hear it we normally do not listen to it:

> Oh, how we lose the habit of responding
> To the pure, quiet hints our hearts transmit!
> Within us, very softly, a god speaks,
> Quite audibly, but very softly, tells us
> What course we should pursue, and what avoid.
> (3.2.1669–73)

Abandoned by the one truthful voice, Tasso, in the claustrophobic fourth act, falls victim to doubts and anxieties, which crowd in on him in his solitude and in the web of lies created by his diplomatic interlocutors, Leonore and Antonio. Tasso's three long monologues trace the path from doubt to delusion. At first (scene 1), left in doubt and ambiguity, Tasso finds himself confused, bewildered by "those ugly beasts ambiguously winged," and lost at the brink of an abyss (4.1.2234–39). At the end of his third monologue he falls prey, as to a fantastic bird of prey, to "despair with iron claws" (4.5.2822) tearing apart his mind in madness. The result is the poet as madman in act 5, when Tasso, in another ironic antithesis to *Iphigenie,* declares to be in possession of the truth: "And if my wretchedness has left me nothing, / Still I can praise it—it has taught me truth" (5.5.3349–50).

In yet another antithesis to *Iphigenie,* love is a central theme, but love is part of the problem, not key to the solution. Love for the Princess impels Tasso toward the conflict with Antonio in act 2, and in act 5 propels him into the final catastrophe when he embraces her. Many-faceted, as in *Iphigenie,* love yet shows very different faces in *Tasso.* In this drama about poetry, love is a variable function of poetry. Pragmatist Antonio states it somewhat crudely: If Tasso were not a poet—otherworldly, irresponsible, perhaps infantile—he would not be so attractive to women (3.4.2085–89). The clearest case among the various love relationships is

Leonore Sanvitale. She elaborates a definition of platonic eros in the first act and, in act 3, plots to play the role of Laura to her new Petrarch, Tasso. In this role, woman adored in the great poet's verse would gain immortality as a perfect self, forever beautiful, forever young (3.3. 1946–51). The love of the Princess is more serious and more complex. Although we may decide that Tasso's fate is not truly tragic—he survives as a poet, after all—the Princess suffers unadulterated tragedy, as the second scene of act 3 demonstrates. Her tragedy is the still-underexplored story of woman as object of the male poet's love. A pendant to the other Leonore's platonic position, the love story of Princess Eleonore would be Laura's story seen from Laura's, not Petrarch's, perspective.

Tasso's love for the Princess, not surprising in this ambiguous drama, has at least two faces. The Princess is his muse; she inspires his creative ardor and she inspires his creations, a fact that marks another difference between subjective modern literature and Tasso's venerated models of the classical tradition. The Muses of antiquity were a plural entity of mythic stature, representative of a divine and distant authority. No matter how hard Tasso tries to elevate the Princess to this level, she reveals herself as a human individuality, fallible and far too close to the beloved poet. The crux of the problem facing the modern poet lies deeper still. The Princess, Tasso repeats endlessly, is the archetype (Urbild) of all his female creations. All the features he bodied forth in his figures—Chlorinde, Erminia, Sophronia, even Armida—he has found in her. She is his fantasies. The Princess as he knows, or rather "mis-cognizes" (ver-kennt) her, is a construct of his poetic imagination.

On the other hand, Tasso exhibits another element of the modern poet's condition: aloneness and the corresponding need for an other who understands, cares about, and loves him. Thrown back onto himself as sole source of his subjective creations, the poet needs an anchorage outside of himself to save him from the threat of entropy, of implosion and collapse within himself, as finally happens to Tasso. Having lost the Princess, his anchoring point, he faces nothingness; he has lost himself (5.5.3409–10).[13] Tasso performs the poet's paradox of necessary solitude versus the horror of imposed aloneness. For him the mild sentence of room arrest is cruel and excessive punishment. He goes to pieces; his mind breaks apart—first into the madness of despair on being abandoned by the Princess and then into the insanity of ecstasy when she once more extends love and understanding.

To keep this ambivalent love tragedy in proper perspective, we should recall the other poet-lover Goethe created at the same time. In

opposition to *Tasso*, the *Römische Elegien* celebrate a happy, uncomplicated love of the senses: "We enjoy the delights of the genuine naked
god, Amor, / And our rock-a-bye bed's rhythmic, melodious creak"
(*Works*, 1:105).[14] The historical Tasso's pastoral play, *Aminta*, similarly
contrasted two kinds of love: spiritual desire in the erudite tradition of
courtly etiquette and, removed to the golden age utopia, love as physical fulfillment of nature's demands.

The contrast between his two works did not escape Goethe. In a letter to Herder (10 August 1789) he emphasized the formal consequences
of the different perspectives: His drama was rigorously composed,
whereas his *Römische Elegien* exhibit the fragmentary nature of erotic
jokes. The evidence of rigorous composition is in the highly poetic language of *Torquato Tasso*. Among its outstanding features are multiple
echoes in which the same word reappears in different formal variations
(e.g., *smile* in the first two lines), masterfully honed lines in which sen-
tentiousness insinuates truth, a rich texture of nature symbolism—light
and dark, sun and moon, fire and water, rock and wave, weather and
plants—in which nature conveys rightness upon the artificial court culture, and extended metaphors and similes—of silkworms and galley
slaves—in which beautiful composition carries conviction despite
doubtful validity.

The seduction of poetry has worked throughout *Tasso* reception history, following the model of the Princess in act 2:

> It [Tasso's poetry] draws us on, and on, we listen to it,
> We listen and we think we understand,
> What we do grasp of it, we cannot censure,
> And so we are won over in the end.
>
> (2.1.1110–13)

The poetic magic worked on other artists, from the romantic poets
who found in Goethe's hero their self-image of *poète maudit*[15] to Thomas
Mann with his unbourgeois and unhappy artist figures. Tasso's language
of seduction has likewise charmed literary critics, who overwhelmingly
empathize with his aestheticized suffering. The most effective stratagem
in Goethe's seductive play, first described by E. M. Wilkinson (1946), is
the poet performing in his symbolic verbal action the genesis of poetry.
Torquato Tasso thus allows us to witness and study the mysterious and
fascinating process of poetic creation.[16]

At the first such occurrence, in act 1, Goethe calls attention to this aspect of his play. Tasso escapes from the coronation into the refuge of an ideal past, where he imagines himself as Narcissus at the fountain. We are explicitly told by the poet and his audience that poetic creation is happening here:

> **Tasso.**   It is the present that exalts me here,
>   Absent I only seem to be. I'm rapt.
> **Princess.** It pleases me, when you converse with ghosts,
>   To hear you speak so humanly to them.
>   (1.3.560–63)

Torquato Tasso, then, is not just a drama about a poet and poetry; it is a dramatic transaction, in negotiations, confrontations, and conflicts and their consequences or resolution of the nature of poetry and the poet.

Chapter Six

Classicism and Revolution

Hermann und Dorothea

Like his classical drama *Iphigenie,* Goethe's attempt in the classical epic genre, *Hermann und Dorothea,* has experienced a contentious reception. Its success at publication (1797) surpassed even that of *Werther,* and during the nineteenth century *Hermann und Dorothea* remained the most beloved and most widely read of Goethe's works. The German bourgeois found in it their ideals of small-town community, family, property, work, and patriotism. The revolution of 1918 put an end to the dominant bourgeois culture and its ideal self-image in *Hermann und Dorothea.* Goethe's epos took a nosedive only to be appropriated by the nationalists (and National Socialists) for its anti-French overtones, a fact that did nothing to rehabilitate the work after 1945.

Criticism today is still divided on how to read *Hermann und Dorothea.* On a serious level, we might take it for a critical analysis of German bourgeois society at the turn of the nineteenth century, with ominous anticipation of the development toward aggressive nationalism. Alternately, the work is read from a perspective of irony: as a mock-heroic epos in which nonheroes and their trivial pursuits are played against the backdrop of the great epic tradition *(Iliad)* and the great historic event of the French Revolution.[1] From the reader's perspective, *Hermann und Dorothea* proffers an intriguing challenge. The reading experience spans a gamut of reactions, from the lure of identification with different figures at different points to the other extreme of outright rejection of the same figures at other moments. This experience suggests a more complex textual organization than the either–or allowed for in the critical tradition.

If we look at the context of composition in the summer of 1796, we find Goethe in a situation of transition, tension, and turmoil. Having just completed the long labor of *Wilhelm Meisters Lehrjahre* and still overflowing with creative energy ("Now that I'm rid of the novel I'm full of a thousand ideas and plans," to Schiller on 17 August), he had to cope with his friend Schiller's voluminous letters—which he had eagerly invited—analyzing and criticizing his novel. Collaborating with Schiller in the Weimar–Jena project to promote classicism, he was also turning out a steady stream of satirical two-liners *(Xenien)* that attacked the opposition. At the same time he was gravely concerned with current political events, in both his official capacity at the Weimar court and on a personal level. The French revolutionary army overran Frankfurt and was threatening to move north on Eisenach and Weimar. Goethe's hometown was bombarded and suffered serious losses from fire, occupation, and retribution. Goethe's mother lived right in the middle of it all, on the central square, across from military headquarters. In lively letters she kept her son informed, and he urged her to supply even more details. The day that brought the news of the happy ending for Frankfurt ("News that Frankfurt cleared by French"[2]) was the first day Goethe began writing *Hermann und Dorothea.*

Goethe's position was straddling the fence between critical distance and empathetic concern. Critical distancing was the inevitable effect of the dissection of literary works: his own *Wilhelm Meister* under Schiller's scrutiny and the work of others for the *Xenien* war. Never before had Goethe been so immediately involved with aesthetic theory as now in close cooperation with Schiller. And never afterward would he share so completely his works in progress with Schiller and so freely invite his criticism. One might speculate that the puzzling blockage of creativity over the remainder of the years with Schiller was brought on by the shock of self-alienation suffered from the Schiller-induced autopsy of *Wilhelm Meister,* a novel with a strong autobiographical subtext. But for the moment Goethe's interest in the formal aspect of literature was at a peak. After the avant-gardist loose structure of the *Meister* novel, he chose a pointedly traditional form—hexameters arranged in nine cantos (three times three, the number of Muses)—for his next work of fiction, *Hermann und Dorothea.*

Hexameters were by then a familiar medium. A renewed study of Homer had led to *Reineke Fuchs* (1794), Goethe's first reflection on revolutionary politics in this renarration of the moralistic beast epic from German folk tradition. Adapting Homeric hexameters to the purpose of satire was a stylistic experiment whose success critics have yet to decide. Additionally, the publication of his *Römische Elegien* in Schiller's review *Die Horen* (1795) took Goethe back to his earlier revival of classical antiquity in the hexameter–pentameter form, the meter (elegiac couplet or distich) he and Schiller chose for their attack-*Xenien.*

Homer, too, was in the news. J. H. Voss's translation of the *Odyssey* and *Iliad* had appeared in 1793, and now Goethe was following the controversy over the multiple or single authorship of the Homeric epics. Most significant, however, was the spectacular success of Voss's rural idyll in hexameters, *Luise,* in 1795. Voss had long cultivated the hexametric pastoral, proving that there was a market in revolution-traumatized Germany for such escape literature: escape not merely into the idyllic peace of a country parsonage but also into the language of a distant time and place, far removed from current confusion and anxiety. *Hermann und Dorothea,* a "bourgeois idyll," taps into the same market, and Goethe was most gratified by its phenomenal success.[3]

Voss's *Luise,* then, supplied the serendipitous form. The substance to be poured into this form sprang from the center of Goethe's own life. And pour it did, as witnessed by Schiller's envious admiration as Goethe produced the first four cantos during a nine-day writing spell at Jena "with a facility and speed incomprehensible to me . . . for nine days more than one hundred and fifty hexameters daily."[4] The source of the poetic flood was Goethe's immediately past experience of the events at Frankfurt, mediated through his mother's letters, which in turn revived his own memories of his old hometown. Not long ago life in Frankfurt had presented itself as a real option. In late 1792 the city invited her lost and famous son to be a candidate for councillor. Goethe declined but made a last visit home before his mother (on his advice) sold his birth house, together with all the memorabilia of life before Weimar (her own decision): portraits of Goethe, family, and friends and the father's prized collections of books, artworks, and old wines. Frankfurt as home, the place of his childhood and youth up to age 26, was irrevocably lost.

Now, in summer 1796, "Frankfurt," place of the mind, was coming back to haunt the poet, as he was made to share from his mother's window the "misfortune of our city": the spectacle of military conquest and retreat, of "emigrants" in chaotic flight with beds piled high on carts; as her letters evoked for him old friends and acquaintances who had all "emigrated"; as she herself finally decided to "emigrate" for a bit to "Mama La Roche" (famous writer and motherly mentor of the young Goethe, whose daughter had coinspired Werther's Lotte) at Offenbach (home of Goethe's former fiancée Lili, whose bravery during forced emigration has long been thought a model for Hermann's Dorothea).[5] Above all, her letters demonstrated indomitable courage based on trust in "God!" (she usually writes it thus), a foundation her son no longer shared; coincidentally, he lacked the courage to visit Frankfurt as planned during these perilous times.

In spirit, however, the son had never been in closer contact with his mother since leaving home. The poetic alchemy of the hometown that had produced *Hermann und Dorothea* became manifest a few months later on an extensive visit to Frankfurt en route to Switzerland. Goethe discovered a new way of seeing, in which objects became "symbolic." In a long letter to Schiller of 17 August 1797 he conjectures that this change of vision has turned him, the supposedly "naive" personality type (according to Schiller's distinction) into the opposite, "sentimental" type. Two places have aroused this new, symbolic vision: the central city square outside his mother's windows and the commercial estate once owned by his grandfather, now reduced to rubble by the bombardment. The answer is given in *Hermann und Dorothea*. Writing it had transformed these places of experience and memory into places of the poetic imagination. One is the site of the citizens' scopophilia, and the other is a site of property accumulation and commerce in the hands of prospering entrepreneurs such as Hermann's father. Goethe now sees these real places refracted through the prism of his fictional creation.

Metamorphic product of memory and imagination, *Hermann und Dorothea*, coming on the heels of *Wilhelm Meister*, is yet another autobiographically inspired work, processed through the formal devices of *Verfremdung*, foremost among these being the Homeric hexameters. Formal distancing, however, does not preclude inner participation or empathy. Goethe had learned that good writing requires "a certain partisan enthusiasm. . . . Pleasure, joy, participation alone is real and can again produce reality, everything else is vain and leads to failure."[6] It is with an attitude of pleasurable participation, or friendly fun, that Goethe tells the story of an afternoon in a small town on the German side of the Rhine during the revolutionary wars, in which Hermann, the innkeeper's son, gets to marry the penniless refugee girl Dorothea against his father's resistance and with the help of his mother, a neighbor pharmacist, and the pastor.

The title of the first canto, "Schicksal und Anteil" ("Fate and Sympathy"), evokes a more serious sort of participation. Most immediately it means the citizens' attitude toward the refugees of the "there but for the grace of God" kind. But *sympathy* also means the absorbing interest that has the Parson elicit the Judge's tale of the refugees' historic experience (fate) and that arouses Hermann's love for the unknown girl. And it means the participation the poetic representation aims to provoke in the reader. As Goethe's narrative unfolds, we see a *Vaterstadt* (hometown) as it confronts historic change and upheaval on the familial, generational, social, and political levels. We witness patriarchy, the rule of the fathers, under assault as sons, mothers, and daughters(-in-law) propose to strike out on new paths, as yet uncertain of where they will lead.

Just as the place of Goethe's private memory has become symbolic (i.e., signifying in a wider field), so too the figures and events of the story have symbolic significance. Their meanings intend the horizon of world history and of archetypal experiences of mankind: Goethe's avowed aim is "to distill the purely human in the existence of a small German town . . . and to reflect from a small mirror the great movements and changes of the world theatre."[7] The fate in which the townspeople participate through their interest in the refugees is world history moving through their private existence and profoundly changing it from its patriarchal traditions toward an as yet unknowable future.

In the simple story (which lasts less than half a day, from midday to sunset) of how Hermann got his Dorothea, we find the established order represented at many levels. Most obviously, there is the Father as paterfamilias, as benevolent despot sabotaged by the plotting of mother and son. Here we find the most autobiographical strain of the epos. The closeness of mother and son—with a subtextual play on *Muttersöhnchen* ("Fourth Canto: Mother and Son"), mama's boy at her apron strings who never kept a secret[8]—and the apparently nonironic, entirely lovable figure of the mother have long been seen in this light. More important, however, is the exorcism of the father performed here: the emancipation of the son from overpowering and finally destructive paternal possession. The Pharmacist's reminiscence of his father's most profound imprint—that all of life is only a waiting for death—shows the disastrous paternal potential, whose effects are evident in this most negative character of the story.

Then there is patriarchy as government, in the apparently progressive role of Hermann's father as City Father. Yet although canal construction may protect the citizens against fire, there is no way the town government can safeguard its people against history. The Father's naive theodicy admits its dependency on divine power for that (174–84). The Judge's report on the destruction of his community through the events of the revolution (1095–1173) likewise testifies to the impotence of government in the face of history. Finally, government cannot even ensure the survival of the next generation, the children and heirs. Dorothea's fiancé was killed for pursuing civic ideals; Hermann sees

death in battle as life wasted because government has failed to create a
unity of purpose (739–41). The future (title of the last canto) opened
by Hermann in the end is fundamentally tragic and defeatist. Even if
government were able to create a common purpose, the people would
still be annihilated in war—and become heroes in literature of the patriarchal tradition, such as the *Iliad*:

They are forever still praised, those peoples who with resolution
Fought for their God and their laws, for their parents, their wives and
    their children,
And at the hands of their enemies perished, still standing together.
                                                                        (2024–26)

Equally failing is patriarchy in the guise of divine authority. The
Father's logic concerning God's intentions with the city is a naive theodicy. The Parson's comment welcomes the subjective attitude but denies
its objective validity: in a worst-case scenario, faith holds out hope
(186–88). The Parson himself, instead of religious principles, represents
a situational ethic of infinite adaptability. In a parody of Kant according
to Schiller, he believes that reason will progress toward moral goodness
by means of baser, natural drives such as curiosity and utilitarianism:

Tell me: if curiosity did not so strongly entice man,
How would he ever have learned of the beauty of ordered creation
And its laws? For first he demands what is new for its own sake,
Then what is useful attracts him and tirelessly he pursues it,
Till in the end he desires what is good, and is raised and ennobled.
                                                                        (88–92)

The Pharmacist represents another late-eighteenth-century type. His
loss of faith has led to existential anxiety, materialism, and egotism.
Goethe marks this feature with an ironic episode. The miser, who leaves
his money at home on principle, makes a gift of tobacco instead of gold
and gets tagged with a deflating line of self-praise: "And the apothecary
launched into praises of his canaster" (1308).
    Crucial to patriarchy are gender relations, which is why Goethe's
assault proceeds by way of a love story. The Father rejects the idea of a
poor daughter-in-law with a stunningly cynical admission that patri-

archy is based on injustice and that love is irrelevant: "Men never treat women fairly, the season of love doesn't last long" (399). He is right to protest, even though he casts a sarcastic light on the Mother's glorifying tale of their own courtship and marriage. For indeed Hermann's bringing the "maid with her bundle" (398) into the house as his fiancée will upend the patriarchal system, the Father's orthodoxy, and the project of accumulating wealth, to which the Father sees all welfare tied.

The two women figures are cast in contrastive roles. The Mother, whose view of love and marriage the Father so mercilessly discounts, is yet his collaborator. In her position of codependency she helps stabilize the Father's rule, even though she is well aware of the chinks in his armor and shrewdly plots to exploit his weak points, which she states just as mercilessly in front of her son. Yet despite all this, Goethe has her assert the inviolability of the patriarchal principle with an axiomatic statement that makes "Fatherhood" an absolute legitimation: "For he is father!" (834).[9]

On the plot level Dorothea is the agent provocateur, instigator of revolt against the Father's rule. But her main function lies on the symbolic level. Of all the figures she is the only one who is not really a character; her "characteristics," recounted by Hermann (1016–23) and repeated practically verbatim by the Pharmacist (1229–37), do not characterize but instead ironically mark her as a topos of *attractive girl*. On the one hand, Dorothea is what her name says: God's gift to men, every man's fantasy object of desire. The worldly wise Parson says it: she is a delight for youthful and experienced men alike (1241–42). But she also has unusual, nontopical attributes that make her a strong woman with leadership competence. It is what Hermann noticed first: the sturdy wagon, the biggest and strongest oxen, and Dorothea's strong steps and efficient guidance of the mighty beasts (235–40). In her role as strong woman she correlates with the male fantasy of not having to carry the load of patriarchy, the man's burden of government and responsibility. And indeed she liberates male desire and aggression in the rapists and in Hermann's final speech. Dorothea's law, conveyed from the dead fiancé, is irresponsibility, a new world order in which love is possible without bonding and history means no more than transience.

Dorothea's symbolic significance extends beyond the confines of the story and into European history. On this stage she is New Woman who as Charlotte Corday killed revolutionary leader Marat or who as Mme de Staël lit up the scene with her radically liberated texts and manners.[10] In the activist and intellectual women of German romanticism, New

Woman surged to public attention and, in a well-known Jena anecdote, jeered the patriarchal view of woman in Schiller's poem *Würde der Frauen.* "Honor the women, they knit the stockings," their parody went.[11] When she conveys the radical message of world revolution from her dead fiancé, Dorothea evokes, finally, the female icon, Marianne with the Jacobin cap, who has stood for New France, the revolutionary drive that had overthrown the patriarchal ancien régime since Delacroix's painting of Liberté leading her people. The grammatically feminine concepts under which the Revolution marched are antipatriarchal. *Liberté, egalité,* and *fraternité* denounce hierarchy; they proclaim the killing of the fathers by the band of brothers, because neither *liberté* nor *égalité* is possible otherwise. Yet Dorothea, too, in Goethe's play between participation and distance, gets her ironic Achilles' heel, signaled, like the Pharmacist's *Knaster* and Hermann's *Kütschchen* ("little carriage," 17), with an incongruous *k* word: "es *knackte* der Fuß" ("she overturned her foot," 1702). Her central dogma of fleet-footed existence ("But even then, as you travel this earth, still tread on it lightly," 2002) has been sabotaged by the reality of the sprained ankle. Dorothea Lightfoot is rather less so at the moment.

What then of Hermann, the focus of everyone's concern, whose name refers us to yet another heroic tradition? The eighteenth century had promoted a Teutonic chieftain, Arminius-Hermann, who had defeated a Roman army in the Teutoburg Forest, to the rank of creator of Germany. Ten years after Goethe, Kleist would reconnect to this tradition with his ambiguous anti-Napoleon drama, *Die Hermannsschlacht (Hermann's Battle)*. In Goethe's epos, Hermann is, after Wilhelm Meister, another empty nonhero, a (Goethean) self as potential, waiting to be filled, shaped, and determined in the process of *Bildung* (formation, education) by others and by events.[12] Characterized with painful clarity throughout the text as exceedingly malleable, an ideal son of patriarchy, the end leaves him, like the novel does Wilhelm Meister, betrothed to a woman who is his opposite and his superior, suspended in inconclusiveness.

Hermann is the vehicle for historical change at the moment of turn, of indecision in the generational succession that will decide the fate of patriarchy. It is this moment that is captured in the most puzzling lines of the poem. We are at a loss of how to react to the overblown rhetoric and artifice of simple Hermann transformed into a marble statue of classic proportions, breathing Kant–Schillerian supremacy of willpower, for no greater purpose than to prevent stumbling Dorothea from falling:

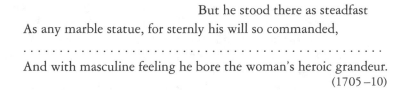

But he stood there as steadfast
As any marble statue, for sternly his will so commanded,

....

And with masculine feeling he bore the woman's heroic grandeur.
(1705–10)

The paradox of verse 1710 holds the key. More clearly in the German original[13] ("Trug mit Mannesgefühl die Heldengröße des Weibes"), the line reverses traditional gender roles and thus designates the moment of overturn as a revolution of patriarchy. In the patriarchal tradition, heroic grandeur belongs to men: Achilles and Hector of classical mythology; Hermann, Robespierre, and Marat of history; and Götz and Egmont of Goethe's own pantheon. By this point the narrative has amply acquainted us with Dorothea as the new, female paradigm of heroism. Hermann so far has been a hero only by default. Humiliated by the Father, he dreamed of heroic action as escape fantasy, easily debunked by the Mother as completely out of character for him (712–16). He is designed to become the New Man of Feeling: feeling the hurt of taunts by the neighbor girls, of rejection by the Father, and of despair over hopeless love. The Man of Feeling does not *fight* for love, respect, or honor; Hermann, "the youth of noble feeling," instead weeps ample tears as Goethe amply confides (660–62, 750–52). Will he then fight for the fatherland, as his closing speech ringingly announces? The jury is still out on this question.

Die Wahlverwandtschaften

In contrast to the popular *Hermann und Dorothea*, Goethe's third novel, *Die Wahlverwandtschaften*, published a decade later (1809), was not well received. The few enthusiastic voices, mostly from among the coterie of Goethe admirers, were far outnumbered by a chorus of condemnation on grounds not merely of immorality or at least ambivalence in matters of morals. More generally the accusation was of elitism, that the author showed little concern for the expectations and capabilities of the reading public. This novel, with its cast of characters weaving hither and yon, alternately arousing sympathy, irritation, and rejection, with its plot running forward during part 1 and then undoing itself in the reverse direction of part 2, with its balancing act between rational realism and super-natural symbolism, with its inconclusive conclusion, and above all with its shifty narrator, was considered bewildering and incomprehensible. It is precisely these features of rich indeterminacy that have made *Die Wahlverwandtschaften* a focus of recent criticism. The past two decades might suggest that Goethe here devised an insoluble textual enigma, a provocation of the very concept of literature: the novel as ironic play of signifiers.[14] As evidence of such a game, critics can point to the names of the four main figures, all variations on the name *Otto,* the name finally given to their combined offspring. More evidence is the chemical allegory highlighted in the title, which changes the four protagonists into literal abstractions, A, B, C, and D,[15] and then proceeds to move them through the plot as on a psychochemical chessboard. The wealthy landowner (Otto) Edward and his wife Charlotte, both on their second marriages, invite the retired Captain (Otto) and young orphan Ottilie to live with them, whereupon each falls in love with the wrong partner. A child, Otto, born to Charlotte and Edward, dies in Ottilie's care. Ottilie starves herself to death, and Edward dies, empathetically, soon thereafter.

The meanings at play, however, are serious indeed. Inspired by Walter Benjamin's seminal essay of 1922, "Goethe's *Wahlverwandtschaften,*" critics have read the novel from a variety of perspectives. The first social novel of the nineteenth century, *Die Wahlverwandtschaften* dissects a world in transition: the crumbling of feudalism under the impact of revolutionary developments at the turn of the century. The psychological novel delves into the complexities of individual souls, exploring the impact of childhood, education, and environment on formation of character and the many faces, masks, and metamorphoses of erotic desire. The novel as culture critique exposes the problematic of marriage and family, with orphan Ottilie as central figure in an evolving vortex and spiritual adultery as its focal event. The novel of ideas examines the tension between the power of nature and the claim to human freedom, engaging with its web of symbols, associations, and allusions the long story of mankind's wrestling match with fate from ancient myths and religious beliefs to modern science and art.

Reading *Die Wahlverwandtschaften* from any of these perspectives makes us realize how much Goethe's world had changed since he penned his good-natured sketch of small-town life in *Hermann und Dorothea.* In political history Hermann's concluding euphoria suffered a crushing disillusion: Napoleon had walked all over Germany, Goethe's own home was invaded, the duke was forced to flee, and both the minister and his sovereign friend were humiliated by having to attend the new emperor's glorification at Erfurt. While Goethe was writing this novel, Napoleon was the uncontested master of Europe, with no end to his reign in sight. Disillusionment likewise followed the collaboration with Schiller in pursuit of a classicist renaissance. The romantic school had carried the day, and Schiller was dead (May 1805). The new century brought a crisis in Goethe's physical, emotional, and spiritual life marked by two life-threatening illnesses and by the traumatic shock of Schiller's death. Benjamin was first to point to the experience of mortality and the fear of death as new features of the eminent man during this, we would say today, midlife crisis. Finally, and most importantly, because it went to the foundation on which Goethe had built and sustained his creative life, his relation with nature had irrevocably changed.

Gone was the harmony between humans and nature, their essential oneness that had still provided the foundation for *Iphigenie*'s "truth." Nature is conspicuously absent from *Hermann und Dorothea*. In *Die Wahlverwandtschaften* nature takes the place of the uncanny, the demonic. Nature is a force inaccessible to rational thought and overpowering both reason and freedom of will, the "realm of serene freedom of reason," as Goethe's advertisement of his novel stated.[16] *Faust Part I*, the long-laboring work finally completed in 1806, had presented this face of nature allegorically in Mephistopheles, the Witch's Kitchen, and the satanism of Walpurgis Night. Faust's quest for knowledge of nature leads astray, away from the desired path of classicist humanism and into crime and (self-)destruction. Instead of higher insight, Faust achieves the defeat of his "Vernunft-Freiheit," this cherished ideal of Kant–Schillerian Enlightenment.

With his work on *Farbenlehre*, in progress since 1790 and published in 1810, Goethe had joined the attempt of scientists, just like Faust, to wrest truth from nature. His position was therefore decisively altered from the erstwhile oneness of human and nature to the division now into man as investigating subject versus nature as investigated object.[17] Moreover, even though a theory of color explores nature's brightest side—light—it yet reveals nature's dark secret: There is no truth to be found, only different interpretations. Goethe's own investigation was driven by the desire to assert a counterinterpretation to Newtonian optics. Goethe of course thought he was right, as he vociferously insisted in his extraordinary and inexplicable anti-Newton polemic. Yet the very assertion that "science" could have been wrong for a century—including

all those contemporaries who now refused to accept Goethe's view—
opens up the concept of scientific truth to skepticism.

Goethe thus has implicated himself in the Faustian dilemma, in the
project of science as a competition of human efforts to nail down nature
in knowledge. *Die Wahlverwandtschaften* demonstrates that such efforts
are doomed. Its characters insist on interpreting, manipulating, and
controlling natural phenomena and contingencies. Symmetrical
headaches, chemical formulas and engraved initials, the lay of the land,
the growth of trees, and a glass that does not break are (mis)read as
expressions of spiritual correspondences. The actions undertaken on the
basis of these readings have disastrous consequences: the deaths of three
individuals—Ottilie, Edward, and baby Otto—within the brief span of
18 months. By the law of narrative logic such behavior must be deemed
wrong*headed*. *Die Wahlverwandtschaften* is the most profoundly skeptical
of Goethe's works, as Benjamin again was the first to see. But what
Benjamin failed to see is that Goethe is attempting something entirely
new in the novel, an approach to fiction that can be seen as forerunner
to what postmodern theory calls magical realism.[18]

In Goethe's novel, nature—inner human nature and the cosmos
within which human life takes place—is an ambivalent force that interferes in all aspects of human existence. Furthermore, nature is essentially
inaccessible, unknowable to humans: a priori other, *alien* in the strong
sense of science fiction. The enigmatic figure of Ottilie is the unwilling
and unknowing carrier of this nature; she is its similarly *alien* representative. The novel's action demonstrates the consequences of this view of
nature. At the end, contemplating Ottilie's coffin, we are told that
"nature's indifferent hand" (*Works*, 11:260) exerts absolute power over
impotent human will, creating with seemingly arbitrary willfulness
good or bad events for humans and thus constituting their lives as ran-
dom mixtures of happiness and disaster. The characters, in turn, because
such is human nature, try to know and to understand these events by an
array of interpretive strategies: presentiments, prophecies, omens,
superstitions, self-deceptions, wishful thinking, divine intervention, and
meaningful coincidences.

One way of trying to understand is, of course, science, the way displayed in the concept of "elective affinities" (i.e., the natural properties
of chemical compounds to switch partners). Working out the implications of this concept, the novel becomes an experiment to test the possibility of human knowledge of nature. The result is negative, and the
novel ends in pervasive resignation: "Nature," what happened to these

lives and why, remains a mystery. But as Faust, too, found out, such experiments have a cost. Three lives are wasted, and one of them (monstrous Baby Otto, pointing forward to Homunculus) was even created for the express purpose of being wasted in order to demonstrate the hypothesis that underlies the experiment.

Die Walhverwandtschaften is marked by strange characters and events denoted as *wunderbar* (strange, miraculous), by apparent magic flowing from provocatively natural causes, by overdetermined rituals and symbols, and by mysterious scientific and "natural" phenomena. The novel is strung out between modern science manipulating nature in an effort to improve creation on the one hand—by new creations of gardens, houses, and lakes or by human betterment through education—and, on the other hand, the dimension of the sacral. The sacral dimension is represented in cemeteries, monuments, mausoleums, and the question of death or afterlife, in religious art and artifice (Nativity stagings), saints, miracles, and the question of faith or make-believe. We can think of this novel as a pessimistic fairy tale told by a disillusioned romantic scientist, Goethe's narrator.

Goethe had participated in the age of fairy tales and romantic nature philosophy. His own *Märchen (Fairy Tale)* of 1795 had spun a romantic fantasy from earth science. His friendship with Jena professor and leading romantic philosopher F. Schelling had made him familiar with nature philosophy and its ambitions. In this school the scientist was encouraged to think he could know the whole of nature because humans, just like the divinity, were part of this whole.[19] Yet by 1808 the heads of romantic nature philosophy had abandoned their lofty goals: Schelling had turned to mysticism, and F. Schlegel had converted to Catholicism.

As the novel assembles its quartet of characters—Edward, Charlotte, the Captain, and Ottilie—the focus turns to "metaphorical language" about chemical affinity and its application to real life (book 1, chapter 4). Divergent interpretations are advanced and, if ever so playfully, contested. Charlotte in particular objects to the analogy between choice among humans and natural necessity in the relations of chemical substances. Her objection highlights the issue of anthropomorphism, or the questionable commensurability of nature and mind and thus the claim of scientific, allegedly objective, knowledge. Goethe's advertisement had made this point: "that in science one often makes use of moral analogies in order to access something very distant from the field of human knowledge."[20] His novel, he continued, merely turns this procedure on its head, leading the reader around the anthropomorphic circle. From the outset, then, the slippery ground of interpretation, of ascribing meaning to natural phenomena or novelistic events, is made explicit.

The members of the quartet represent distinct positions within the human-to-nature relationship. Charlotte stands for the Enlightenment ideal of reasonable partnership. Supremely rational, she shows understanding, moderation, and tolerance toward the most extravagant vagaries of human nature; she approaches nature as environment with incremental reformism. Her new creation in the park is really a mere tinkering with nature, as seen from the Captain's perspective. Although her fortitude and resolve never waver even in the face of severe provocation and disaster, she nevertheless fails to achieve any of her goals. Her life, over the course of the novel, is a steady stream of incremental diminishments. The narrator's endorsement of this admirable character cracks open only once: perhaps, because her own standards are so high, she expects too much of others (*Works,* 11:161).

The Captain is cast as *homo faber,* the can-do man of science and technology, who, with his complete set of graphs and instruments, is equipped to reconstruct nature on the grand scale. The perfect tool of friends, patrons, and other masters who make use of his eager and efficient services—the word *tüchtig* (efficient) characterizes him best—he is also the perfect loser. When he enters the novel he has just lost his career. In the game of elective affinities he first loses Edward to Ottilie and then Charlotte to her moral principles. His attempt to build a life away from the doomed foursome fails when his prospects of an advantageous marriage disappear and he is sucked back into the services of friend Edward and beloved Charlotte. He emerges most clearly as the loser from the inserted novella, *Die Wunderlichen Nachbarskinder (Curious Tale of the Childhood Sweethearts; Works,* 11:224–30). He was the fiancé who lost the damsel to his rival. To add insult to injury, even this story is no longer his story: It has been expropriated to focus on the lucky winners named in the title. The story simply forgets him; the ending says not a word about the man who lost his girl. In the telling of this narrative the Captain has become—just as in the novel—the nonhero, an "unperson." *Homo faber,* man the maker, is unmade in his own story.

Edward, who moves his attachments around among the members of the quartet and who likes to gamble and to bet, now represents free will at the absolute level: arbitrariness. He does only what he wants, he does all he wants, and he expects to get what he wants. Edward embodies desire in its paradigmatically human form: eros.[21] He is human desire also insofar as he is the unconscious bearer of drive. He, and the reader with him, thinks he is free because he chooses his goals and acts on his choices. But in the new Goethean universe desire means drivenness by one's nature, which in turn is shaped and thus predetermined by forces outside the individual's control. The narrator lets us in on this secret very late, in one of his sly asides. Man, he tells us in the penultimate chapter, is essentially unchangeable because every individual is at any moment the product of his agglomerated experience consisting of "character, individuality, inclination, disposition, place, surroundings, and habits" (*Works*, 11:254).

Although we are deceived along with Edward, we are undeceived before he is, when the narrator, in telling about Edward's decision making, keeps correcting his modals, those signifiers of the subjective aspect of an action, from "he only hoped and desired" to "he had to . . . he was compelled to" (*Works*, 11:249). Edward reaches insight, perhaps, only after Ottilie's death and shortly before his own, when he has to engage his will to overcome his "nature" in the difficult "martyrdom" of ascesis (*Works*, 11:262). But then again, perhaps the irresistible attraction between the two fated lovers retains its "almost magical" (*Works*, 11:254) power even beyond Ottilie's death. The narrator does not say, but clearly narrative logic demands that Edward follow Ottilie. His ascesis would thus be determined by necessity, not free will.

The admission to the household of Ottilie, representative of alien nature, is prepared with presentiments, omens, and "intuition . . . that doesn't augur well," felt, of all people, by enlightened Charlotte (*Works*, 11:97). Competing interpretations of contingencies, such as Charlotte's ink blot and the shared name Otto, are advanced by Edward and that bearer of misfortune and mixed messages, Mittler. The anticipation of Ottilie opens the game of contested meanings. Ottilie is introduced as *wunderbar* ("strange," but also "miracle bearing"); her mere presence has profound effects on the other three and provokes the need for interpretation. Her amazing correspondences with Edward—headaches, music making, and handwriting—must mean something. Edward reads it as love. The narrator's explanatory model is the first explicit pointer to the dimension of magic (i.e., the interpenetration of inanimate nature and spiritual forces). Beauty, he says, is a healing power lodged in minerals, humans, and saints: in emeralds, Ottilie, and her name saint, who bears the sobriquet "Augentrost" (*eye comfort*, which translates to "joy to behold," *Works*, 11:121).

Ottilie's power over Edward climaxes in the fateful night of spiritual adultery, which captures all four characters in mystery and magic.

Edward seeks out Charlotte but in the subjective reality of his fantasy makes love to Ottilie, and so Charlotte to the Captain. Coming on the heels of the mystifying foundation ceremonies, the event is steeped in the uncanny and surreal. At the stroke of midnight, phantom hour, Edward resuscitates the past, inspired on his lover's quest by a joint reminiscence with the Count. The gothic staging of Edward stealing through dark halls, winding staircases, and secret doors marks the act as transgressive. The idea of transgression carries over into the fetishism of kissing her shoe. The phantom mood ("all this seemed ghostly," *Works,* 11:150) lingers on when the hidden love between the two new pairs erupts into the light of the next day; Charlotte's "strange premonitions" (*Works,* 11:151) confirm the narrator's foreknowledge of the "monstrous rights" (*Works,* 11:147) of biology: her pregnancy.

In contrast to activist Edward, Ottilie is merely a conduit, passive and unconscious, of the alien power she represents. Like Edward and unlike Charlotte and the Captain, however, she suffers a wrenching impact from their separation. She metamorphoses into her own opposite. She now seeks the outdoors, especially in solitary boating on the treacherous lake, and engages in exorbitant daydreaming. Both fated lovers experience a heightening of perception beyond the physical dimension; their visions of each other keep them insolubly linked. Concurrently, fed by absence, loss, and fantasies, their misreadings of apparently significant events abound and mislead them into wrong actions. In the last pages of part 1, such misdirections, mediated by busy go-between Mittler, come to a head.

Edward reads the letters *E* and *O* on the glass, which, luckily or unluckily, did not break, as his and Ottilie's initials intertwined to signal that fate wants their union. But we should remember the narrator's earlier underhanded remark that the two letters were Edward's own initials (*Works,* 11:135). In a similar move Charlotte overinterprets the synonym for *pregnant,* "guter Hoffnung" ("of good hope") to authorize new hope for the future of her marriage on the basis of divine intervention. She takes steps to preserve the marriage on the perverse argument that the morally illicit conception was "ordained by heaven" (*Works,* 11:173).

Baby Otto, the child of quadruple parentage, brings about revelation in an almost biblical—or magical—sense. Truths about the entangled relationships must be faced, and decisions must be made. Yet the truth looks different to each of the four, and so do the consequences they draw for their actions. The truth is, there is no rational way to deal with an impossible fact such as "Wunderkind" Otto. Again, language plays games, first with the name so blatantly yet necessarily given: "he could hardly have any other name than that of his father and his father's friend" (*Works*, 11:215). The language game continues, as the child's unnatural resemblance to the Captain and Ottilie reveals itself under the key term *Wunder* ("miracle"). This "Wunderkind" is to be understood in its literal meaning, not as *child prodigy* but as *offspring of miracle,* or rather, in tune with the unholy circumstances of the conception, *child of magic.* Finally, then, the fairy-tale figure of the changeling is called up.

The child of magic is a powerful agent who determines events. In the physical being of Otto, the four are now chained together really and materially. Escape attempts initiated by Edward, Charlotte, and Ottilie fail, and the Captain is drawn back into the fold. The true meaning of their enigmatic offspring, so frantically denied in the interpretations attempted by the parents, is death. The parson who performs the blasphemous baptism of "Otto" is the first victim. The child's death, assisted by Edward and Ottilie and staged as high melodrama, locks the chain among the four. From now on, they will live together in suspended animation till death do them part. Otto's power and meaning, to be the bearer and signifier of death, has passed on to Ottilie, who through her suicide threat makes death the only way out of the quadrangle.

Ottilie's deathlike sleep on Charlotte's lap after Otto's death marks a threshold and reveals her true essence. She returns from her faint with a message from the dimension of the sacral or demonic, which has appointed her to be the conduit of life-governing power. This power is as real and material as, for instance, electricity, and just as morally indifferent. Ottilie, we now hear, is a lucky or unlucky star (*Works*, 11:243) that bears happiness or misfortune according to no perceivable moral categories. The apparent miracle performed on the young girl, Nanny, after Ottilie's death is cast in ambiguity. The narrator explains the phenomenon of faith by the general human need to believe (*Works*, 11:261), just as Edward had believed in omens and correspondences. In the end, we readers need to believe that nature is on balance beneficent. The malignant face of ambivalent nature has prevailed in the novel, particularly in the later parts. The ending rights the balance to present nature as no more or less than ambivalent: death bearing and life bearing both.

Chapter Seven

Wilhelm Meisters Lehrjahre or Abdication of the Subject

Goethe's second novel, when it appeared in installments from January 1795 to October 1796, found an enthusiastic reception, particularly among the nascent romanticists at Jena. Friedrich Schlegel, in a long essay on the work in his programmatic journal, *Athenäum* (1798), went so far as to proclaim that together with the French Revolution and Fichte's philosophy, Goethe's *Wilhelm Meister* constituted the intellectual and historical mainstream of the era. As writers during the nineteenth century imitated and emulated Goethe's novel, a new genre came into being: the bildungsroman (novel of education or development). This tradition, however, has created a problem in interpreting *Wilhelm Meister*.

Recent critics find the term *bildungsroman* a misnomer. They contend that the concept of *bildung* was read into *Wilhelm Meister* in order to uphold the German ideal of a classical education. According to bildungsroman tradition, Goethe's novel would trace the organic development of a well-rounded character toward the goal of individual autonomy. Today's readings tend to focus on aspects outside of the hero's self, including social and historical relations and other characters in the novel insofar as they represent an other for Wilhelm, with the enigmatic figure of Mignon the undisputed favorite. Instead of an idealization of individualism, the novel is seen as analysis and critique of individualism. For these readings, *Wilhelm Meisters Lehrjahre* explores the limitations of individualist projects such as self-realization, self-autonomy, freedom, and the pursuit of happiness.[1]

Writing this novel must have presented Goethe with unexpected difficulties: no other work except *Faust* took him so long to complete. The interrupted genesis and substantial differences between the two extant versions indicate a major break in thematic conception. Goethe started his second novel soon after getting settled at Weimar, in early 1777, but writing slowed down to a snail's pace and he finally abandoned the project when he left for Italy. Discovered in 1910 and known today as *Wil-*

helm Meisters theatralische Sendung, the fragmentary result of this work phase was preserved despite the intention of the author, who had destroyed his earlier manuscript. In early 1794 Goethe returned to the novel after reconceptualizing it during the French campaigns. With new friend Schiller's encouraging support and critical advice, and under the self-imposed pressure of seeing the early volumes in print before he had finished the entire novel, Goethe completed the renamed *Wilhelm Meisters Lehrjahre* in two years.

Like Goethe's first novel, *Werther, Wilhelm Meister* springs from a strong autobiographical source. This origin is especially clear in the childhood segment, a fact gleefully commented on by Goethe's mother, who eagerly awaited each shipment of her son's new novel. Unlike *Werther,* however, there is no lure of identification. The omnipresent narrator, like a film director, views and manipulates his characters from retrospective distance. In retrospect, or rather in two different retrospectives in the two versions, Goethe imagines alternative life stories for his fictive self. In the first version it is the life as a poet and proactive creator of new German theater, the story of the artist who can shape his world according to his subjectivity: a German Shakespeare in the image of Goethe's Prometheus. Such a life, *Wilhelm Meisters theatralische Sendung* hypothesizes, might have been Goethe's had he not opted for a Weimar government career.

In the final version, *Wilhelm Meisters Lehrjahre,* the possibility of a career in the arts constitutes only the beginning, a beginning that is explicitly rejected as a wrong path. Instead of the first version's triumph of subjectivity reveling in the fullness of life created from the artistic individual's desires, *Wilhelm Meisters Lehrjahre* presents life as a sequence of options and choices. Each choice inevitably diminishes the remaining options. Life is thus a progressive narrowing down, a process of increasing limitation. The subject, instead of molding a world in his fashion, is constrained more and more to adapt to a world of givens. In the final analysis, as the end of the novel reveals, the hero, far from creating his own choices, has been following a plan devised and supervised by others: the collective of the Tower.

Wilhelm, a young man with a solid middle-class background, has a love affair with actress Mariane, whom he abandons pregnant. When his father dies he leaves home to become head of an itinerant theater troupe and picks up two strange members of a mountebank group: a young dancer, Mignon, and an old man, the Harpist. After many love and other entanglements and a position as actor and dramaturge with a resident theater, Wilhelm joins a group of aristocratic entrepreneurs (the Tower) and finally finds his son, Felix, and his destined bride, aristocrat Natalie.

Abdication of the subject is the fundamental reason why *Wilhelm Meisters Lehrjahre* is Goethe's anti-*Werther,* as many critics have noted. Even though he plotted a catastrophic story, Goethe with *Werther* opened the modern era of the subject, in which literature explores subjective interiority, with the romantics the immediate successors of the *Werther* approach. Goethe himself, a mere two decades later, closes up the reign of subjectivity and proposes, in his second novel, a—dare I say it—postmodern view of the subject as a culturally constructed, multiply mediated self. If we agree that "the literary crisis of the self may finally reach closure as subjectivity is equated with having options" and no more, then *Wilhelm Meisters Lehrjahre* is indeed a novel for our times.[2] Small wonder the romantics in their own novels of development soon turned away from the Goethean model. Far less known than Schlegel's encomium is Novalis's argument, developed "against 'Wilhelm Meister's Apprenticeship,'" ending in a series of devastating judgments, which one hesitates to quote without comment: "dismaying and silly, pretentious and affected . . . ends as a farce . . . pilgrimage to the certificate of nobility . . . A 'Candide' against poetry" (*HA,* 7:664f).

Novalis's allusion to Voltaire's *Candide* links Goethe to the picaresque tradition. Basic features of this genre indeed inform the structure of *Wilhelm Meister,* while thematically the novel redefines the meaning of picaresque. The plot proceeds through a series of encounters, with very few significant events or actions to drive the story. Encounters with men present the hero with choices to be made by the intellect, on the basis of rational evaluation and judgment. Hearing their stories, Wilhelm is to consider each as a positive or negative model for his own life and behavior. It is a structural technique Goethe developed further in his successor novel, *Wilhelm Meisters Wanderjahre,* in which the slenderest possible thread of a plot is spun between formally independent stories. Wilhelm's far more numerous encounters with women follow a romance plot, with two major differences. Wilhelm's is a course of multiple romances, intertwined and shifting the goal of the quest between several very different women. More significantly, after his first love for the actress Mariane, Wilhelm's emotional response to the women he meets does not fit the conventional understanding of "romantic" love.

The introduction of a narrator, too, moves *Wilhelm Meister* away from *Werther* and toward the picaresque convention. Werther's editor stepped in only after the hero's monologic voice was silenced. In *Wilhelm Meisters Lehrjahre*, an impersonal narrator handles Wilhelm's affairs throughout. His third-person narrative is interrupted only occasionally by a few letters, by the autobiographical manuscript of the Beautiful Soul (book 6), and by the written account of the Harpist's and Mignon's stories. The narrator maintains his position outside the hero's experiences, reminding us of his ironic distance in frequent judgmental or humorous asides. His self-references in the first-person plural, *we*, subtly draw the reader onto his territory, suggesting a collusion of superiority between narrator and reader vis-à-vis the hero's unsatisfactory behavior.

In distinction from the typically chatty picaresque narrator (e.g., in Wieland's *Don Silvio de Rosalva*, which is often mentioned as one of *Wilhelm Meisters Lehrjahre*'s forerunners), Goethe's narrator demonstrates a marked reticence. He consistently underexplains and thus incites the reader's own imagination to produce the missing links. As Goethe's first reader, Schiller, complained, the ideas behind the figures and events remain unclarified. Goethe's reply was: leave it to the reader.[3] So if *Wilhelm Meisters Lehrjahre* is not a bildungsroman for the hero, perhaps we might consider it a bildungsroman for the reader.

If we trace the abdication of the subject through the novel, one phenomenon becomes immediately apparent: the lack of interiority. Characters, including the hero, are portrayed from the outside, through their actions and words. "A certain realistic tic," was Goethe's seemingly apologetic explanation to Schiller.[4] We are denied access to the figures' innermost thoughts, their "true" motivations, their souls. Occasional glimpses of Wilhelm's thinking are just as likely to be misleading down the primrose path of his self-deception. The narrator frequently reflects and comments on his hero's acts or mishaps, but always in terms of general experience ("It is well known that a first love . . ."), never in respect of the unique individual Wilhelm. "The history of every human being is his character," states the radical pragmatist, Therese.[5] To judge from the regularity with which all the characters come equipped with their particular histories, the novel subscribes to the same principle.

Subjectivity does play a large role in the novel but is regularly downgraded, rejected, or shown to be pernicious. In the beginning Wilhelm is completely immersed in subjectivity. Trying to realize his childhood self-image in a vicarious life in the theater through a love affair with actress Mariane, he insists on his own dreams despite and against bourgeois everyday reality. Yet here, and later in his masquerade as Shakespeare's Prince Harry or in his Hamlet performance, he demonstrates sheer narcissism. He only plays himself, which is, as skeptic Jarno cruelly enlightens him, proof that he has no acting talent. Narcissism likewise rules his love for Mariane. Old Barbara's bitter accusation that he had no idea of his beloved's true circumstances, that he did not care, hits the mark. Wilhelm's image of Mariane is a projection of himself. His ecstatic happiness in love, as is generally the case with a first love, according to the narrator, is subjective exuberance, love of self. Wilhelm is entirely full of himself, filling page after page with his talk of himself, while Mariane and Barbara fall asleep from exhaustion or boredom. He does not have a single question to ask Mariane about herself (book 1).

Wilhelm's life in the theatrical sphere, which extends over more than half of the novel, is marked as illusionary, hovering between half-admitted guilty conscience and good-natured self-deception. More often than not Wilhelm, who fancies himself in control, is duped or victimized by clever manipulators or by his own overblown self-confidence. "Playing for empty nuts with empty nuts" (*Works*, 9:102), he chases after grand illusions. His theater mission would bring culture to the debased populace. As exalted artist he would command the respect of the frivolous aristocracy. The climax in his career of theatrical delusion is reached in the Hamlet performance and the subsequent ensemble orgy. So great is Wilhelm's willingness to suspend disbelief that he accepts with barely a question the pleasures of an unknown woman in his bed. It is hard to imagine how he could be unable to tell the difference between the two likely candidates, Philine or Mignon (*Works*, 9:198–99).

The story of the Beautiful Soul (book 6) reveals subjectivity as self-limitation from fear. Every decision the admirably pious lady takes is a defeat, a step inward and backward, a retreat out of reach of a life that is too much for her to cope with. Similarly, Wilhelm's deliberate choice of Therese for a wife (book 8) is motivated by fear. Her uncomplicated clarity holds out the promise of an escape from the complexities of life. Her life story tells Wilhelm that she always knew precisely what to do and did it. She seems an ideal person to aid with the frightening new responsibility of parenting Felix. Finally, Wilhelm asks Therese to marry him out of fear of facing his love for Therese's friend, the seemingly unattainable Natalie.

In the terms of Goethe's second novel, radical subjectivity cannot survive. Subjectivity without compromise informs the two most fascinating figures, Mignon and the Harpist. Wilhelm's closest companions during his life as an aspiring artist, they represent the dimension of art separate from the reality of life to the point of alienation. In a much-imitated innovation in novel writing, Goethe has them find their authentic expression in poetry; in the language of normal human communication they are as good as mute. For the Harpist, defiant reliance on the dictates of his own nature had led to incest, exile, and insanity. Mignon, the offspring of this incestuous spirituality, grew up an autistic child in a life of solitude and silence. Wilhelm does not dream of understanding her, nor can we, narrator and reader, make such a claim. When Wilhelm and his well-meaning friends put the two mysterious solitaires on the road to social integration and common sense, both adapt willingly, but they cannot make it. Mignon pines away, and the Harpist kills himself.

Subjectivity, in this novel, is restricted to a far more limited role. It means making choices according to one's identity. The title of Wilhelm's only completed work from his youthful poetic practice, "Jüngling am Scheidewege" ("Youth at the Crossroads"), is a leitmotif. The novel consists of offering options—encounters with men for intellectual models and with women for objects of desire—and it is Wilhelm's primary task to choose among them. More often than not, Wilhelm makes the wrong choice or he cannot decide. His story, and thus his character, according to Therese's dictum, is an accumulation of errors. The reason is that he does not know himself; he has no clue to his identity and therefore to his true desires. He lacks self-reflection and self-consciousness because Goethe denies him interiority. His wrong choices fill the novel from beginning to end, from the theater career and the misjudged friends (Melina, Laertes, and Serlo) to his marriage proposal to Therese. If Therese is his most egregiously wrong choice, the choice of his ersatz family, Mignon and the Harpist, causes the most heartbreak. Once Wilhelm decides to join the rationalist community of the Tower his wrong choice of Mignon and the Harpist has to be corrected. He gives them up, they die, and Wilhelm is given his own family of son Felix and fiancée Natalie in return, neither of whom he had chosen himself.

Some of Wilhelm's wrong decisions result from his impulsive temperament, and some are the result of pressure: an obligation, promise, or merely the pressure of circumstances, as in his morally objectionable willingness to help kidnap Lydie, Lothario's cast-off love object. In yet other decisions there is no pressure, and Wilhelm merely goes along with others' initiatives. The worst of these decisions, with a lasting burden of guilt as a consequence, is his playing along with the impersonation of the Count, who will be forever haunted by this apparent specter of himself. His bonding with Felix and accepting him as his son is a decision that follows a series of others' (Mariane's, Barbara's, Aurelie's, and Mignon's) initiatives who have brought him Felix. Yet the novel declares this the most crucial choice of his life, the magic formula of initiation from apprenticeship to membership in the band of the chosen, the Society of the Tower.

In view of Wilhelm's lack of self-knowledge, it is not surprising to find him prey to endless confusion and indecision when faced with a choice. This quandary intensifies after he quits the theater, and it is to escape such anxiety that he feels attracted to Therese: her clarity is to compensate for his own lack. Anxiety and indecision reach a climax when his choice of Therese meets with the challenge from the Tower group. Wilhelm's passivity here contrasts most vividly with Therese's determination and defiance. She comes to take possession of her fiancé, whereas he stands helpless and merely complains of manipulation. The only way Wilhelm can help himself in this conflict of loyalties and desires is to explicitly yield up his own will, first to Natalie's and then to the Tower's guidance. To get to this point, however, Wilhelm first has to go through a rupture of identity, a loss of self similar to his breakdown after his separation from Mariane. That earlier crisis had changed him utterly, from theater enthusiast to hardworking businessman.

This time the rupture happens through the loss of Mignon. Mignon collapses and dies the moment Therese steps in to claim Wilhelm with a shower of kisses. Wilhelm's mind is a thoughtless void, fluctuating between the images of Mignon and Natalie, two contrastive objects of desire that signal his split identity. A prey to despair, he fails in the task "to test and to choose" that is specifically assigned him (*Works,* 9:339). Over the long, drawn-out funeral of Mignon Wilhelm remains emotionally paralyzed. When all is over, after Mignon is finally *out of his life,* he is ready formally and on principle to renounce his own will, to sign himself over to command and control by the Tower: " 'I consign myself entirely to my friends and their direction,' said Wilhelm, 'for it is useless trying to act according to one's own will in this world. What I most wanted to keep, I have to let go, and an undeserved benefit imposes itself upon me' " (*Works,* 9:364). There is yet a last episode of despair from indecision, when Wilhelm cannot make up his mind to admit his love for Natalie or else to depart. Again, "his friends" have to act for him. This time it is gadfly Friedrich who provides the concluding spectacle—Novalis called it a farce—of Wilhelm being led to the goal he did not know was his.

Wilhelm's path through the novel, his quest or development, leads him from individualism to integration in a collective. He starts out as a flamboyant individualist who flouts convention and intends to break with his bourgeois community in joining Mariane and theater life. After his impulsive false start fails, and after a host of mixed experiences in different realms of life, he decides yet again, this time with deliberation and on principle, as set forth in the programmatic letter to friend Werner (book 5, chapter 3), to create a personality and a life for himself, of his own design and choosing. In contrast with model capitalist Werner's cozy bourgeois family, Wilhelm collects his queer family of Mignon, the Harpist, the oddball Friedrich, and the arch individualist Philine. The Society of the Tower, which he finally joins, is built on the family model, too, but of a very different brand.

The Tower subscribes to a collectivist ideology that has been judged socialist by some critics and totalitarian by others. In the center stands not man the individual but man as collective, as mankind. In this view the individual is merely part human, each representing an aspect of total humanity. Only together, acting in common, can these individuals attain to human nature, to fullness of life. Each of the four founding siblings, Lothario, Friedrich, Natalie, and the Countess, represents a specific human feature to excess. Their family ties consist in symbiosis and supplementarity: each has an excess of something that another member lacks. Natalie literally illustrates this principle of supplementarity. She leads a vicarious emotional life through brother Lothario's love exploits, and in the end she supplies the bride whom the newly inducted member, Wilhelm, lacks after having ceded Therese to Lothario's older claim.

Everywhere we look the Tower denies the projects of individualism. Instead of equality, democracy, and autonomy there is leadership and tutelage in an idealized tradition of aristocracy. The Tower's self-image is of an educated elite, who appoint themselves guardians of others who are only too happy to be led. " 'It is beyond belief what a cultivated man can achieve for himself and others, if, without trying to lord it over others, he has the temperament to be the guardian of many, helping them to find the right occasion to do what they would all like to do, and guiding them toward the goals they have clearly in mind without knowing how to reach them' " (*Works,* 9:372).

The brotherhood Wilhelm is invited to join holds progressive views on economics, politics, and global cooperation and exchange, based on a strong foundation of statism, all of it in contrast to Wilhelm's erstwhile individualist beliefs. Wilhelm's path to collectivization is a long and rocky road through resistance, wrenching pain, and sacrifice. His resistance to manipulation, however, is halfhearted, in contrast with Lydie's and Therese's protest and active rebellion. The temptation to be accepted by the powerful and wise aristocrats is too strong for the petty bourgeois and failed stage impresario. To earn admittance Wilhelm has to submit to the hierarchical order, and he must acknowledge the special rights and privileges of the exceptional person, leader Lothario, to the point of ceding him his fiancée, Therese. Most significant, he has to sacrifice his elective family of idiosyncratic individuals. He consents to both Mignon's and the Harpist's institutionalization in an effort to assimilate them to the new order. The Harpist's suicide confirms his recurrent nightmare in which Felix, the beautiful boy with the blond curls, was the cause of his death. Wilhelm has traded in his old family for his new one: son Felix and the Society of the Tower.

The abdication of the subject plays out the most striking scenario in the innermost field of human experience, love. As Wilhelm moves from Mariane to Natalie, the course of the novel changes the definition of love from subjective expression of individual desire to a universal supplement of need. Mariane, who lives and dies for love, embodies the tragic romance of Western literary tradition all the way to the illegitimate and abandoned mothers of Sturm und Drang drama, including Goethe's own Gretchen in *Faust,* or the male fantasy of total female dedication and submission. Natalie denounces precisely this tradition: "What we read in books about love, and what the world shows us of what it calls love, has always seemed to me idle fancy." Love is a matter of definition, which is why she can say that she has been in love "never—or always" (*Works,* 9:330). The love she represents is closest to the Christian concept of *caritas*: the desire to give to all according to their need, to make people whole, and to supplement their wants and lacks. Her love for Wilhelm, then, has nothing to do with his individuality, with who or what he uniquely is. It has everything to do with what he needs, and he, ever since his first auratic vision of her in a moment of gravest need after the robbers' attack, has built up his need for her unknown image in dreams and fantasies. Madcap Friedrich's flippant remark to his sister is a joke on the surface only: "I don't believe you will marry until some bride or other is missing, and you, with your customary generosity, will provide yourself as a supplement to someone's existence" (*Works,* 9:346).

On the way from Mariane to Natalie the novel proffers to Wilhelm and the reader the many faces of love, most of them deterrent, in the women he meets and the stories he is told. The love stories are generally disastrous, and they all sound like we have heard them before: small wonder, because they draw on the rich thesaurus of love literature in

Western culture. Aurelie's reenactment of Countess Orsina from Lessing's tragedy of love and betrayal, *Emilia Galotti,* is only the most blatant instance of life imitating literature. Particularly repellent are the stories of love in marriage and among the parental generation. The message of these texts seems to be that it is high time to discontinue the Western love tradition, that the rising generation—Wilhelm's—must not follow in the steps of their fathers and mothers. Madame Melina's stepmother coveting her daughter's lover, Therese's parents conniving with adultery, Aurelie's prostitute and exploitative aunt, Laertes' cuckoldry, and the Harpist's incest are warning signs, deterrent examples.

Among the love options Wilhelm is offered by the women he meets after Mariane, three are so far outside the tradition as to challenge our very comprehension. Although the concept of *caritas* supplies a frame of reference for understanding Natalie, we are at a loss how to categorize Philine and Mignon. We might see in Philine a provocation to all attempts at categorization, a defiance of logic and understanding in matters psychological, because her character consists explicitly in not being a coherent character (*Works,* 9:55). Similarly, her love for Wilhelm goes against all expectations the hero and the reader might bring to a lover's behavior. Arguably the most quoted sentence in the novel is her astounding: "And if I love you, what's that to you?" (*Works,* 9:139). Philine is the one truly free and autonomous individual in the novel, a female countermodel of individualism to the finally complaisant hero.

Mignon's love defies understanding in other ways. Her hermaphroditic nature, indeterminate age, unknown past, and refusal of normal communication all translate into so many obstacles to comprehension. Unlike other figures and in contradiction to Therese's axiom, her history does not explain her character. Even after we know about her origins and childhood we still have no clue to the enigma of her being. The mystery that is Mignon can be represented in dance, music, or poetry; it cannot be narrated or explained. Like poetry—authentic poetry, not what the world according to Natalie calls literature—Mignon's love and Mignon's being resist rational analysis.

This is why her songs, and above all her signature poem, "Know you the land . . ." (*Works,* 9:83),[6] have so powerfully captured readers' (and composers') imagination and affection. Goethe himself plays on this real-world effect of his fictional character in the second *Wilhelm Meister* novel, in which a Mignon fan movement has taken hold. And yet it is precisely Mignon's signature poem that makes explicit the contradictions inherent in her person and her love. Wilhelm is for her at one and the same time beloved/lover, protector, and father, roles that in the normal ken of human relations are incompatible. Thus, although the abdication of the subject is inscribed in the life path of the hero, Wilhelm Meister, the novel yet saves subjectivity in translating it to a dimension of mystery and enigma figured primarily in the woman.

Chapter Eight
Wilhelm Meisters Wanderjahre or Going Beyond

The notion of difficulty has clung to *Wilhelm Meisters Wanderjahre* like no other Goethean work, including *Faust Part II*. Biographers routinely apologize for the "elusive" text to justify their highly selective discussions of Goethe's last novel. Conrady advises readers to forget about genre or unity and instead consider the alleged novel a "Prosabuch-Reservoir" for readers to fill in with their own thoughts (Conrady, 2:515).[1] Reaction to the first edition of *Wilhelm Meisters Wanderjahre* in 1821 was disappointment bordering on anger. The reading public felt cheated because it was not the kind of sequel to the first *Meister* novel they had so long awaited. More particularly, critics protested that practically all the inserted novellas had been published before and that the so-called novel around these stories lacked cohesion, ideas, and closure. The second, considerably expanded, edition of 1829 was as good as ignored.

Precisely the features that bedeviled nineteenth-century readers make up the fascination of *Wilhelm Meisters Wanderjahre* for today's critics, who consider this the most avant-garde of Goethe's works, one that could only be appreciated with the advent of the modern and postmodern novel. For, in yet another Goethean first in the history of the novel, *Wilhelm Meisters Wanderjahre* skips the era of realism to offer a panorama of multiple perspectives on a multidimensional, "virtual" reality. The narrator splits in a number of authorial and editorial functions, as various sorts of texts compose the texture of the novel, including diaries, letters, speeches, archival material, a social science field report, translations and adaptations of other literary texts, novellas, and even fairy tales that cross over into the "real" space of the novel, and conversely events of "real" literary history (the Mignon phenomenon) invading the present fiction. This text mixture is structured in an apparently arbitrary fashion: 3 books of 11 to 18 chapters, some of these ultrashort, laced with a total of 8 novellas, and a collection of aphorisms at the end of the second and third books.[2]

In content, too, *Wilhelm Meisters Wanderjahre* goes beyond genre tradition to open the novel up to a horizon of themes and thought heretofore assigned to nonfiction writing. Economics, politics, history, education, and science—from geology to cosmology and astronomy—are given extensive consideration and motivating force in the development of the action. Goethe's last novel is revolutionary, too, in the treatment of themes within the traditional purview of the genre, such as love, generational relations and family structure, and that successful theme launched by *Wilhelm Meisters Lehrjahre,* individual growth and development. In fact, Goethe's title hints at the general idea behind the work. *Wilhelm Meisters Wanderjahre* presents the view of life as a journey, but not in the romantic sense of *wanderlust,* of being driven by inner longing for whatever hardly defined goal. The essence of *wandern* here is an obligation imposed from outside—Wilhelm must not stay longer than three days in any one place—of always going on and going beyond whatever is accepted as known. The novel is a guidebook to the unknown, an introduction of the reader peering over Wilhelm's shoulder to the new, ever-changing and ever-expanding world Goethe saw emerging around him.

The post-Napoleonic era in Germany, when *Wanderjahre* was written, was an age of uncertainty in the social, political, economic, and cultural spheres. Eighteenth-century certainties had gone down in the Napoleonic debacle. What remained of eighteenth-century structures was profoundly unstable; much was coming to an end, but new beginnings were yet barely perceived. Goethe had made autobiographical writing his main occupation and, while surveying his individual past, maintained at the same time a steady gaze on developments at home and abroad. It is this outlook on life that we find mirrored in the *Wanderjahre* structure or, more precisely, in the novel's procedure of scrolling through space and time, where instead of a cohesive plot or a sequence of decisive encounters we find a series of temporary way stations with changing views on human lifestyles and events. We might think of a Chinese journey painting, in handscroll or wall hanging format, that offers ever-different views of a wide landscape and of tiny temples, huts, and people drawn in corners here and there, as we scroll forward and backward, viewing and reviewing the unfolding panorama.[3]

The underlying principle of the *Wanderjahre* structure is a view of life not as an organic process of growth and development or as a deliberate construction according to the idea of progress toward a goal. Rather, life is seen as a problem in the mathematical sense: a task given to the individual to be worked out. Unlike math problems, however, in the late Goethean conception real problems have no solution; their only possible outcome is a new problem. Or, applied to life, chaotic entities cannot be transformed into ordered structures. *Wanderjahre* represents life as an "aggregate"; as in life so in the novel, "the complex of the whole contains necessity and contingency, intention and opportunity, success and failure. The result is a kind of infinity which cannot be wholly comprehended or encompassed in reasonable and rational language."[4]

Mindful of Goethe's warnings on comprehension and comprehensiveness, I will try to provide an access path to *Wanderjahre* that follows the novel's own procedure. After an introductory survey of how *Wanderjahre* steps beyond traditional borders of genre, culture, and thought, I will scroll along these border crossings through the three books of the frame narrative. The main novellas in each book are considered as they highlight problems posed in the framing journey. In book 1 we need to examine two novellas, *Die pilgernde Törin (The Deranged Pilgrim)* and *Wer ist der Verräter? (Who Is the Traitor?),* because they anticipate major themes of the novel through the mirrors of female and male counterparts. For books 2 and 3 the main novellas are *Der Mann von fünfzig Jahren (The Man of Fifty Years)* and *Die neue Melusine (The New Melusine).*[5]

In the thin plot of the frame, Wilhelm sets out on his travels with his son, Felix, but soon places him in the Pedagogical Province to be educated. Wilhelm pursues his journeys alone. After training to be a surgeon he joins a group of emigrants to America that developed out of the Tower associates. Finally, Wilhelm can use his surgical skills to save Felix' life, who had attempted suicide from unrequited love.

Love and family are a staple of the traditional novel, and they figure prominently in *Wanderjahre,* too, but in significant distortion. The nuclear family, which Biedermeier culture was just then promoting to normative status, is replaced by far looser kinship patterns. Mothers are nowhere to be seen. Fathers are a rare species, with fatherhood a daunting task beset by unending problems, a task preferably delegated to professional educators. Uncles and aunts take the parents' place as heads of families and guidance providers to the younger generation; Aunt Makarie is the novel's most exalted figure. Generational relations, with father and son at the center in the figures of Wilhelm and Felix, undergo drastic revision. Paternal despotism and filial submission are cast as the root of destructive developments in some of the novellas (*Das nußbraune Mädchen {The Nut-Brown Maid}* and *Wer ist der Veräter?*). Other novellas, like the frame narrative, feature father–son rivalry instead. The traditional love triangle is gradually replaced by various bridge constructions, shared love develops into a new bond between father and son, and brotherhood finally displaces the paternal relation. Love is where the most radical transformations take place. Love is no longer the scene of romance, defined by the exclusivity of twosomeness and aiming toward a happy ending in sexual union. Love is part of the chaotic aggregate of life, and in the course of the novel the conventional concept of love is redefined along an expanding track until, in the end, love encompasses a host of diverse experiences and configurations. This novel explores the many faces of love: blindness and insight, trauma and reparation, conversion and religious rebirth, intimacy and distance, trust and betrayal, individuation and socialization, and passion and friendship involving two or more lovers and including homoerotic attraction. It is here that the novel's subtitle, *Die Entsagenden* (*The Renunciants*), reveals its relevance. In a deliberate move beyond desire, *Wanderjahre* links the expansion of love to renunciation. Western tradition reserves the step beyond desire to the exceptional existence of saints. *Wanderjahre* challenges this tradition: it does not take a saint, only a sage, and everyone can get there—even the most unlikely candidates, Lydie and Philine of the *Lehrjahre* cast.

Gender roles and relations, while obviously involved in love and family contexts, come into view on their own, most explicitly in the novella *Die pilgernde Törin,* an experiment in feminist revisionism. In the frame narrative Hersilie, a complex and ambivalent figure in need of closer scrutiny, foregrounds the gender issue. She is allowed her own voice as one of the letter writers, but she ends up paralyzed in action, suspended between father and son in an emotional chaos worthy of Kleist's Alkmene. Then there is the tomboy turned leader of *Das nußbraune Mädchen* and its sequels in Lenardo's diary: the emancipated woman among tradition-bound men. Other novellas (*Wer ist der Verräter?* and *Der Mann von fünfzig Jahren*) aim barbs at female education; note that the Pedagogical Province is for boys only. And finally, there is superwoman Makarie. Anchoring point for family and society, source of truth through intuition and insight, and reconciler, peacemaker, and energizer, the human ideal appears in the feminine gender.

The *Wanderjahre* challenge goes beyond the private sphere of love and family to the very foundations of its cultural context. The intellectual bases of Enlightenment, classicism, and romanticism come under questioning in the events and figures of the novel. Cartesian rationalism, the view of reason as essence of humanity and hub of the universe, is left in the dust before the triumph of irrational powers: Makarie's cosmic existence and the woman who "feels" subterranean minerals,[6] humanoids and their magic in Melusine's realm, and the truth of dreams and the insistence on terminal secrets locked into a mysterious box from the netherworld of mountain caverns.

Classicism, the movement spearheaded by Goethe himself, had placed European antiquity at the center of present cultural efforts as the paradigmatic model. In *Wanderjahre,* classicist Eurocentrism is superseded by the proposal for a new culture on the American continent. Yet the American venture is not the preferred alternative, but another option to be explored besides an ambitious European experiment; the future remains open to new horizons. In a still more decisive postclassicist turn, the use of the past as model is shelved in the Collector episode (1.12), in which heritage has become curio and tradition a house full of collectibles awaiting an uncertain future.

After witnessing the abdication of the subject in *Wilhelm Meisters Lehrjahre,* we should not be surprised by the principled deconstruction of subjectivity, source and anchor of romanticism, in *Wanderjahre.* The hero is removed from the center, as attention shifts to the protagonists of the novellas and increasingly to Wilhelm's son, Felix. The heterogeneity of the text material prevents any unified self from emerging in the author role. Instead of authoring his own story, Wilhelm collates others' writings and mediates communication between others— Lenardo, Hersilie, Felix, Hilarie, and the beautiful widow—as he carries out their requests and as he carries their mail in their search for partnerships and identities. His own self-clarification, too, needs the mediation of others: Wilhelm sends his childhood memories of the fisherboy to distant Natalie to help him explain himself. Dominant subjectivity is revealed as the wrong way in the ironic tale *Wer ist der Verräter?* Here the solipsistic hero of *Werther* days indulges in the pathetic fallacy of making the world a self-projection and ends up as his own traitor.

The widest sweep of *Wanderjahre*'s transgressive gaze reaches to principles of Western thought: the project of theoretical knowledge, the binary structure of thinking, and the teleological perspective on history. History is an important topic, because the economic and political situation in the novel reflects the development of capitalism, technology, specialization, and industrialization in early-nineteenth-century Germany. Yet instead of the historical idea of progress, the plans for American and European utopian states offer, as does any utopia, a way out of history, a life beyond historical necessity: we can always start again from the beginning. Right on the heels of planning these hardworking utopias in the first five chapters of book 3 follows the lure of the idle rich in the fairy tale *Die neue Melusine.* The alleged "novel of work ethic," embodying the new religion of the nineteenth century (*HA,* 8:691), turns back on its tracks. The ending, finally, returns history to myth and progressive future to cyclical movement, as father and son transform into twin brothers Castor and Pollux, interchangeable and forever exchanging identities and positions.

Binarism, the dominant Western tradition of thinking in opposites, is passed over in a number of ways. At a moment when Hegelian dialectics was placing its binary grid over all of reality, *Wanderjahre* proposed to get out of the binary constriction. A pattern of imbalance and rebalance, instead of opposites, structures the revisionist fairy tale *Die neue Melusine,* most visibly in the variable sizes of its characters. Generational opposition is replaced by exchange and rebalancing in the frame narrative between Wilhelm and Felix and between the father–son pair in *Der Mann von fünfzig Jahren.* We have seen how the binary structure of love is reconfigured in triangles and quadrangles. In what is surely the most striking innovation of the novel, the dualism of inner and outer is integrated as the spiritual becomes physical in Makarie's journeying into interplanetary space.

Along with binarism *Wanderjahre* abrogates the two-dimensional structure of human reality with its opposites of inner and outer, upper and lower. The novel introduces a three-dimensional world that consists of above, beside, and below. The three kinds of respect *(die drei Ehrfurchten)* taught in the Pedagogical Province offer the most explicit statement of this three-dimensionality. There is a ubiquitous emphasis on the triadic direction of the world: the above in Makarie's realm, the below in Montan's geology and in subterranean explorations, and the beside in the prevalent social orientation in groupings and associations. The novel promotes a new way of perception in the traveler-reader, who must keep looking in at least three directions at once. In their perpetual motion, with changing perspectives across the lake in mountainous Mignon-land (2.7), Wilhelm and Hilarie model the learning experience needed for the new *Wanderjahre* vision. Through Hilarie's painting and Wilhelm's memories as author-creator of Mignon, they undergo an aesthetic education that moves them and readers to a new level of understanding life, the world, and the individual's role as part of the world.

Wanderjahre ultimately takes us beyond theory and the acquisition of knowledge for its own sake, the paradigmatic Western ambition that

Goethe was just getting ready to critique in *Faust Part II*. Goethe's last novel sweeps aside the project that had engaged the best minds from Enlightenment and idealism to postromantic philosophy and science. Through his friends Schiller and Schelling, Goethe had been closely associated with philosophical developments that by the late 1820s had led to the dominance of Hegelian systematics. In his *Farbenlehre* he had proposed an empirical approach to optics in opposition to the predominance of theory (he called it mathematics) in science. In the mountain festival of *Wanderjahre* (2.9), guests nearly come to blows over geological hypotheses. Montan, the practicing scientist, demands praxis in tandem with theory ("Thought and action, action and thought, . . . neither should occur without the other," *Works*, 10:280), and in the Pedagogical Province the goal is *Ausbildung* (professional training) instead of *Bildung* (education). Accordingly, Wilhelm's life goal, instead of becoming a well-rounded personality, now is the practical calling of a surgeon, whose function is to repair broken bodies. Knowledge, that all-encompassing Faustian desire, is pushed back within close borders, as any number of mysteries and secrets are kept off limits, under lock and key.

Book 1

The first book opens on a wide scope, with Wilhelm viewing the world from a "significant spot" (*Works*, 10:97) high up on a mountain. We meet nearly the entire cast of characters of the novel. Four inserted novellas, the most of the three books, offer a rich array of life stories. All the boundary crossings outlined earlier are engaged in the course of book 1.

The emphasis of this journey novel is on views and viewpoints. The first chapter opens with a subtitle that presents a picture: *Die Flucht nach Ägypten (The Flight into Egypt)*. The first novella into which this opening image leads is likewise focused on images. *Sankt Joseph der Zweite (Saint Joseph the Second)* happens at the visual level; one might consider it a *Bildergeschichte* (a story in images), a movie after a comic strip. The carpenter Joseph is modeling his life on the chapel fresco paintings that represent the legend of Saint Joseph.

The opening chapter, with its significant if misleading title (*Die Flucht nach Ägypten*)—pretending to be a novella—sets the tone and sets forth important themes. We learn how images work, linking perception with deception and cognition; we see the spiritual interwoven with everyday life; and we witness tradition anchoring and shaping the present. The chapter begins and ends with Wilhelm writing as he ponders his own and his son's future. Felix's troubled future is forecast when he is pictured between the light and the dark child. We also note how first impressions can mislead. Wilhelm sees his son between these two children as "among dear little angels" (*Works,* 10:99), but he soon finds out that the dark one, fey Fitz, is anything but an angel. In this consists indeed Wilhelm's task to be fulfilled in his journeyman years: to correct the errors he is prone to falling into—misled by traditions, assumptions, and first impressions—and to correct his errors by experience: live and learn. We are told the reason of Wilhelm's exile, his flight into Egypt, only belatedly, at the end of the chapter. Like biblical Jacob, he must first earn Natalie, whom he had so undeservedly found at the end of his apprenticeship years. Belated information is a frequent feature of *Wanderjahre,* a teaching device in this essentially didactic novel. Like Wilhelm, the reader must learn to revise views and visions continually, to correct or discard earlier assumptions and judgments as new facts come into view and different perspectives open up.

Chapter 2, with the first (previously published) novella, *Sankt Joseph der Zweite,* asks the question of classicism, the question of whether imitation and emulation are the right use of the past. The answer is no. The conditions for it to work in carpenter Joseph's case are too idiosyncratic to be generalized. There is "irresistible inclination" of a particular individual: growing up under the domination of the chapel images so that his imagination was mimetically shaped; the coincidence of significant names (Joseph, Maria, and Elizabeth) suggesting identities; the unbroken continuity of tradition through grandfather, father, and son; and the idyllic mountain life in which livelihood is guaranteed and change nonexistent. Mimesis means the peace of stagnation; it can produce beautiful images, rituals, and stagings but fails at productive change, at creation. The proof is Fitz. In the very bosom of the "holy family" this child remains a denizen of the dark realm, enigmatic, dangerous, and eminently seductive. Fitz, his name a pointer to "Felix," brings out the dark side in Felix. What the father must realize is that there is a lot of Fitz in his own Felix. The question of how to cope with raising a son becomes an urgent problem.

Chapters 3 and 4 take us to the mountaintop and the scholar-recluse Montan (*Lehrjahre* Jarno's new persona). The elevated viewpoint promises help in the search for orientation after the rejection of classicism in the Joseph story. What we get, however, is another negative. The project of learning in order to acquire knowledge, pride of Western culture and basis of progress, is declared pointless. Only what can be experienced and practiced immediately is worth knowing. Montan's polemic against theory contains a radical deconstruction of textuality. Language misleads, and linguistic signs consisting of letter, sound, and meaning fall short of the real. Even dialogue, that venerable Socratic path to learning, is degraded as "miserable junk of empty words" (*Works,* 10:116). The only true, unambiguous language is nature itself, and it can only be learned through lifelong practice. Montan has become a geologist from working with miners. Wilhelm reluctantly disavows his goal of all-around education, for his son as well as for himself. For himself, in a flash of insight, he discovers a professional career after Montan's heart, of which the reader, however, will only be informed belatedly, as the narrator explicitly holds out on us again.

Negation is not the end of the journey into Montan's mountains. The geologist opens the door to the first of the three dimensions of *Wanderjahre* reality: that which is below, the physical universe. Appropriately, it is mysterious Fitz who initiates the voyagers and exposes them to the innards of the earth and the dark side of human existence in the body and its desires, the passions and betrayals, the unconscious and the uncanny, the incomprehensible and the secret. Fitz introduces a group of criminal friends huddling around a charcoal kiln at night. Wilhelm and Felix's venture into the caverns of the Castle of the Giants is a mythic transgression fraught with danger. Ariadne's thread is needed to lead the way out of the maze. Felix underground turns into another Fitz, finder and keeper of secrets, secretive, and a liar now himself (*Works,* 10:123). When Fitz's betrayal has trapped them in the tunnel of the Uncle's plantation, Felix reveals an entirely new side. He erupts in self-destructive rage, ready to hit his head against the wall, a sinister omen of his passionate future.

In chapters 5 through 7, in the domain of the Uncle, we enter the second *Wanderjahre* dimension: that which is beside us, fellow humanity. The horizon is wide enough to offer fresh views on a full range of living together, from everyday routines such as eating habits and family structure to social, political, ethical, and global concerns. To emphasize the revisionary nature of these views, they are attached to the eccentric Uncle, whose eccentricity is based on experience in the Old World and the New World, America. Eccentricity, therefore, is really a revision of Eurocentricity. In the private sphere, the avuncular family subverts the tight bonds of bourgeois nuclear family life: "the horrors of family dinners" (*Works,* 10:143) are abolished. The Uncle's own opposition to his emigrant father had brought him back to Europe; nephew Lenardo will later supplement the Uncle's conduct with a principled warning against paternal despotism (*Works,* 10:192).

Gender issues, too, come under review, with niece Hersilie. Reversing the conventional older-man–younger-woman pattern, the adult Hersilie becomes the object of preadolescent Felix's passion. Hersilie reveals decidedly feminist views in her criticism of male arrogance in "men [who] arrive from foreign parts" and of male privilege ("spoiled nephew," *Works,* 10:146–47) and masculinist ideology in the Uncle's cherished slogans. From a woman's perspective, she declares, "men's maxims," such as "From the Useful by Way of the True to the Beautiful," would read very differently (*Works,* 10:139). Finally, her story of *Die pilgernde Törin,* with its counterpart in the novella *Wer ist der Verräter?* offered by the young (male) manager, presents a sustained questioning of traditional gender roles and relations.

At the next level, that of social organization, it has been noted how the Uncle's "higher philanthropy" (*Works,* 10:126), his way of helping people do well for themselves in an agrarian economy, regresses to the eighteenth-century welfare state. Yet the difference from traditional norms is marked in the Uncle's push for progress and increased productivity and in his eccentric administration. A sort of liberal avuncularchy has replaced feudal patriarchy; individual employees at every level have a high degree of autonomy. Most significant and frankly amazing is the Uncle's central motto, "Possessions and Common Property." At first glance contradictory—"do not those two concepts negate each other?"—the slogan is carefully explained to the visitor as a way to achieve balance between individual and collective happiness: "and thus everything balances out" (*Works,* 10:140–41).

The highest level of the world beside us is reached in the global horizon. Images of world geography adorn the Uncle's abode, their comparable yet contrastive message following the sedentary Saint Joseph pictures. The Uncle, too, strives to realize an ideal. One of the reasons he returned from America, we hear belatedly (again), was that he found William Penn's principles compromised by the treatment of the Indians. The strange religious observances in his domain represent an Old World interpretation of Quakerism; his German colony is an experimental utopia of natural and cultural synergy. It is only fitting that the entertainment of the Uncle's extended family, which includes an unrelated management team of father and son, should be the study of world literature. Each member of the family circle is in charge of one national literature; their conversations aim to bring about a global perspective on national cultures.

For all his practical competence and global ken, the Uncle's vision is not sufficient to deal with the more troublesome aspects of life. Faced with problems, he consults a wise old woman, also part of the extended family, Aunt Makarie. Her authority is described in extraordinary terms: "as if the voice of an ancient sybil, now become invisible, spoke pure, divine words of the greatest simplicity about human affairs" (*Works,* 10:138). Frail of body and strong of spirit, Makarie is a new kind of mystic. She represents the third dimension of *Wanderjahre* reality: that which is above us, spirit and cosmos. Entertainment in her circle is the higher wisdom of thought and stargazing under the direction of an astronomer. In contrast with the flow of information about the Uncle's philosophy, the Makarie dimension is presented with reluctance and with an emphasis on silence. After-dinner conversation, we are told, bears on the abuses of mathematics, but the discussion is not reported. No one even in her own family knows the most astounding thing about Makarie: her innate integration into the planetary system. Wilhelm is told only after a wondrous dream in which he visualized Makarie's true nature.

In the refusal to explain the inexplicable Makarian dimension, the novel's insistence on the limits of understanding is most evident. In addition, mathematics, the modern method of scientific understanding, is ostracized as abusive. Instruments, the indispensable keys to scientific perception, are shunned as unnatural, distorting, and damaging. Instead, another path to knowledge is proposed: through experience and intuition. Not every kind of experience will provide access, however; it has to be of an order above normal human existence: the sublime and miraculous. Wilhelm is overwhelmed by the starry sky viewed from Makarie's observatory. And then his dream reveals to him Makarie's stellar existence. This "strange spiritual intervention, [his] unexpected comprehension of [the] deepest mysteries" (*Works,* 10:182), is the miracle that admits Wilhelm to the small circle of the chosen who share Makarie's secret. Only now are we informed, again belatedly, about the incredible coincidence in Makarie of vision and reality, of knowledge and existence: "that she not only carried the entire solar system within her, but also that she moved within it spiritually as an integral part" (*Works,* 10:183).

The two novellas at the center of book 1, *Die pilgernde Törin* (chapter 5) and *Wer ist der Verräter?* (chapters 8 and 9), highlight central themes

of the novel, which just begin emerging in the frame narrative. Foremost among them is love. The Saint Joseph story played out a first variation of the novel's professed theme, renunciation, in the field of love.
Wilhelm's letters to Natalie are steeped in love on hold, and Felix's
explosive love for Hersilie threatens to tear down any and all limitations.
Gender relations and roles, obliquely addressed by Hersilie, are reflected
in the mirror arrangement of the paired novellas and call into question
the convention of "What behooves the male does not behoove the
female." Another theme is subjectivity, which is shown to mislead self
(Lucidor) or others (Revanne father and son), to alienate and liberate the
self (Pilgrim), or to subjugate the self to the decisions of others (Lucidor). Finally, both novellas reveal reality as a construct that depends on
the relativity of deception or truth, reason or folly.

Die pilgernde Törin

For all its lighthearted mood and ironical frivolity, *Die pilgernde Törin* is
a subversive tale. It forces us to view accepted values and lifestyles from
a radically other perspective and to review our assumptions on gender,
sex, family, codes of behavior, and standards of judgment. Unsettling,
in the first place, are the multiple perspectives Goethe has built into
the story. Presented to Wilhelm as a translation from the French by
Hersilie, the story is told partly by a first-person narrator, who reports
what M. de Revanne Sr. told him and who occasionally inserts his own
opinions. In addition, the heroine herself is the author of an important
part of the narrative: the ballad of the unfaithful lover, which we are to
understand as an account of her own past and an explanation of her
present behavior.

The wandering lady's project, as she unequivocally states from the
outset, is to be her own woman. She insists on being taken on her own
merits, she denies the usual guarantees of family and class, and she
defends her own space against invasion by the men's desire to know and
to possess her. The men's reaction is utterly conventional. They interpret her strange behavior along categories of romance, and they behave
according to a romance plot: falling in love, trying to seduce her,
promising marriage, father and son fearing each other's rivalry. During
the two years the stranger spends in their household, she plays the game
of society and conventions, but with her own rules. She works for her
living—once in the male career of wandering minstrel—yet eats at the
masters' table. When pressed for information about herself she replies

with generalities. She repels any talk of love. In sum, she refuses to be domesticated, after two years still strange, unknown. The narrator is a friend of Revanne Sr., and the reader expects him to take the side of the duped men. Although ostensibly objective, the narrator surprises us at crucial points with comments that endorse the weird stranger. M. de Revanne considers her parting ruse the strangest of her "follies"; the narrator corrects his friend by suggesting "that folly is often nothing but reason under another aspect" (*Works,* 10:135). She, on the other hand, reads her situation correctly as being in the power of two desirous men, whose promise of marriage legitimates in their eyes any unscrupulous behavior. With the briefest of statements in this elegantly styled text the narrator confirms her view: "Thus it was, and thus she perceived it" (*Works,* 10:136).

The most radical revolution in perspective, however, comes from the stranger's own lips. Father and son have just condemned each other for committing the evil deed each had desired to commit himself: getting her pregnant with—in the son's words—a competing son-brother and heir. Her retort is precisely not what we expect, not a denial of pregnancy but a denunciation of the male and of mankind in the male image. "It is neither your son nor your brother. Boys are wicked, I did not want one. It is a poor little girl whom I will take away, far far away from people, evil, foolish, faithless people" (*Works,* 10:137). This is patently not the factual truth; she is not pregnant. But it is truth of another order: the truth of this story, of the stranger's experience from her perspective, whose "folly" in the narrator's opinion is merely reason from another point of view. The hints at her possibly supernatural origin—a water sprite "who appeared as fleetingly as an angel" (or demon according to the son) (*Works,* 10:138)—emphasizes the estranging effect of this other perspective.

Wer ist der Verräter?

Protective in the pilgrim novella, subjectivity turns destructive in the counterstory, *Wer ist der Verräter?,* told in chapters 8 and 9. The pair of novellas are an explicit example of exposure to multiple views and reflections. The purveyor of the second story, the junior manager in the Uncle's home, instructs the reader—Wilhelm—to view the novellas in a compare and contrast mode. The key to the intent of the second story is the prominently displayed mirror motif. The mirror in the garden pavilion, a garden that also contains an amusement park, functions like a

funhouse mirror: it distorts and deceives by apparently reflecting truth-
fully. The human mind, we are to understand, is an inherently distorting
mirror as it interprets what it perceives as reality. It is more distorting
yet if left to its own devices, as is the case with the protagonist Lucidor,
who preferably converses with himself.

Narrative techniques illustrate the mind's distortive potential. The
pathos of Lucidor's monologues, ostensibly authentic thus truthful yet
increasingly caught in self-deception, contrasts with the narrator's irony,
when he tells us after the first such "heartfelt and passionate soliloquy
[that it] will take many words to explain" (*Works,* 10:153). The denoue-
ment is presented in the form of a dramatic dialogue (i.e., unmediated
speech) between the two protagonists, Lucidor and Julie. Julie clearly
dominates this exchange as she readjusts the perspective from Lucidor's
misperception to the correct viewpoint. The recurrent mirror motif
keeps reminding us of the theme of perception and point of view, most
explicitly in its last appearance: in the pavilion mirror others can see us
where "we cannot see ourselves" (171). Ostentatious artificiality marks
the narrative style, with an overabundance of descriptive adjectives,
repetitive synonyms, and frequent wordplay. The result is exaggeration
and caricature. These characters are meant to be types, not individuals,
as signaled in the case of Lucidor's impossible father, the anonymous
"Professor N. of N." (*Works,* 10:153).

On the literary level, this is parody with a host of referential texts.
Anton Reiser, F. Schlegel's *Lucinde,* and Goethe's fragment *Der ewige Jude*
(*The Wandering Jew*) are quoted in the text of the novella. Other views of
Lucidor are more subtle (Goethean self-)parodies: of young Wilhelm as
Hamlet, who does not dare and is always too late; of young Werther the
subjectivist, blind victim of his own fantasies; and of young Goethe the
government official, "who is to administer justice" and yet is wrong
about everything and everyone (*Works,* 10:172). As part of Wilhelm's
learning experience in his journeyman years this is social satire. Offered
in all seriousness by the Uncle's young manager to demonstrate the rec-
titude of the German middle class, the novella, even as it exaggerates
and distorts, reveals the failings of precisely this, Wilhelm's own sphere
of life. It shows a despotic father who first neglects and then subjugates
his son to the point of annihilating his identity; an educational system
that molds and rewards rubber-stamped nonindividuals; and a family
structure in which wives, mothers, and daughters are used and disre-
garded yet in which, in effect, the women manage and manipulate the
men. The only good place to be is away from home: Julie's wanderlust

ends up with the highest valuation. And the only wise man is the non-family man: the old bachelor in his separate abode, hidden away among images of an eccentric past.

Book 2

After the wide open spaces and the many vistas and issues traversed in book 1, book 2 concentrates. Concentration occurs in a number of ways, most prominently in the quest motif. In addition to Wilhelm, more figures go journeying, and more types of journeys and goals come into view. In consequence, more stories and open endings are created and clamor for closure. The second means of concentration is a narrowing of focus on one major issue: education, the task of becoming an adult. Very few new characters enter the picture; instead there are reencounters with the figures of book 1 in different settings: revisions from new perspectives. Finally, only one novella interrupts the framing journey, but it is all the more substantial. *Der Mann von fünfzig Jahren* takes up one-third of book 2, without nevertheless coming to conclusion. Instead the novella opens up into the frame, and its characters enter Wilhelm's own story, joining his quest for a span and waiting for closure in book 3 with the rest of the novel's cast.

The novella is integrated into the frame thematically as well. It provides a view in future perfect subjunctive on the main issue: from a back-to-the-future perspective, we see the disastrous results of a misguided education. The story of the 50-year-old major and his lieutenant son might happen to Wilhelm and Felix if they do not find new ways of upbringing, of parent–child relations, and of formal education. The novella offers a gendered counterweight to the exclusively male Pedagogical Province, where most of the frame narrative takes place. Female education, too, needs reform if catastrophic mistakes are to be avoided. At the end of book 2, Wilhelm will have reached one certainty, his career goal as a surgeon. But he has not found a solution to his larger problem: the meaning of love and death, of inner and outer world, the purpose of an individual's life—his own and his son's.

Wilhelm journeys through the Pedagogical Province in two stages, separated by a time span of several years and by the novella. Revision in the light of the novella's critique is thus built into the presentation of this central region of the second book. The first visit shows character development through general education; the second follows up with professional training through specialization. The Pedagogical chapters have received much scholarly attention and approval. Only recently have critics warned not to see here a rendition of Goethe's own educational philosophy. Rather, like the proposals for new government in book 3, the Pedagical Province offers variations on the persistent nineteenth-century theme of educational reform. Goethe's variations play in a gamut of modes from the rational and experimental to the iconoclastic, satirical, and utopian.

As the students move up in years they move through distinct spaces and places; education is an anticipative journey through the varied scenes of life. Basic to education is an attitude of awe and respect *(Ehrfurcht)* toward the whole of life. (Wilhelm is told that he is still remiss on this score.) The role of religion, traditional place of *Ehrfurcht,* is exchanged for a syncretist civilizing primer. Goethe's revision of Christianity excises the Passion story; his radical historicization anticipates the work of philosophers D. F. Strauss and L. Feuerbach. Indeed religion serves to exemplify the revisionary process of learning itself as a journey through time and space that changes views and perspectives. Strolling through galleries of pictures from the Old Testament, Wilhelm "perceived some new purpose" and gained "new insights. . . . In the end, he looked at the pictures entirely with the eyes of his child" (*Works,* 10:207–8). Traces of secularized religion inform the principles and methods of the first educational phase. Wilhelm hears of the insistence on secrets, silence, and taboos; of emphasis on the visual, aural, musical, gestic, and ritual over the verbal; of the priority of the performative before the conceptual; and of the hierarchical social structure based on discipline and authority.

By the end of his second visit Wilhelm has learned the revisionist stance expected of the *Wanderjahre* reader and endorsed with explicit irony by the narrator. The guide through the arts departments recants classicism in favor of a *Bauhaus*-type universalism. Imitation of the great works of antiquity is considered useless; exhibitions and prizes, Goethe's own strategy in his past campaign for German artistic renewal, are superfluous. Dramatic art alone is excluded from the Pedagogical Province, with damning words for its corrupting effect. Wilhelm and the empathetic narrator (here an obvious stand-in for Goethe) ruefully reflect on their own past efforts at education through the theater, but the position to be taken is left in no doubt. The unregenerate acting talent, we hear in the most sarcastic simile of the novel, is sent away to a good theater "so that, like a duck on a pond, he can be initiated on the boards without delay into his future of waddling and quacking" (*Works,*

10:277). The reader, familiar with the failure of Wilhelm's theatrical education from the *Lehrjahre* novel, is to draw the conclusion that the son, in his own quest of adulthood, should avoid following in the father's footsteps.

Der Mann von fünfzig Jahren

A long and complex novella, *Der Mann von fünfzig Jahren* takes up chapters 3–7, which constitute the interval between the two visits to the Pedagogical Province and thus form the centerpiece of book 2. Any brief reading must fall short of the wealth of meanings created in this tale, which dates back to the very beginnings of *Wanderjahre* writing in Goethe's own 50s. Here it is read as a story of perversions, or, in the German equivalent closer to the journeying spirit of the novel, *Verirrungen* (going astray). Its characters have taken the wrong road in the erotic field, with disastrous effects for their psychic balance and for the stability of their social world. An accumulation of mistakes—misguidance, misperception, misunderstanding—destroys relations among family, friends, genders, and generations, threatening individual despair and social disorganization.

Each of the five main characters—the major and his son, his sister (the baroness) and her daughter, and the beautiful widow—shares two basic mistakes. They do not pause to reflect but merely react to the momentary situation, and they see things only from their own point of view, which leads them to wishful thinking and self-delusion. The narrator calls attention to the failure to reflect on the part of the major and the baroness, representatives of the parent generation responsible for the well-being of their children, by telling us that he does not know what they were thinking, if anything, at critical moments. "What the major thought, we do not wish to enlarge upon" (*Works,* 10:226). "[The baroness] would not have bothered to analyze the reasons" (*Works,* 10:230). There could hardly be a more damning judgment on the behavior of these two adults than their own reasoning after the catastrophe: that they were all "misled by the mistake of an inexperienced child" (*Works,* 10:249).

The central figure is this inexperienced child, Hilarie, not the titular 50-year-old hero. Although the story sets out from the major's perspective and in a comic mode, a radical change of view occurs with the distraught son's bursting in on Hilarie's bridal idyll (chapter 5). From now on, Hilarie occupies the foreground of a near tragedy; it is the story of her wounding and healing that continues into the frame. This young daughter and niece, who almost married her uncle while falling in love with her cousin, is the innocent ("inexperienced") victim of misguidance. Both parental adults fail her, the uncle for shifting responsibility to the mother: " 'If this should turn out badly,' the major said, 'the fault is yours. If well, we shall be forever in your debt' " (*Works*, 10:222). The mother is indeed responsible, for projecting her own lifelong desire of her brother onto her daughter. Family ties have come dangerously close to incest; "natural" sibling and avuncular relationships are perverted to "something so unnatural" (*Works*, 10:214).

The *Wanderjahre* context, in which the avuncular is to replace the patriarchal family, makes such perversion all the more reprehensible. This explains Hilarie's overreaction to the idea of replacing the uncle by the cousin. She calls it criminal. It is from this self-indictment that Hilarie needs to be redeemed. In true *Wanderjahre* fashion it can only happen through a readjustment of perspective, a cleansing of vision that leads to revision and to revaluation of self and world. Hilarie's old values represent a patriarchal exchange economy, in which women see themselves as commodities ("wares") to be traded in the courtship game. This is what she learned from her mother, the baroness, as stated in the bluntest terms in a narrator's aside (*Works*, 10:230–31). The primary interest of the parent generation is in family property; children, particularly daughters, are chips to be placed so as to keep that property together.

Hilarie's moral crisis is really a crisis of identity, which explodes in her face when her distraught cousin and prospective stepson calls her " 'Sister.' The words pierced her to the heart" (*Works*, 10:239). From an alienated self who could be assigned the successive functions of belonging first to the cousin, then to the uncle, then to the cousin again, she must become a true self. She must discover her own individuality and learn to make her own choices. One path toward this goal was followed by the beautiful widow, who achieved independence and individuality precisely by becoming a wealthy widow. Her "female wiles" of playing the erotic market and playing the men, including father and son, against each other, prove the success of female education, for example, in the art of needlework. Her artfully stitched satchel, from the major's perspective, is a spiderweb used to bag men. For the beautiful widow it represents a profoundly alienating practice. Made for someone else, to be used as a gift, the work yet contains all the thoughts and feelings that accompanied its making. Giving it away means giving away "part of my self" (*Works*, 10:228).

The widow's path disqualifies itself by its destructive results, which only a Makarie can be hoped to undo. Hilarie happens onto another path accidentally: aesthetic education. She learns landscape painting from the artist who accompanies Wilhelm on the visit to Mignon's homeland. Artistic practice, in Goethe's view, is first of all training to see, to perceive aright. Hilarie now learns to correct her vision and, in the selection necessary for aesthetic representation, to develop her own point of view and the power to implement it. It is for this reason that aesthetic education is also moral education. In artistic production, the artist creates her own self: an individuality that can choose and has the courage to realize her choices. Moreover, artistic production can repair the damaged relation between self and world. The victim of tragic mistakes, Hilarie learns to love again the world she sees and represents with a joy that expresses the metaphysical power of art to transcend the boundaries of self and world. "To see the glorious world spread out before her for days on end, and now suddenly to experience a fuller power to represent it! What bliss, to approach the inexpressible through lines and colors!" (*Works,* 10:263).

After following fellow questers Hilarie and the beautiful widow for a while, the focus returns to Wilhelm; after exploring the role of the arts in education, it is the turn of science. A reencounter with Montan (chapter 9) promises answers to Wilhelm's questions about the value of knowledge, which Montan had refused at their earlier meeting. The answer is given in the negative: five camps of geologists fight over their hypotheses on the origin of Earth's surface, a topic of impassioned debate at the time. Theoretical knowledge, according to Montan, is not just pointless, it is detrimental because it is mere subjectivity and thus threatens to disturb the essential balance of mind and life. "Thought and action, action and thought" informing each other is the only way not to "go astray"; it is "the right path" through life (*Works,* 10:280). With his career choice Wilhelm has taken the right path, but we will only find out what that choice was at the very end of book 2, in yet another flashback to the first encounter with Montan.

In the meantime, in chapters 10 and 11, more questions open up and more characters join the search for identity and for the meaning of their lives. Hersilie, over a message from Felix delivered by the mysterious Fitz, is plunged into uncertainty about herself and about her relationship with Felix. She turns to Wilhelm for help in understanding; he in turn seeks Natalie's help in explaining to himself the mysteries of life,

love, and death, of reality and subjectivity, and of outer and inner world
in his memory narrative of the drowned fisherboy (*Works*, 10:285–91).
The second book, then, closes with nonclosure. In demonstration of
Montan's axiom, all efforts at understanding can at best lead to a
restatement of the problem, never to the truth (*Works*, 10:280).

Book 3

Whereas book 1 unrolled all the issues and book 2 concentrated on
quests, questers, and the question of education, book 3 narrows the
focus on what might be considered the theme of the novel as a whole. It
is the relation between individual and other, between that which defines
an individual, which is claimed as one's own, and all that is not of one's
own, be it of another gender, family, class, nation, country, or continent:
the world. The horizon widens far beyond family and society to include
the Old and New Worlds in economic, governmental, cultural, and
geopolitical perspectives. The novel explores the individual–other relation on many levels, from the personal to the political, spiritual, and
cosmic. The examination, in the frame narrative and all three inserted
novellas (*Die neue Melusine, Die gefährliche Wette {The Perilous Wager},* and
Nicht zu weit {Not Too Far}), reveals antagonism between one's own and
the foreign and with struggle for control in consequence. Far from
deterministically accepting this state of the world, the novel structures
events and the lessons they teach in such a way as to demonstrate the
need to overcome that antagonism, to find a new balance that would
enable the coexistence—even the integration—of individual and other,
without one absorbing or usurping the other.

Integration proceeds at a steady pace on two fronts: Wilhelm's career
change from self-representing actor to service-oriented surgeon and the
association of emigrants. Wilhelm's individual journeying in search of
himself is over. Except for a short side trip to take leave of Felix (chapters 16 and 18), he has joined the emigrants, all strangers except for the
two leaders, Lenardo and Friedrich, to depart in search of another life on
another continent. Chapter 3 reports on his progress through his surgeon's training in a particularly alienating phase: the study of anatomy
with the problematic task of dissecting the arm of a known individual.
Goethe's solution to this much-debated dilemma of his time is innovative but as yet, the novel suggests, possible only in the New World. A
sculptor, in yet another other-directed career change, undertakes the
construction of anatomic models. After the third chapter Wilhelm

recedes into the background and functions mainly as passive recipient of Hersilie's ever more disturbing letters until he steps forward again in the final chapter. In the meantime, he and we the readers are made to observe the coming together of disparate individuals in the emigrant group: their practice of togetherness in ritual, work, and song; tales of their turbulent pasts (the novellas); and plans for their future.

From the first to the penultimate chapter, the story of emigration develops in skillfully managed stages. At a rather late point (chapter 13), Lenardo's Swiss travel diary reports on the economic origins of the migratory movement. Overpopulation and the advance of technology and capitalism threaten the mountain's home industry, leaving no alternative but poverty or emigration. It is this future that weighs on the mind of the regional leader, Lenardo's long lost love, Nachodine-Susanna, heroine of the unfinished novella from book I, *Das nußbraune Mädchen*. "The increasing dominance of machine production torments and frightens me: it is rolling on like a storm, slowly, slowly; but it is headed this way, and it will arrive and strike" (*Works*, 10:396).

Earlier, however, in chapter 9, Lenardo's inspirational speech had proposed a very different, positive reason for emigration. In the style of a manifesto Lenardo here presents an ideology of migration that declares that to be human means to keep moving. By destroying the Tower of Babel, God has ordained it. The emigrants' hymn says it succinctly: "For us to disperse in it, / Therefore is the world so vast" (*Works*, 10:369). The novel's theme of going beyond unfolds in a social anthropology of migration. Page upon page (*Works*, 10:365–68) fills with Lenardo's evidence of humanity on the move, be they students, scientists, tourists, craftsmen, traders, salesmen, artists, musicians, actors, professors, missionaries, pilgrims, pioneers, soldiers, diplomats, conquerors, or exiles. The Jewish people, though not named, serve as paradigmatic instance of a nation whose millennial history of migration ("blessing of eternal wandering," *Works*, 10:366) has enabled their overtaking of the more sedentary parts of humankind.

The American utopia, the emigrants' planned community, has aroused much critical interest, in contrast with Odoard's rather bland German development project for those who would eventually shy away from the step across the ocean. Only recently has the provisional character of the American proposal been acknowledged. Much is left unstated; experience on-site, we are told, will revise and fill in policy as needed. Overall it is no surprise that Goethe is skeptical of democracy ("majority rule," *Works*, 10:380) and prefers incremental improvement to revolutionary change. The American venture thus appears rather traditional. It is nevertheless interesting to view the group's statements on social policy—religious freedom within Christianity, no capital punishment, no liquor, no lending libraries—in the context of nineteenth-century Europe on the one hand and of early mainstream America on the other. Three features deserve special notice: (1) government needs to be proactive but prevented from becoming a central power; (2) religious policy is purely pragmatic, and Christianity is selected because it serves the community's goals best; and (3) most interesting, the work ethic, which constitutes the supreme value in the new community, is redefined as a time ethic. For time, "the highest gift of God and Nature," is life, and to do truly good, "useful" work takes "circumspection . . . attend to the task as well as to the hour" (*Works*, 10:379).

The orderly development of the emigration theme is interrupted by three novellas—tales of passion and excess of individualism—located in the past to be sure but presented as warning parables of future dangers. The passions are not limited to the traditional sphere of love; they include self-love, honor and ambition, lust of power and need to control, addiction and greed. We are shown the disastrous impact of unchecked individualism, or the other side of the hero coin. The novellas deconstruct the heroic ideal of Western tradition, the ideology of greatness that entails the sublime experience of tragedy. In the real world of *Die gefährliche Wette* and *Nicht zu weit*, tragedy means shame, guilt, and unmitigated and irreparable suffering for everyone, including the innocent children in *Nicht zu weit*. The third story, *Die neue Melusine*, exposes the heroic ideal to the ridicule of the average man in a comedy that could only happen, we are made to understand, in a fairy-tale world.

Die neue Melusine

A rich tale, *Die neue Melusine* is the result of a long incubation period that extends back to the beginning of Goethe's creative life at Strasbourg. During his classicist period Goethe thought of it as his *Reisemärchen* (travel fairy tale), a tale of unrest and perpetual motion in contradiction to classicist quietude. Yet neither is it a romantic text despite the romantic subject matter and a wealth of fairy-tale motifs. The irony of its double perspective and unheroic protagonist consistently undermines the romantic dimension. And, finally, with its consistent refusal to accommodate logic and the desire for rational understanding, Goethe's *Melusine* stands in opposition to the tradition of Enlightenment.

The story takes up a host of themes from the earlier part of the novel. All address the essential and problematic human condition; some, such as love and gender relations, have been extensively treated before. Other themes are new; after the *Melusine* tale in chapter 6 they will play out through the rest of book 3. They concern control of others and self, or the lack thereof; the power of passions and addictions; money as an object of desire, equally as or more important than the erotic object (see the giveaway sentence: "Finally she pressed a purse of gold into my hand, and I pressed my lips onto her hands," *Works*, 10:345); and the role of the body in identity and self-consciousness. At the heart of the narrative, however, is the issue of going beyond, that fundamental move practiced in *Wanderjahre* as a whole.

Going beyond appears under three aspects. First, radical otherness in humans is to be not merely tolerated but accepted in the most intimate way possible: love. The crucial question is whether love will survive the discovery that Melusine is a dwarf. Second, another, radically different reality is to be allowed next to and interacting with reality as we know it. The other reality, Melusine's world, is not just a smaller version of our own; it has an alternate history and mythology, too. In that other Genesis narrative, God created dwarfs, dragons, giants, and knights with well-known (we are assumed to be familiar with this utterly strange story) consequences of power struggles among the different humanoid races. There is, finally, the ultimate challenge of metamorphosis, the need to change one's identity. The hero has to join the race of dwarfs, to shrink down to Melusine's size if he wants to live happily ever after.

Today's reader, weaned on science fiction and Star Wars mythology, might find little to worry about Melusine's triple challenge. Not so her chosen champion, the average male of the nineteenth century, with its fervent belief in scientific truth and progress. The hero-narrator proves inadequate to the challenge. He can make the leap intellectually; he accepts the fact that Melusine is real, even in her dwarf shape with all the magic of her box palace. After all, her money is real enough, and perhaps that is what matters most in this subversive fairy tale of exchange value magic. Melusine's lover can leap across his shadow emotionally, at least for a while. Desire for continued bliss—erotic and monetary—overcomes his hesitation at moments of decision. But he fails the challenge experientially; he cannot live with his decisions. Not with his beloved of the variable size: he betrays her with other women. Not with the truth of her other reality: he ridicules it and humiliates her. And not with his downsized identity: he explodes it to return to his own, habitual, average humanity.

Goethe's sustained irony ensures that this hero never becomes an identification figure. Instead the reader is to be tempted, just like the hero, by the beyond: to take the step across the final frontier of the utterly other, to overcome alienation by that which is foreign in order to appropriate it as one's own—one's love, one's child (Melusine is pregnant), one's homeland and kingdom, and one's new identity in the ultimate magic of transfiguration. And, finally, the irony of casting such an egregious nonhero in the champion's role aims to make the reader imagine that he or she could do it: take that step across because he or she is so obviously superior to that recidivist wretch of a protagonist.

After the novella interruptions, including the conclusion to Lenardo's Nachodine-Susanna story (chapter 13), the emigration theme achieves closure from the highest possible perspective. The emigrants unite once more and depart with the blessing of Makarie, that modern saint based on science and nature rather than faith and metaphysics. Chapter 15 describes in sober terms her astounding cosmic existence. Yet her effect on others is very much like that of Christian saints on pilgrims, the seekers of help and insight. Chapter 14 draws toward her all the wandering characters, including some from the *Lehrjahre* novel who had yet to show up in *Wanderjahre*. At the apex of the Makarie effect, hysterical Lydie experiences an epiphany and is healed forthwith. Makarie's spiritual power has disentangled (almost) all confusions, and settled (almost) all the knights and damsels errant in marriages or productive occupations. From her flow peace and renewed energy into the band of emigrants.

The exception to Makarian closure is the Wilhelm–Hersilie–Felix triangle, which over chapters 2, 7, and 17 has become ever more of a tangle. Hersilie's letters to Wilhelm are another source of interruptions (besides the novellas) in the smooth progress of Wilhelm and the emigrants. Because Wilhelm never responds, the letters are a persistent irritant of mounting urgency. The confusion that baffles Hersilie is her ambiguous position between father and son and her ambivalent attraction to both. The mystery box with the still more mysterious key symbolizes this confusion. Beyond that, this object symbol (Goethe includes a drawing of the key, *Works,* 10:321) stands for the enigmatic nature of human life at its deepest level. "Such secrets," counsels a wise old gold-smith, "are better left untouched" (*Works*, 10:416).

Through Hersilie's letters we follow Felix's development into an ever more passionate young man, clearly on the opposite track to that advocated by the novel. The last three chapters bring the son back into focus, casting a strong light on his all-or-nothing, self-destructive nature. Without Makarie to mediate or even Wilhelm to advise, catastrophe arises from confusion: Felix seeks death by dashing himself from a cliff into the river. Fortunately, his father the surgeon just happens to pass by and brings him back to life. The final chapter sketches a dramatic, symbolic, and poetic ending but no conclusion. The Wilhelm–Hersilie–Felix triad persists, without a clue as to the next shift in the interrelations. Felix's turn from beloved Hersilie to his father ("If I am to live, let it be with you!" *Works*, 10:417) is valid only for the moment. Hersilie, after all, is not there, nor is her problem solved: she is left holding the famous box. What Goethe's inconclusive conclusion does is to reassert, after Makarie-induced peace and quiet, that passions will ever be reborn, making of life an alternating path of destruction and production.

Chapter Nine

West-östlicher Divan and Other Late Poetry

The task at which Melusine's champion failed is precisely the task Goethe sets himself and his readers in his volume of poems and prose *West-östlicher Divan*: going beyond, crossing the border from the familiar to the foreign, transcendence in many dimensions. As the title states, this is to be an encounter—a conversation and negotiation—between West and East.[1] Most of the poetry, 240 pages in the first edition, about half that in modern editions, was composed in the short space between spring 1814 and autumn 1815. Yet right up to its publication in 1819, Goethe kept writing an even longer prose segment, *Noten und Abhandlungen*, to follow the poems, under the original title "Besserem Verständnis" ("for better understanding").

He presents himself to his readers as a traveler and a tradesman. In the poems he is a traveler seeking to adapt to foreign ways of life and to appropriate the foreign tongue as far as possible. In the *Noten* he is a tradesman who exhibits and advertises his imported wares to best advantage ("Einleitung").[2] Thus the *Noten* offer an introductory course in Persian cultural studies: history, government, daily life, religion, and literature, complete with references for further study, as Goethe in conclusion discusses Orientalist scholars and sources. At a deeper level the essays reflect on the nature and function of culture in a wide range, encompassing relations of power and submission, tradition and innovation, love and war, God and man, spirit, intellect, and the arts. There is in particular an entire poetology in these *Noten,* a view of literature radically different from the classicist version that Goethe had previously espoused. The imaginary excursion into the Orient gave the Western author a new vantage point from which to evaluate and revise his own theory and practice.

Goethe's project of cultural mediation developed over time. Like his Chinese studies, his interest in Persia originated in an impulse to escape from the chaotic end of the Napoleonic Empire. The very first lines of the poetry cycle point to this origin: "North and West and South are breaking, / Thrones are bursting, kingdoms shaking: / Flee, then, to the essential East" (*Works*, 1:203, lines 1–3). When his publisher, Cotta, gave him a translation of poetry by the fourteenth-century Persian Hafis, it was to serve as diversion in the small-town spa close to home, Bad Berka. Here Goethe had withdrawn while the European powers were sorting out Napoleon's future after his resignation from the throne in April 1814. And then the unexpected happened. Hafis hit like a flash of lightning, reigniting Goethe's lyric genius that had lain dormant for decades and that now began pouring forth poem after poem. The strange new voice, speaking from afar in time and space, captivated the acknowledged grand master of German poetry to the point of identification. *Unbegrenzt* (*Unbounded; Works*, 1:205) presents in Goethe's new, witty style the relation between the German poet and his Eastern model and "twin" (16), Hafis.

The opening poem, *Hegira* (*Works*, 1:203), tells how and why the twinning came about. Although the impulse was indeed one of flight, the flight takes direction toward origins: the poet's origin in the time of youth and lyric poetry ("youthful bounds . . . spoken word," 15–18) and humankind's origin in the Eastern cradle of faith. From rationalist sophistication ("brains racked and riven," 12) of aged Europe, the poet turns back to seek pure beginnings in the East, in a quest of rebirth, renaissance. The fifth stanza recalls Mignon's song of longing, reminding us of that earlier escape in search of renaissance—Goethe's Italian journey—but with a decisive difference. This time the goal is not classical Rome and Greece, the homeplace of European culture. The fourth stanza evokes the exemplary foreign: oases, deserts, and caravans trading coffee and spices. The spring of classical poetry, Helicon, has been displaced by Khizr's spring (6). Goethe's readers, educated in the classical tradition, would be utterly bewildered; they had no idea who or what Khizr was.[3] And instead of the moving pathos of Mignon's lines, we find the hallmark of the new poetry Goethe had discovered in Hafis: the intellectual play of associating incongruous elements, the sublime with the ludicrous. Poetry serves "for the stars to hear, / Robber bands to quail with fear" (29, 30).

Incongruity pairs the sacred and the profane in the sixth stanza: Saint Hafis and the tavern, holy poetry and the lust of wine and women. And the last stanza proclaims that precisely this is Goethe's new poetological program. Poetry claims to be a higher discourse, a discourse on spirit enabled by ecstatic experience, in particular the ecstasies of love and wine. The difference from classicist doctrine is apparent. Instead of ascetic abstraction and separation of the ideal and sublime from the real and sensual, this poetry finds the sublime within the sensual, in the real and banal of everyday life: the holy poet in bars and spas and paradise in a woman's hair and perfume.

The poetological program structures the volume in its 13 titled segments or "books." The two first books on poetry and the poet (*Buch des Sängers {Book of the Poet}* and *Buch Hafis {Book of Hafis}*) lay out the orientation, as the Western author responds to his Eastern model, Hafis. Two books on love (*Buch der Liebe {Book of Love}* and *Buch Suleika {Book of Suleika}*) mark the main body of the volume, framing four shorter books of reflections on the wide horizon of life including politics, power, and a poet's peeves (*Buch der Betrachtungen {Book of Reflections}, Buch des Unmuts {Book of Distemper}, Buch der Sprüche {Book of Proverbs}*, and *Buch des Timur {Book of Timur}*). A chapter on the ecstasies of wine and desire in the shape of a beautiful boy *(Schenkenbuch)* leads to the final sphere: paradise *(Buch des Paradieses {Book of Paradise})* through another set of reflections on religious matters (*Buch der Parabeln {Book of Parables}* and *Buch des Parsen {Book of the Parsee}*).

The most famous poem of the entire cycle, *Selige Sehnsucht (Blessed Longing; Works,* 1:206), states the poetic program in poetic terms. Despite its place in conclusion of the programmatic first book on poetry, *Selige Sehnsucht* is commonly read as a love poem. Love, however, is here merely metaphor and way station on the progress proper: the path of poetic transformation. Goethe here reworked a Hafis poem of similar length, which is indeed a love poem.[4] The change of theme must be taken seriously. Love is the central trope, a poetic aid to understanding spiritual transformation. Goethe also recycles two recurrent symbols of Persian poetry: the candle or lamp and the moth burning. For Western culture, where sun or fire worship is unknown and fire instead signifies damnation and annihilation, the meaning of emancipation and transfiguration intended in these symbols might be inaccessible. Goethe makes it accessible by presenting the sun–fire religion of ancient Persia in the *Noten* and in the poems of *Buch des Parsen.*

The poem *Selige Sehnsucht* and the transformative process it enacts pass from paradox, from juxtaposition of contrasts—"bliss" and "longing," "alive" and "death by fire"—to synergistic union. The heart of the poem, the site of that union, is the sexual experience of passion, procreation, and renewed desire for ever higher union in stanzas 2 and 3. The lyric *thou,* differentiated from the *I* of the speaking voice (3), seduces the reader to identify with the subject of this central experience: we all love to love. Then hits the shock of line 16: "Moth, you meet the flame and die." Instead of glorified human life at its highest, literally flying high in stanza 4, *thou* is a moth burned to death. "Schmetterling," however, also refers us to the butterfly law of metamorphoses, from caterpillar through pupa to winged creature: model of transfiguration. Death is one more metamorphosis in the chain of life.

And it is an unending chain, a cycle in which every end is a new beginning. "Die and dare rebirth!" in the last stanza is a radical restatement of the truth hidden within the tired concept of rebirth. Every true change presupposes death; it means the ultimate and absolute giving up of whatever there is now: identity, our living self. The imperative form makes it a challenge and turns the death wish of the beginning (4) into obligation. Radical change is the only way toward being truly alive, toward being of this planet and knowing it as our home. Otherwise humans will remain bewildered strangers in a world they do not see through (19–20). For it is ever the essential human task, and particularly the poet's task, to enlighten, to make life transparent to truth, a task that can be completed only through transcendence and transformation.

That there are far more who will not take this view and this step is stated in the first stanza. The poem is a word to the wise, not to the crowd. The encounter with aristocratic and meritocratic Persian culture could only reinforce Goethe's elitism in postrevolutionary Europe. He gives it ample rein in the poems of *Buch des Unmuts*, for which he offers nice apologies in the *Noten* but no excuses. The Eastern model of unabashed self-esteem appeals to him far more than the hypocrisy of the Western virtue of "Bescheidenheit" (modesty, self-denial, *HA*, 2:199, line 10). Immodesty is a necessary corollary of being a poet; the very act of creating poetry is what the Greeks would have called hubris. But Goethe is no longer in the classicist mold; thus he brashly proclaims the overboldness of poetic speech in "Dichten ist ein Übermut" ("Writing poetry is an arrogance").[5] In the Eastern world Goethe has found once more the proud assertiveness of *Prometheus,* the signature poem of his Sturm und Drang days.

If in *Selige Sehnsucht* love was *only* a metaphor, it was, however, to signify a central theme of the work: poetry, like love, is creative power. The *Divan* as a whole demonstrates that love is a most fertile soil for creativity. The largest group by far are the love poems in *Buch der Liebe* and *Buch Suleika*. More than that, the book owes its very existence to love. For when Goethe, captivated by Hafis, had decided to compete with his

twin in "love, drink, and song"[6] there happened to him, after a summer
of wine, partying, and poetry on the banks of the Rhine and Main, an
extraordinary love experience. The story of Goethe and Marianne Willemer deserves to be read on its own. Glorified for generations as a tale of
the power of mutual inspiration between congenial partners in passion
and poetry, for today's readers, and not just women, the story holds a
deep ambivalence. In the end, Goethe included four of Marianne's
poems, edited of course, in his volume.[7]

For Goethe's own program in the *Divan,* love played a dual role: (1) in
providing the ecstatic frame of mind requisite for the higher discourse of
poetry and (2) in acting as a most malleable phenomenon, infinitely
sprouting words, poetic speech, and imagery. One of the features that so
attracted Goethe to Eastern poetry was its wealth of associations, com-
parisons, and symbols. Everything associates with everything, he states in
the *Noten* (*HA,* 2:179). "What makes you great is that you cannot end"
begins his praise of Hafis in the poem *Unbegrenzt* (*Works,* 1:205). Love is
the site of boundless potential for speech: the paradigm of poetry and
playground for spirit. Goethe had long used nature to speak about love,
but now he has found a new way of looking at nature, a new attentive-
ness with the focus on the natural rather than the emotional phenomenon. The bridge between the two, nature and love, is made by spirit: in
explicit reflection by means of pathos or irony or in implicit equivalence
anticipating the poetic realism of the later nineteenth century.

Another famous *Divan* poem, *Gingo biloba* (*Gingko Biloba; Works,*
1:208), uses one tiny detail of nature, "this tree's leaf," to explore the
concept of unity and division. Philosophers had meditated on dualism
and dialectics from Saint Augustine to Hegel, who just then was at the
height of fame. Goethe's brief three stanzas distill centuries of thought
in a lucid statement, which nevertheless includes the Eastern inspiration, the esoteric gesture of love—only the two lovers will understand
the secret—and the essential nature of this love that exists (only?) in
these poems ("my songs," 11). The poem *An vollen Büschelzweigen* (*On
Laden Twigs; Works,* 1:210) also takes a close look at a bit of nature, but
from a different perspective. Here it is a chestnut kernel, growing,
ripening, and finally bursting from its shell. By anthropomorphic sleight
of hand the "fruits" of nature (3) come to mean both the swelling of passion to consciousness and insemination ("Schoß" [16] means lap and
womb), as well as the process of poetic production: "my songs" (15).

Goethe is at his most playful in a poem that bears his pseudonym for
its title, *Hatem* (*Works,* 1:212), in the game of mythical Eastern lovers he

was playing with Marianne-Suleika. *Buch Suleika* is arranged as a dialogue, in which the pair exchange poetry over a period of meetings and separations. In this poem Goethe has encrypted himself in the "Hatem" of verse 11. The rhyme requires a response to "(Morgenr)öte" (9): *Goethe*, of course. The play of self-irony expands over the entire poem and includes grand features of nature evoked in snow-capped summits and volcanoes. The stern mountain face ("jener Gipfel ernste Wand," 10) and snow on the peak poke fun at his advanced age in contrast with the "snakes" of her youthful tawny "curls" (he was 65, Marianne 30). Only in Goethe's Oriental poetology was it acceptable to compare snakes with mountains. In a radical change of style, the last stanza explodes the sophisticated language game by taking the metaphoric volcano literally. A little pile of ashes is all that is left of the aged lover who thought he was an Etna of passion.[8]

Wiederfinden (*Reunion; Works,* 1:212), the longest poem of *Buch Suleika*, is in a different register. Crafted in stanzas of twice the usual *Divan* length, it maintains a consistently serious tone with a rhetoric of the sublime. Again nature on the grand scale is the setting. Love is part of a cosmic spectacle: the creation of the universe; or, rather, the creation of the universe is part of a love story. The lovers' "reunion" in the first and last stanzas, framing the cosmic scene, is the individual event that first calls forth and in the end replaces universal creation ("Creators of his world are we," 40). It happens merely in the mind, but it is precisely the claim of this poem that the mind of the poet can be the source of creation. And so Goethe rewrites the creation myths of biblical and classical traditions. To the biblical story of "Become!" (13) he adds the pain of division from original union, in a version of the big bang theory (14–16). For the music of the spheres in Platonic cosmology he substitutes his own *Farbenlehre* ("of hues and harmonies a game," 30): light and dark can enter into relationships through the colors, just as "Trüben" (opaque) rhymes with "lieben" (love, 29–32).

The last poem in *Buch Suleika* takes the boldest step yet from love to the divine. *In tausend Formen* (*A Thousand Forms; Works,* 1:216), disarmingly playful and elegant, practices idolatry; religious fundamentalism would have to condemn it as blasphemy. Goethe plays on the first syllable of the divine name in Islam, All(ah), and on a ritual of enumerating Allah's names, to place the beloved in *all* the imaginable functions of the divinity: from the conventional "Allerliebste" (2) to extraordinary word creations such as "Allbuntbesternte" (14) and "Allherzerweiternde" (20). Goethe's religion of the beloved proves superior even to its model, at least in the mind of the poet. Islam gives God many names but does not allow images. Poetry visualizes the word, and the poem realizes names as "forms" in a profusion of images, two to each stanza. In the penultimate stanza, the *All*-beloved fills up all the world and constitutes the totality of outer and inner life: earth and the sky/heaven (*Himmel* means both), light and air: "I breathe you" (20). Because breath turns air into soul, as in the Genesis story, or into heart, as in Goethe's "Allherzerweiternde," the poem's last line follows naturally. God, "Allah," under every one of his names, now means the beloved.

The last *Divan* segment, *Buch des Paradieses,* confirms the link of love and the divine. The higher discourse of poetry, inspired by love, leads to the highest state of human existence: pure spirit in a life beyond this world. The most meditative poem of this group announces the upward dynamic in its title: *Höheres und Höchstes* (*Sublimer and Sublimest; Works,* 1:218). Composed in retrospect, three years after the *Divan* experience, the poem offers a summary in conclusion. At a level of abstraction unusual for the *Divan,* it imagines a vision of the afterlife. Goethe attempts to state suprahuman, metahuman ideas in human, imaginable terms and to express religious content in poetic form. At the same time, this is a test to validate the *Divan* program. Is poetry really a higher discourse able to speak on matters of spirit? Have readers of the cycle learned to understand this new language? The challenge goes to Goethe, too, the tradesman who now asks himself whether he succeeded in selling his foreign wares: did he enlighten, did he teach well enough so that now he can speak in these "sublimer and sublimest" terms?

Following a basic *Divan* principle, the beyond is linked to this world, the spiritual to the sensual. The first half of the poem chats in comfortable language on familiar topics: my self in this life: my needs, desires, limitations, likes, and dislikes. This self is not the subjective individual, Goethe, or a Werther self of romantic definition; it is everyone—"der Mensch"—because everyone is his own "liebes Ich" (6, 9). And everyone, says the first half of the poem, wants to remain an *ich,* clings to his or her identity in this and any other world (8). But, says the second half, that is not possible. Any truly other world is utterly foreign, as foreign as East is to West. The East–West theme closes the first half and opens the second half with the most densely written and abstract verses on language as central metaphor. The language of the beyond is far more foreign than "German" is to Islamic paradise (19–20), with many dialects and a secret grammar whose declensions we hear but cannot understand.

To achieve understanding, the human will have to remain a sensate being, but the five senses operating separately and thereby failing to comprehend will have to become one unified sense. Such radical change is possible only by means of transsubstantiation: "der Verklärte" ("in Glory," 32). The finite body has become infinite desire, action, and motion directed toward God. God, focus of all desire, is love and the force that links all—everything and everyone. Finally, of course, there is no more everything or everyone. The exclusive identity of the *I,* last seen in verse 37, is displaced by the inclusive *We* of the last line, and this *We* disperses, disappears in the All of divine love.

Urworte Orphisch

Written in autumn 1817 but published only in 1820 in Goethe's house journal, *Zur Morphologie, Urworte Orphisch (Works,* 1:231–33) has acquired near cult status, quite in keeping with its title, one might say. Goethe's later poetry tends to be philosophical but also rather brief: a reflexive moment in verse, a variation on his ubiquitous prose *Maximen und Reflexionen (Maxims and Reflections). Urworte Orphisch* is an exception. It is far longer and far broader; it is a meditation on the principles that structure human life. In his study of Near Eastern culture Goethe came upon the Orphic cult in Egypt and preclassical Greece, which continued to exist as an underground, archaic religion during the classical period. The stanza titles refer to the gods that in Orphic myth surround a newborn, similar to the fairies in *Sleeping Beauty*: representations of the powers that determine human destiny.

As the Orphic myth attempts to explain the enigma of life—the interrelation of character, behavior, and destiny—so Goethe's poem tries to answer the basic question after what drives and controls an individual's life: What makes people act the way they do? What in particular explains exceptional persons such as Napoleon, who never ceased to fascinate Goethe, or, for that matter, Goethe himself? In 1817 Goethe was still working on the *Divan Noten und Abhandlungen*; exploring culture, history, and individual life; and hoping to write some more poems for the *Buch des Timur,* representing Napoleon. He had not yet returned to his autobiography. After the dramatic and traumatic events of the recent past in the public and personal spheres, he was still reorienting himself.

Public events included Napoleon's amazing hundred-day return and final exile, the postrevolutionary turn to antirevolutionary reaction, the shifting power relations in Europe and within Germany, and the accelerating emergence of economic factors in the destiny of nations. Closer to home, in 1817 Goethe had finally resigned as director of the Weimar theater, thereby breaking the last link with Schiller and his own classicist epoch. On the personal side there had been the passion and renunciation of the *Divan* experience, the horrible death of his wife (1816), and the marriage of his only son (1817). The emphasis on the generational sequence and on family and marriage is remarkable in the explanatory remarks on *Urworte Orphisch,* which Goethe published in his other house journal.[9] Even more remarkable is the deep ambivalence of his comment.

The form of the poem signals its superior status. Goethe cast only his very important poems in the long iambic stanza with its constricting rhyme scheme: *ababab cc (ottava rima).* The Greek strophe titles erect a ceremonial threshold, proclaiming esoteric and archaic meaning. The style is elevated, predominantly abstract and conceptual, with scant imagery except for the middle strophe, "Eros," which elaborates an allegory of love. Here, style is message. Goethe translates the ancient way of viewing the world figuratively, in myths and gods, into our ways of thought, into nineteenth-century concepts developed to understand life's phenomena. The attentive contemporary of German idealist and romantic philosophy had learned this conceptual language well.

But it is more than a question of language. The poem replaces the old, static worldview with the modern, dynamic view of the world as a field of energies and forces in constant change. The question now is of history: What drives humans as individuals and collectives? What controls our directions? What obstructs or accelerates our course? Goethe here sees human life as a grid of vectors that reinforce or weaken each other's effects. The poem plots the course of a life like a graph through a field of interacting vectors, with the individual a bouncing ball drawn, pulled, kicked, blocked, or diverted hither and yon. Far from offering a new orientation, let alone a certainty in the bewildering modern world, the poem declares human life on principle a system of errors. Goethe's comment is amazingly pessimistic: "Man who has lost his way is lured into new labyrinths; there is no limit to going astray: for *the way is an error*" (*HA,* 1:406; emphasis mine). Dynamic drive versus blockage is the overall design of the poem, in the sequence of topics and strophes as well as within each strophe.

The pattern is prominent in the first strophe, "Daimon." Static forces prevail: the sun standing still, the inescapable law of identity, the individual indelibly minted by origins. Among the factors that shape a personality, the constellation of planets and sun merits special note. Scholars may disagree on Goethe's view of astrology; the least we can say is that the opening image denotes the historical time and place of an individual's life. It matters when and where Napoleon, or Goethe, was born; the historical moment decides to a large degree who a person can become. The accumulated counterforces of growth and development seem preset within eternal limits, foretold by prophets and sybils. But precisely here is a way out of the determinist bind. Truths told by prophets and sybils are myths; the modern truth valid for us will be modified by all that follows in the rest of the poem.

"Tyche" in the second stanza brings immediate change. In direct opposition to *daimon, tyche* is the not-I: what befalls a person from the outside. (In Goethe's usage "Das Zufällige" [coincidence] connotes "that which befalls" a person, in life events as well as in encounters with others.) Humans do not grow up in isolation; they develop through parenting and education and through chance encounters with mentors, friends, and lovers or with strangers and the foreign who become relevant in the way that Italy and Hafis did for Goethe. Tyche is a mobile force that interferes with the essentially stable daimon: self. The first big jolt of tyche signals a leap in development: the exit from self-enclosed childhood and adolescence (Freud's narcissistic period) through love arriving in the next stanza.

In the third stanza, "Eros" is not merely erotic desire but all desire that has the force of eros, that excites enthusiasm and promises ecstasy. It includes ambition to attain a goal, the lust of power, or an artist's desire to create. It means reaching out toward an other, wanting to possess and shape what is outside the self. Love here is a metaphor for self-aggrandizement and for intensified pleasure of the self by expansion into other territories and appropriation of other selves. Such expansionist drive carries the danger of dispersal and dilution. The last line introduces a countermove of concentration to refocus desire so that an individual's highest potential may be achieved. This concentrated effort in turn entails the next stanza, "Ananke-Necessity."

The fourth stanza, "Ananke-Necessity," is the most abstract in style and teems with provocative paradoxes. It poses the question that drives the poem as a whole: how free are we really? Kant and his disciple Schiller had spent their lives trying to save human freedom; Goethe's answer is highly skeptical. All our efforts at liberation, all our actions to try to prove our free will amount, ultimately, to narrower space in the prison of our existence. The elaborate play with modal verbs reflects on the real-life impact of action. No action is experientially neutral. All our acts circumscribe arbitrariness (*Wollen* and *Willen* versus *Willkür*, 2–4). Whatever we choose to do will limit our choices of future action. It is here, in this interaction of modalities, that ethics, morals, and laws originate ("sollten," 3, and "Muß," 6). Freedom has to be negotiated with the irreducible conditions of human life.

"Necessity" ends, logically, in total blockage. The last stanza, entitled "Elpis-Hope," begins in a world of iron walls, locks, and rock-solid barriers of eternal duration. But then, in the fourth line, the locks fall away. The figure of hope is Goethe's addition to the Orphic tradition, which knew only the four gods of the previous stanzas. In this, more than in anything else in the poem, consists the modern turn: there is always hope. Remarkably, Goethe's comment is silent on the last stanza. Except for implying that ethics and religion could not exist without hope, he leaves it to the reader to reflect on what hope means: "every fine mind will gladly undertake to formulate a comment in moral and religious respects" (*HA,* 1:407). A final comment on the poem as a whole might point out that hope emerges, ultimately, as the crucial tool of empowerment and liberation. It took the course of history from Orphic antiquity to Goethe's modern era to discover hope as the defining glory of being human: the ability to always again believe in new beginnings.

Marienbader Elegie

The great elegy generally known as the *Marienbader Elegie* (1823), may well be Goethe's most astounding poetic feat; its power is evident in its reception history. For Goethe scholarship the *Elegie* stands as an uncontested summit and a continuing challenge to interpretation. The poem's exceptional standing stems from three factors: its sheer length of 23 six-line stanzas, the immediacy gained from its origin in an intensely personal experience, and the artistry that translated this experience into a universal dimension. The old poet's last love story, his unrequited attraction to the very young Ulrike von Levetzow over three Bohemian spa summers and his rejection, need not be elaborated here. When he received the final no, after having resolved for his part—at age 74—to embark on a radically new life should he be accepted, he composed the *Elegie* on the long journey home, and he composed himself by doing it. This is part of the *Elegie*'s unique character and a large part of its powerful impact: here language is action, and the poem enacts a healing process.

The *Elegie* (*Works,* 1:246–52) presents three major aspects. It is a poem about love; it represents the experience of a tremendous loss; and it is a performance of mourning. The poet speaks in personal and particular terms about his love for a childlike girl, yet he also says what all love is, can be, and can do. Love in the *Divan* was quite different. Stylized after the Hafis model, love was at bottom impersonal and instrumentalized in the service of aesthetic ecstasy. In the *Elegie* love is onesided, an activity solely of the poet's soul. Poetic love does its usual life-intensifying magic: time disappears (stanza 3),[10] absolutes become reality (stanza 2), and desire finds total fulfillment (stanza 2) or, when denied, creates total misery (stanzas 4 and 5). But beyond that, love reveals a potential special to this poet—Goethe, surely one of the most thinking poets we know—at this stage in his long, productive life.

Love has the power not merely to inspire (*begeistern*) but to inspirit ("begeisten," 11.5): to revitalize, to motivate, and to give the gift of spirit as in the miracle of Pentecost. The lover is newly aware of himself (stanza 10), but also—and more importantly—released from the rigid enclosure within the self ("Selbstsinn," stanza 15). His imagination is freed from the bonds of anxiety imposed by past experience (stanza 12); being in love means living entirely in the present moment, to the fullest possible extent (stanzas 16 and 17). At its farthest reach love is religion. In stanzas 13 and 14, Goethe attempts a definition of religiosity and equates it with love. What stands out is the simplicity of the feeling on the one side (stanza 13; end couplet of stanza 14) and the complexity of the explanation on the other. Love shares with religiosity an essentially enigmatic nature. In love as in religion we become aware that we do not understand ourselves, which is precisely the challenge of love and religion: we attempt to "unriddle" ("Enträtselnd," 14.4) ourselves in the presence of and through an other.

All of this—and much more—is lost when love is lost. This more is what the *Elegie* describes when it explores how a tremendous loss affects us. There is, of course, the general misery to be expected: "gloom, remorse, self-mockery, clouds of care" (5.5), indifference to the splendors of nature (stanza 6), haunting by the beloved's image (stanzas 7–9), and the body's protest in tears and life-threatening torment (stanzas 19 and 20). But again, as in the poet's love, there are aspects of loss that go beyond the conventional to the tremendous, the exemplary. In the last four stanzas, after the accumulated details of love and loss have been spelled out, this side emerges as loss of reality and loss of self: "I've lost it all, earth, heaven, self" (23.1). The poet, whose talent it is to speak his pain (the *Elegie*'s motto evokes *Torquato Tasso*), has lost the power of speech (19.2). In exploring why he cannot speak he finds that he has lost the essence of spirit: willpower and the ability to think, to go beyond mere images to concepts (20.6, stanza 21). Thus he has lost access to the world: to his friends, whom he sends away; to the rest of humankind, who still are connected to each other and to the world; and to all of nature: the universe. Nothing makes sense anymore (stanza 22).

How does Goethe resolve the contradiction between what the poet says and the fact that he can still say it? The poem, despite the poet, makes magnificent sense. The solution lies in the third major aspect of the *Elegie* as a performance of mourning. Psychoanalytical views of mourning emphasize four points. First, to achieve healing over time, the mourner must keep going through his or her loss over and over again. Second, it is the work of mourning to retell in detail the story of lost happiness in order to commit the events to memory, to take them out of the present and place them in the past. Over its 138 lines the *Elegie* probes into past bliss and present misery. The difference between past and present ("nun") is emphasized repeatedly, as required in mourning. A third requirement is the telling to someone: the reader of the poem or, explicitly, the "good companions" who have listened to the narrative (stanza 22). Finally, mourning is a ritual, a performance with formal requirements. Poetic form in itself, with its demands on style and meter, meets this requirement. The *Elegie* is particularly formal in using the ceremonial stanza *(ababcc)* that Goethe reserved for special occasions (see *Urworte Orphisch*), in its demanding synthesis of affective and intellectual abstraction, and in its rhetoric of high seriousness. Translating feeling into form, this poem traces a path from the personal to the universal dimension.

Chinesisch-deutsche Jahres- und Tageszeiten

Goethe's cycle of 14 short poems, *Chinesisch-deutsche Jahres- und Tageszeiten* (1827), deserves to be better known. Once more, now 77 years old, Goethe ventured out toward a foreign culture and created from the encounter, as he did in the *Divan*, a new type of poetry. He started the year 1827 by reading Chinese novels (in French translation); then he reviewed a volume of Chinese poetry (in English translation) and offered prospective readers a sample by translating two poems into German. Next, like the Chinese sage of his cycle, he withdrew to his garden cottage outside the city for a very productive summer. Part of the harvest were the 14 poems, which transplant the Chinese model into German nature and culture. Each poem, in an average eight lines, presents one impression, reflection, or dialogic exchange of thought in Goethe's new style, which he called "geistig schreiben" (writing with spirit) (I).[11] We might call the new poetry emblematic, where meaning is immanent in the emblem, inscribed in the phenomenon depicted. Like bamboo or peach trees and blossoms in Chinese pictorial poetry, plants are the favorite emblems here. White, star-shaped daffodils with red hearts wait for spring (II). A field of wildflowers bursts into extravagant fireworks of verbal virtuosity; desire is fulfilled at the apex of the sun's course in June: "Wunscherfüllung, Sonnenfeier, / Wolkenteilung bring' uns Glück!" ("Wish-fulfillment, sun celebration, / Cloud division bring us luck!" III.7–8) Throngs of thistles and nettles—very unpoetic plants these—crowd out the poet's vision in summer (VI). The rose, by contrast, is the flower of flowers, emblem of emblems in the German tradition from the Baroque mystic Angelus Silesius to the modernist R. M. Rilke.[12] In Goethe's cycle the rose is the anchoring point. Present in 3 of the 14 poems (IX, X, and XI), the rose stands for absolutes (X) and for the eternal law of growth, bloom, and waning that governs all being through passing seasons and time: "Es ist das ewige Gesetz, / Wonach die Ros' und Lilie blüht" ("This is the eternal law / directing the bloom of rose and lily," XI.8–9).

The outstanding poem is VIII: "Dämmrung senkte sich von oben" ("Twilight Down from Heaven," *Works,* 1:260). Twice as long as the others and placed at the center of the cycle, it marks a long moment of balance, when spring and summer turn into fall. The first strophe balances downward with upward movement as twilight descends and the evening star ascends, as fogs rise and the darkness of the lake draws the gaze into its black depth in another extraordinary word creation: "Schwarzvertiefte Finsternisse" ("darkened deeps more black than ever," VIII.7), all coming to rest and balance in the reflection on the lake's surface: "Widerspiegelnd ruht der See" ("mirroring calmly lies the lake," VIII.8). The second strophe similarly balances distance and closeness between the faraway moon and the nearby water, until the moon's image, "Luna," joins the reflected twigs in a shadow play on the lake.[13] Finally, outer and inner worlds interconnect in the closing lines: "Und durchs Auge schleicht die Kühle / Sänftigend ins Herz hinein" ("Through the eye the coolness sliding / Touches with a calm the heart," VIII.15–16). Here visual perception, physical sensation, and emotion are all at one, in calm equivalence. Man, having opened his eyes to take in what the previous lines depicted, is in perfect balance, at peace.

Chapter Ten

Faust or Recycling Myth

Anyone who writes on *Faust* today must begin with a disclaimer acknowledging the incommensurability of the work, especially if writing less than a book. Let me state that I do not claim to offer an interpretation of this vast text that is, in anyone's book, a paragon of superlatives.[1] Instead I want to suggest an approach that may be expanded or abbreviated to accommodate different interests, methods, and time constraints. *Faust* is, among all the other things that have been said about it, an agglomeration of myths—one might say a mythology of its own—rooted mainly in the Judeo-Christian and Greek traditions. Yet *Faust* reaches beyond the mythological mainstream to pre- and postclassical and even esoteric myths and includes myths derived from history (e.g., ideas of empire and colonialism). Goethe changed, actualized, and revitalized myths so that they could carry new meanings—the meanings of his own, modern time—in addition to and interaction with their traditional meanings.

It is precisely this interaction that makes *Faust* a never-ending challenge to interpretation. Far from offering a smoothly syncretist eclecticism, *Faust* is a "coexistence of contradictions" with which the reader has to come to terms on his or her own.[2] The meaning of myth is by its very nature undefinable, because myth represents the attempt to explain the inexplicable, such as the origin of the world, the nature of man and woman, the purpose of life, good and evil, happiness and suffering, success and failure, love and desire. Myths as explanation strategies vary with time and place; they are functions of a particular culture in a particular era. Myth is or does what the final *Chorus mysticus* proclaims: acting out in the form of a parable what defies understanding.

> All that is transitory
> Is only a parable;
> What's unrealizable
> Here becomes event;
> What's indescribable
> Here it is done.[3]

Myth is what Kafka's *Prometheus* parable demonstrates: four versions of a story and the conclusion that the inexplicable is inexplicable.

Faust was already a myth when Goethe chose his topic; Goethe's Faust in turn has become an evolving myth with variations and valuations that span the extremes of positive and negative. Oswald Spengler's Faustian man as paradigm of Western mentality has had a fascinating career of ups and downs during the twentieth century.[4] When we read of a Faustian bargain being struck we shiver in anticipation of some enormity or other. The "eternal feminine" has as many meanings as users of the phrase. Writers, composers, painters, and filmmakers have found in *Faust* an inexhaustible source of inspiration.[5] Before Goethe made him *the* modern myth, the fortunes of Doctor Faust had sunk very low from his sudden rise in the era of Renaissance and humanism.[6] A German antihumanist chapbook about the dreadful fate of a scholar who sold himself to the devil for unlimited knowledge (1587) was immediately translated into English and inspired Marlowe's best-known tragedy, *Doctor Faustus*. Goethe did not know Marlowe's work until 1818. He was a child when he first met Faust in a bowdlerized version of Marlowe on the popular marionette stages that toured German cities.

Over the almost 60 years that Goethe spent writing *Faust*, from 1773 to 1831, the work became his life myth. With long pauses to reflect and revise, he cast his experience of life—from the individual and private to the political and historical—into *Faust*. The three main periods of composition, at great time and thought intervals, account for the different meanings of the continuing Faust saga: the much-discussed heterogeneity of the work. There was first, in the Urfaust version, the Sturm und Drang Faust, a tormented man overreaching toward divinity and sinking to diabolical debasement instead. The author's interest has clearly shifted to the victim of his diabolical hero to show us in Gretchen the corruption and destruction of innocence.[7] Next came the classicist Faust with a major work period around 1800 and published as *Faust. Der Tragödie erster Teil (Faust. Part One of the Tragedy)* in 1808. The focus is back on Faust and in particular on the questions of how and why he concluded his pact with the devil. Spiritual despair and hope take us deep into the individual soul. At the same time, however, Goethe placed the excruciating soul search at a metaphysical and aesthetic distance by adding a triple frame with "Zueignung" ("Dedication"), "Vorspiel auf dem Theater" ("Prelude on the Stage"), and "Prolog im Himmel" ("Prologue in Heaven").

We will never know what made Goethe resolve to write the second part promised in the title of the 1808 version. Perhaps it was the jubilee year 1825, celebrated on the 50th anniversary of his coming to Weimar, that occasioned a retrospective on life and work from the vantage point of wise old age. Among the many fragments scattered along his career there was the beginning of a Helen of Troy scene from his classicist era pertaining to the most gigantic fragment of them all: Faust. From the Helen text Goethe wrote what is now act 3 of part 2, and published it in 1827 under the titillating title *Helena, klassisch-romantische Phantasmagorie, Zwischenspiel zu "Faust"(Helena, Classico-Romantic Phantasmagoria, Interlude to "Faust")*. Now, with this interlude, there was a new commitment to continue work, and he did: first acts 1 and 2 leading up to the Helen center, then act 5 as second nucleus, and finally act 4.

Heterogeneity extends to the genre of *Faust*. Parts 1 and 2 are both radically new in form, but in different ways. Part 1 is a monologic–dialogic parable with lyric and operatic interludes, arranged in episodes of varying length. It resembles what we would call filmic structure today. Part 2 consists of five long and scenic acts, each closely composed but only loosely connected with each other. There is nothing conventionally dramatic here; rather, the huge spans of space and especially time—3,000 years, Goethe boasted—make this an antidrama of epic proportions. It might best be called an allegorical spectacle staged in the dimension of Spanish baroque theater of the world: each act a *jornada*, a day's worth of sight and sound.[8]

Is *Faust* a tragedy, as the 1808 title states? Part 1 certainly is. Gretchen perishes and Faust "goes to the devil" (in the German phrase), as he follows Mephisto's call: "Away, with me!" (4611). Faust rejects the option, offered in Gretchen's example, to give himself up to secular justice as Valentin's killer and ask God's mercy. His fate at the end of part 1 seems decided. We do not need to assume that Goethe knew what he was going to do with Faust's future, but he did give himself an opening for the salvation of his problematic hero. In a crucial change of *Urfaust*— where the last word on Gretchen was Mephisto's "She is judged!"—he added the Voice from Above: "She is saved!" (4611). So although Faust here has damned himself, he too may yet be redeemed. And there is no question but that he is saved at the close of part 2, despite cries of foul from Mephistopheles and large parts of the critical community.

Faust Part I

Our first myth, in "Prolog im Himmel," is the biblical story of Job with the bet between Satan and God over God's exemplary servant Job. The

Book of Job, the first of the didactic or moral books in the Old Testament, is a theodicy. Despite all the undeserved suffering visited on humanity, God is right. His justice must not be doubted even though human reason protests against the incomprehensibility of his action. Goethe's *Faust* in the epoch of Enlightenment replaces God in the center with man. Man is responsible for his own life; his free will must decide the success or failure of his earthly existence—"Lord: Men err as long as they keep striving" (317)—and he will be judged precisely on what he made of his life. The passive figure of Job is replaced with hyperactive Faust, who has done or seen everything and not been satisfied. Job's temptation is suffering. Faust's temptation, offered by his devil, is a surfeit of pleasure: knowledge, action, and fun. It is the temptation of modern man who sees everything potentially within his reach and who needs only empowerment—tools, brainpower, maximum potential—to seize it all.

Faust certainly does not believe in God the way Job did; times have changed, and for Faust God is an enigma. Goethe calls on the myth of the God seeker to explore Faust's spiritual self and to explain the split consciousness of modern man, who hopes to find the answer to the riddle of his own existence in solving the enigma of God. Like Luther, the paradigmatic God seeker in German tradition, Faust wrestles with the meaning of the word of God—*logos*—in translating the Bible (1224). During a moment of transcendence he contemplates the macrocosm sign in a mystical volume on cosmology, and the spirit of creation comes to life for him in the image (429–53). Easter chants, celebrating the resurrection of Christ, save him from suicide despite his protest of nonbelief. At sunset on his Easter walk he longs to soar up and fly, godlike, over the Earth, overtaking time: the wish to be like God, Wagner (1126–41) and Mephistopheles (2048) remind us, is the original temptation of hubris leading to perdition. Finally, the famous "Gretchen question" about Faust's religious belief elicits an emotional tirade full of Sturm und Drang pathos and the Faustian definition of God: God is feeling, God is love (3426–58).

The obverse of the God-seeking self is represented by the devil, a myth of great variability. Goethe's Mephistopheles is less a religious than a philosophical devil. Early admirers such as Hegel considered *Faust* a philosophical tragedy; Mephistopheles speaks by far the most philosophical lines. Against the Lord of creation and life, he is the principle of negation, of annihilation, and of death. Against Faust's emotional and spiritual nature, he is cool intelligence—relentlessly rational, indefatigably resourceful, and thus ideally serviceable, the incarnation of instrumental reason. And, in opposition to Faust's idealistic, God-seeking striving, he has a down-to-earth side: Mephisto is materiality. The Earth Spirit is his ally, and animals are his attributes. He is the lord of gold and worldly treasures (Gretchen's jewels) and of flesh and blood (the carnal side of man). His magic works through bodily chemistry in the rejuvenating potion, he requires a signature in blood, and his understanding of love is sex.

At the center of the Faust legend is the pact with the devil: the myth of each era's defining desire. For Marlowe's Faust it was power, for Goethe's it is knowledge and experience, and for both it is a way of self-expansion, of appropriating others and the world. Goethe's Faust, Enlightenment man on the threshold to modernity, defines himself as desiring to know. Emancipated from the bounds of religion, secular man refuses to acknowledge limits to knowledge, as science extends the reign of the human mind over an ever-expanding universe. And what he has found he wants to know not just in the abstract but to experience his discovery in control, possession, and enjoyment. The world is his oyster: walk on the moon, travel in space, harness energy from nuclear to solar or, in Faust's project, tidal power. This is the summary of Faust's creed: "Whatever we understand we can seize" (11448).

In addition to redefining, Goethe altered the pact myth in a substantive way. Traditionally the contract runs for a definite time of 24 years, after which Faust will die and become the property of the devil. Goethe leaves the term of the contract open and makes its fulfillment contingent on a bet. Death and the devil shall get Faust when he declares himself satisfied. Faust's wager is based on the nature of desire as understood by modern man: desire is by definition unsatisfiable. As long as man lives he will desire, and as long as there is something outside of man he will make it the object of his desire, if not in reality then in the limitless wealth of his liberated imagination. Man can dream, and his dreams are creative, producing fantasy objects of desire ad infinitum. The wager makes a second point: happiness for modern man exists as an object of desire; it is always only the pursuit, not the possession, of happiness. The contract-wager that Faust offers Mephisto contains a definition and an anticipation of modern, postreligious humanity.

The Gretchen story is Goethe's original addition to the Faust legend. In it he uses the most powerful myth of them all, the myth that tries to explain the attraction between humans in love and sex. In Faust tradition the answer was beauty in the figure of Helen of Troy, who became

Faust's paramour. For the late eighteenth century, the age of sentiment and emerging social consciousness, love played a different role. Goethe's Gretchen originates in the novels of Richardson and in the social tragedies of Goethe's Sturm und Drang companions: female innocence victimized by the superior male lover. The Sturm und Drang dramatists in their social class crusade, above all J. M. R. Lenz in *Die Soldaten (The Soldiers)* and H. L. Wagner in *Die Kindermörderin (The Infanticide)*, had unmasked Richardson's ambivalent "love stories" as sexploitation. Goethe does not follow suit. Far from pointing an accusatory finger at bourgeois or aristocratic male malfeasance, his Gretchen drama raises love back up to mythical stature and cloaks it with poetic beauty of overwhelming persuasiveness. The Gretchen part of the Faust myth has proved its mystifying power over nearly two centuries. Gretchen still charms and moves us despite our objections as critical readers today.

For Goethe has created in his Gretchen myth a male fantasy of the perfect love object. She is the ideal of purity, innocence, and naïveté. Young, pious, uneducated, a simple girl from authentic folk culture, she is for the debauched and disillusioned intellectual Faust a long-lost dream come true. Goethe has given her two immortal songs to express this ideal: "Der König in Thule" ("The King in Thule") and "Gretchen am Spinnrad" ("At the Spinning Wheel"). Her home situation is the perfect setup for seduction: no male presence, a strict mother who enforces modesty and obedience to convention, and a rehearsal of loving in the substitute mother role with her infant sister. The other characters that make up her world are stereotypes, almost caricatures, of figures in a seduction story: the procuring neighbor, Madam Martha, and the honor-obsessed soldier-brother, Valentin.

But Gretchen is more than a male fantasy. In Faust's new life under the auspices of the double wager, she is the first significant event; the love story is Faust's only significant experience in part 1. Thus, in the contest playing in Faust's split self, she incarnates both God and the devil, the spiritual and the material, soul and body, love and sex. Faust's love story is prepared in the Witch's Kitchen and ends among the witches of Walpurgis Night. Engineered by Mephisto, this frame casts the entire love episode under the spell of sex. The myth of the witch at work here defines the feminine as sexuality; Faust remains bewitched until the bitter end of his romance in Gretchen's prison. The reader, however, also sees the other side, the God side, in Gretchen. Two episodes that draw on powerful Christian myths place her in a religious context. The first, her prayer before a Mater Dolorosa statue, calls on the myth of the grieving mother of Christ in her role as redeemer. Goethe reproduces and adapts to Gretchen's situation one of the best-known set pieces in Catholic liturgy: the *Stabat Mater* (3587–3619). The second, in the cathedral (presumably at her mother's funeral), translates the Latin text of the traditional requiem mass into the voice of Gretchen's guilty conscience. The topic of the requiem segment chosen is the Last Judgment, and judgment will be the last topic of Goethe's first Faust drama in Gretchen's dungeon.

For it is in the prison scene that Gretchen leaves the frame of the male fantasy to become a self-defining figure in her own right. Her voice dominates absolutely, with Faust being progressively shut down and shut out until she finally rejects him at the price of her life. It is instructive to observe the changes to the *Urfaust* version. Far more than merely versifying a prose original, the classicist Goethe of 1800, no longer captivated by the male fantasy of his Sturm und Drang 20s, created a new persona for Gretchen. He expanded brief sketches or mere phrases in Gretchen's original text into dramatic-lyrical solo passages of exquisitely haunting poetic power. Gretchen in her visionary madness composes six fantasy scenarios, whereas Faust's role is reduced to bit player or completely written out of her script.

In the first scenario (4453–69), Gretchen recognizes her lover and welcomes him as the dashing hero who saves her from hellfire and brimstone. In the second (4475–80), memory sets in to recall the happy days of their love before the fall into sin and guilt. But memory continues, and the third scenario (4507–17) remembers her and Faust's murders: of her mother, of their child, and of her brother. The fourth (4520–28) is memoriography—the planning of burial sites—and this is where Faust gets excluded. He will not be allowed to join her and hers in death: "No, you must go on living!" Gretchen assigns him instead the job of executor of her will. The next, most hauntingly vivid, scenario (4551–71) sends shivers down everyone's spine. Here Gretchen's guilt rises up out of the memory of the past as she relives the drowning of her child and sees her undead mother blocking her way out into any conceivable future, except for the one visualized in the last scenario: judgment day (4580–95).

The chilling tones that depict Gretchen's execution, in contrast with the breathless intensity of the haunting passage that precedes it, demonstrate the consummate artistry Goethe employed to give Gretchen a new identity. She creates this identity by remembering and accepting her past as her history. She is now who she has become in the experiences and actions she recalls. She is also the one who questions identity, Faust's and her own: Do you know who you are? Do you know whom you want to rescue? she asks (4501–5). Faust, by contrast, refuses to accept his history as identity: "Let what is past, be past," he pleads (4518). This is what separates, what liberates, her from him and why she can step into the new role that Goethe is preparing while he rewrites the final scene. In Gretchen's new text of irremediable pain we have witnessed "all mankind's miseries" (4406). Gretchen now is ready to assume her third mythical role, that of exemplary sufferer and sacrifice in the place of another—Faust who refuses to suffer for his guilt. At the end of *Faust Part II* Gretchen will reappear as Christ substitute: the sacrificial redeemer.

Faust Part II

The second part of *Faust* is a veritable feast of myth, especially act 2, which requires a mythological guidebook on its excursion from the Sphinxes of ancient Egypt to the hypotheses of Earth's origin in Goethe's own time. Our discussion is necessarily highly selective.[9] A brief overview of the five large and disconnected acts reveals a broad field of myth recycling but also the occasional creation of new myths, such as the Mothers in act 1 and Euphorion-Byron in act 3. Part 2 opens with a transition scene that places Faust under the healing powers of nature personified in the elves and fairies of literary tradition. The action at the imperial court plays with the myth of empire, pointing out the cracks and flaws in the glory as myth is translated into real history. The empire game continues in act 4 and explores myths of power and war. Act 3, the germination point of part 2, is openly self-reflexive. The nature of myth, its modes of existence, and our uses of myth are explored through the figure of Helen. Act 5 is thematically split, weaving the defining myths of the modern age—economy, government, and technology—into a meditation on death.

Not surprisingly, since Goethe wrote the two works during the same period, the structure of *Faust Part II* shares basic features with the *Wanderjahre* novel: plot is marginalized as frame, and what matters are the inserts. The plot concerns Faust's career in the emperor's favor, leading to the award of sovereignty over coastal territory, including any land reclaimed from the ocean. Three inserts constitute the action proper. There is, first, the quest of Helen, arranged like a set of Chinese boxes tracing a path to the interior. Faust's magic journey to the Mothers at the close of act 1 models this path. There is next Faust's expansion of self into the outside world in his pursuit of effective action in his role as warrior, ruler, and creator of a new world. And there is finally the quest of ending, of closure in the attempt to find the meaning of death. Students of Goethe's biography agree that death was his deepest irritation.

The three quests correlate with and lead to questions concerning three basic coordinates of human existence: time, space, and the void. Time as interior space is directed toward origins, to questions such as where we as individuals come from and how it all began: identity, history, civilization, life, and the universe. Space directs us toward the exterior, drawing us to explore and appropriate others, nature, and the world in its real, tangible existence. The void, nothingness, of death is hardest to imagine. This is where myth steps in with its explanatory function. Myth offers ways to imagine and represents to the imagination and thus enables us to apprehend at least metaphorically what time, space, and death mean. This is what Goethe attempts in *Faust Part II.*

The play opens with the founding myth of New Man. The rainbow symbol at the end of the first scene links Faust's recovery from his catastrophic experience in part 1 with the biblical deluge, the myth of rebirth, of a second chance for mankind shared by many cultures. In a spectacular performance of poetic show-and-tell at the moment of daybreak and sunrise, Goethe places his New Man within secular space. Nature, not God, is the ground on which Faust can recover and project a better future life; "sky" and "earth" are his safeguards of vitality (1.4679–89). Faust will direct his future efforts not toward reaching the absolute but toward a limited goal of achievement within the real world. He turns his eyes away from the blinding light of the sun to rest them in observing the sun's image in the quasi rainbow above a waterfall, for "what we have as life is many-hued reflection" (1.4717). More difficult to accept in Goethe's New Man is the condition of forgetting. Faust's plea with Gretchen in prison to let bygones be bygone is realized here. "Bathed in the dew of Lethe's waters" (1.4629), Faust becomes a man without memory, without and outside of history. For the nineteenth century, the age that invented historicism and psychoanalysis, this is an amazing concept.

Surely the most intriguing myth in *Faust* is that of the Mothers at the close of act 1. Although the figures of the Mothers are Goethe's invention, the journey toward them goes back to the fertile myth of the underworld visit. From Orpheus and Christ to Ulysses, Virgil, Dante, and the heroes of German fairy tales recently popularized by the Grimm brothers, a return trip to the underworld meant victory in crossing the ultimate frontier. Two distinct features stand out in Goethe's revision. First, the Mothers represent a taboo; penetrating their space and their essence is a transgression. The mere thought makes Faust shiver, and when he touches the figure of Helen he stole from them, he is punished by an explosion. For the second point, Faust's return is a hollow victory. The figures he brings back are mere imagoes, nothing but empty form. Touched by reality they vanish. The Mothers' realm, as Mephisto states, is the void, pure emptiness; Faust's magic journey there is his first encounter on the death quest. His falling unconscious from the explosion is only a warning but a genuine one. The void, although undefined and thus full of unlimited possibilities, as Faust sees it ("In your Nothingness I hope to find my All," 1.6256), cannot produce life.

The end of Faust's conjuring trick shows that the shortcut of magic is mere illusion, not effective action. To affect reality, an action has to happen within time and space. Acts 2 and 3, quest and conquest of Helen, translate geographic space and historical time into the inner space and time of spiritual creation. From the collective memories stored in myths, the three questers, Faust, Mephisto, and Homunculus, produce answers to their different needs. Faust, who desires beauty, discovers and brings forth Helen in a productive union that results in their offspring, Euphorion, allegory of poetry, or beauty in language. The male devil Mephistopheles, principle of negativity, finds his place and form in Helen's opposite: a female figure of utmost ugliness, Phorcyas. And Homunculus, mind in search of a body, takes the advice of Proteus, god of all shapes: he disperses in water, the element and origin of life.

Goethe here plays an explicit game with time. In act 2 the prophetess Manto, who sees the future as well as the past, asks us to imagine circular time when she states: "I stand still, time circles around me" (2.7481).[10] In act 3 time skips 2,000 years when Helen returns from the Trojan war to step into the courtyard of Faust's medieval castle. If Helen is transported forward, Faust travels back in time from his early modern sixteenth century to the era of the crusades. Goethe locates Faust's life with Helen in Arcadia, mythical place of timelessness and unchanging beauty. From standing still in Arcadia, time shifts to fast-forward with the birth of Euphorion, who grows from infancy to adulthood, from birth to death, in a matter of minutes in the imaginary time and space of 300 verses (3.9599–9900).

Helen herself, object of Faust's desire since he glimpsed her image in the Witch's Kitchen and germinal cell of *Faust Part II* in Goethe's writing, is the emblem of myth. This figure explains what myth is and how it works. How myth is missed and abused was shown in the conjuring trick at the emperor's court: the shortcut via magic produced fantasy, not myth. Myth is not individual property; it is a concentrate of culture, stored in a place of collective memory such as Hades, where the "shades" of past existences dwell. To revive a myth means exactly that: to fill with life a "shade," the outline of a memory. Such restoration requires labor, the labor of art. Myth in the modern age exists as art in paintings, statues, and literature. Acts 2 and 3 are commonly read as representation of the creative process of writing: this is how Goethe discovered the imaginative dimension of his Faust poem. How myth is brought into existence ("Dasein," 3.9418) through and in art is the statement of a key passage, in which Faust teaches Helen how to speak in rhyme. In and through language art, Helen comes to live and love: these rhymed lines realize her mythical essence (3.9365–9418).

At this crucial moment and earlier, prodded by the bearer of negativity Mephisto-Phorcyas, Helen realizes another aspect of myth: its fragile and multiple—because imaginary—mode of being. Memories of her past existences in different versions of myth destabilize her identity— "Was I all that? am I that now?" (3.8839)—and destroy her grounding in reality. Haunted by her own self as phantom, she faints: "become a shade to myself too" (3.8872–81). These fits of negativity, however, are far outweighed by the positive functions of myth, above all its productive power. In *Faust Part II*, myth is a major force of inspiration. The main actions of act 3 illustrate myth's productivity through allegories of creative epochs in the history of civilization. Western courtly culture of the middle ages developed from the pursuit of Eastern beauty and ideals in the crusades: Helen takes refuge in Faust's castle. Conjoining ancient Greek heritage with early modern energy and power drive resulted in the Renaissance: Faust creates riches and a realm to safeguard and glorify Helen. Goethe's own era of classicism and romanticism reenacted a renaissance, if of short-lived duration (in Goethe's view): Eyphorion-Byron is born from the union of Helen (antiquity) and Faust (modernity).

The final setting of act 3 in Arcadia exposes the basic paradox of myth. Myth, because it is timeless, is at the same time transitory and eternal. Arcadia is idyllic landscape, a golden age topos since the Renaissance. It is place without time, outside of history, and withdrawn from change and, of course, death (3.9550–53). When Euphorion disrupts the spell, Arcadia and Helen vanish. Yet precisely their evanescence makes them endure. Myth is regenerative. If conditions are right, Arcadia can be reproduced anywhere and anytime. The anonymous chorus girls in Helen's retinue metamorphose into nature, ready to reemerge as Arcadia again. Individualized beings such as Helen and the leader of her troupe, Panthalis, have eternal existence in mythical memory, in mythology. As memory image, represented in the gown and cloud, Helen will continue to inspire Faust's grander enterprises (3.9950–53).

Act 5, the second focus of *Faust Part II*, is an extended meditation on death, somewhat in the manner of a musical composition taking us through changes, allusions, and variations that end, in fact, with a sequence of hymns and a *chorus mysticus*. Death was much on Goethe's mind during the writing of this act (1830–1831). The duke, eight years his junior, had died in June 1828. The duchess, to whom Goethe had been very close, followed early in 1830, and late that year Goethe's only son died. Goethe, now 81 years old, suffered a collapse that brought him close to death for days. The question of how to end his Faust play was inscribed in the very beginning with the open-ended contract. The way the contract was written required that the ending include an evaluation of Faust's lifetime achievement. Part 1 ended with a judgment scene, in Gretchen's imagination and in the Voices from Outside and Above her prison. The theme of judgment is woven through the death meditations of the final act in part 2.

The opening scene with Philemon and Baucis invokes a death myth and invites comparison with Faust's approaching death. In the classical story from Ovid's *Metamorphoses*, the old couple's desire was focused on death. Granted a wish by Zeus, they wished to die at the same time and were metamorphosed into two trees. Goethe has them, instead, pronounce the first judgment on Faust, who denies and defies everything they believe in. He denies the march of time, old age, and the reminder of death in their bell's tolling (5.11258–68). He denies and defies the announcement of death carried by the phantom women Want, Debt, Care, and Distress, sisters of Death (5.11384). Offspring of the Parcae or Norns, who set the end of life for humans, the four Grey Women do call forth a retrospective self-evaluation in Faust (5.11433–40). Physically blinded, in a play on the Oedipus myth, Faust finally gains the insight into his own self and life that he had lacked in his hyperactive drivenness: "I've never tarried anywhere" (5.11433).

Judgment on Faust is not limited to his past actions. At death's door, in another play with difference on the Philemon and Baucis myth, he too looks forward into the future. Faust's desired afterlife is not vegetal

continuity in a tree; his prospective, cast in his last great monologue
(5.11559–86), produces a vision of perfect life for a community and
immortality for himself as the creator of this life (5.11583–84). Faust
has reached yet another insight, which he announces with great emphasis, and it is on the basis of this insight that we are called on to judge
him finally:

> To this idea I am committed wholly,
> it is the final wisdom we can reach:
> he, only, merits freedom and existence
> who wins them every day anew.
>   (5.11573–76)

Faust's view of the value of his or any life is immediately contradicted by
Mephisto's radical nihilism. Life is a zero-sum game. A spent life, no
matter how full or how long, is worth absolutely nothing: "What's over,
and mere nothing, are the same. . . . things might just as well have
never been" (5.11597–601).

We are to ponder these opposing judgments during the following
burlesque interlude of angelic and diabolic hosts fighting over Faust's
soul. Here Goethe stages a central myth of the Christian middle ages
popularized in paintings of the Last Judgment, which typically adorn
the wall behind the main altar. These paintings elaborate the myth with
a profusion of imaginative activity, including the soul escaping from the
deceased's mouth and being pulled up or down by angels or devils. The
most famous example, Michelangelo's Sistine Chapel fresco, is a beauti-
fied Renaissance version of the medieval grotesqueries that provided
instruction and diversion to the faithful during the worship ritual.

The final change of scene to Mountain Gorges transports us to yet
another myth: redemption as exemplified in legends and images of
saints and sinners. Goethe's staging is again intensely pictorial, but this
time the images remain in perpetual motion. Combined with the
singing voices of individuals and groups, the result is a choreography for
a celestial ballet, the libretto for a surrealist opera. One might imagine
the performance of a redemption oratorio in a baroque church. At the
highest point of the cupola Mary *(Mater gloriosa)* would be painted in
apotheosis. All around and beneath her on the wide ceiling and on the
wall paintings between the windows, a host of saints and supplicants

would be shown rising toward her, carried aloft on the sound of sacral words and music, following their individualized paths toward redemption.

The last Goethean *Faust* myth, one that keeps feeding critical speculation more than any other aspect of the work, remains to be discussed. It is the idea of the "eternal feminine" on which the play ends. The position *in conclusion* gives this concept additional weight. All through his course on Earth woman was the driving and shaping force for Faust: Gretchen in part 1 and Helen in part 2. The ending of part 1 prepared for Gretchen the role of sacrificial sufferer, of Christ substitute. When she reappears now it is to initiate the feminization of the divine. Instead of the Lord Father of "Prolog im Himmel," now the Supreme Mother *(Mater Gloriosa)* holds the highest place. The standard invocation, "God, have mercy upon us," appears revised in the feminine gender: "Virgin, Mother, Queen, / Goddess, keep mercy upon us!" (5.12102–3). All the penitent supplicants, whom Faust is to join, are women. Conversely, the singing male saints on their upward path are in various states of desire or love for "heaven's High Queen" (5.11996), whom the highest among them, Doctor Marianus, glorifies.

It is not, however, a question of gendering, let alone of a feminist agenda. What is at issue here is the necessity for Faust to attain full humanity. The old sinner, jaded but rich in experience, will first have to be integrated by and assimilated into the band of innocents: the *Blessed Boys* who died soon after birth. By the same token, to become fully human, the paradigmatic male overachiever will have to absorb or be absorbed by the feminine, whatever that might be, provided it is his, the Faustian male's, missing complement.

Notes and References

Preface

    1. Nicholas Boyle, *Goethe: The Poet and the Age,* vol. 1, *The Poetry of Desire (1749–1790)* (New York: Oxford University Press, 1991), x; hereafter cited in the text as Boyle 1991.
    2. Richard Friedenthal, *Goethe: His Life and Times* (Cleveland: World Publishing, 1963).
    3. Karl Otto Conrady, *Goethe: Leben und Werk,* 2 vols. (Königstein: Athenäum, 1982–1985); hereafter cited in the text.

Chapter One

    1. Goethe to Lavater, 1780. Cited in Conrady, 1:352.
    2. Goethe to W. v. Humboldt, 17 March 1832.
    3. In the long essay "Goethes *Wahlverwandtschaften*" ("Goethe's *Elective Affinities*") of 1921–1922, in *Gesammelte Schriften,* vol. 1, ed. Rolf Tiedemann and Hermann Schweppenhäuser (Frankfurt: Suhrkamp, 1977), 123–201; hereafter cited in the text.
    4. After their break, Charlotte had her own letters to Goethe returned and destroyed them, so we can only see the relationship from Goethe's side.
    5. See the poem "Ilmenau," for the Duke's birthday in 1783.
    6. Goethe to Herder, 4 September 1788.
    7. Jean Paul in a letter, 1795. Cited in Conrady, 2:282.
    8. Goethe to Carl August, 27 May 1820.
    9. Conversation with Eckermann, 21 February 1827.

Chapter Two

    1. *Goethe's Werke. Hamburger Ausgabe,* 14 vols. (Hamburg: Wegner, 1949–1960), 12:22; hereafter cited in the text as *HA.*
    2. The essay *Von deutscher Baukunst (On German Architecture)* is quoted from *Collected Works,* 12 vols. (Boston: Suhrkamp/Insel, 1983–1989), 3:3–10, here 6; hereafter cited in the text as *Works.*
    3. The version discussed here is the original version (printed in *HA,* 1:27–28) to illustrate the poem's threshold character. *Works,* vol. 1, *Selected Poems* prints the second version. The selection of poems in this chapter, as in chapter 9, follows the *Works* edition. The interpretation refers to the German text, because in poetry the body of a word matters. The English text provided

on facing pages of the *Works* volume should make it easy to follow the discussion. Numbers in parentheses refer to lines.

4. See Herder's 1774 essay "Übers Erkennen und Empfinden in der menschlichen Seele," in *Sämtliche Werke,* vol. 8, ed. Bernhard Suphan (1892; reprint, Hildesheim: Olms, 1967), 236–62.

5. In the decisive encounter with Lotte the word *Klopstock* is code for the emotional experience expressed in "Frühlingsfeier." The Klopstock moment of epiphany and bonding seals Werther's fate.

6. *Mailied* is quoted from *HA,* 1:30–31, here line 25. Numbers in parentheses refer to lines.

7. See Nicholas Boyle, " 'Maifest' und 'Auf dem See'," *German Life and Letters* 35 (1982): 18–34.

8. *Wandrers Sturmlied* is quoted from *HA,* 1:33–36. Numbers in parentheses refer to line.

9. Harold Bloom, *The Anxiety of Influence: A Theory of Poetry* (New York: Oxford University Press, 1973).

10. Goethe's short lyrics *Heidenröslein* and *Das Veilchen,* famous in compositions by Schubert and Mozart, are counterfeit folk ballads.

11. Goethe to Fritz Jacobi, 31 August 1774.

12. "Ein Ärgernis," Herder declared. See Karl Eibl, in *Sämtliche Werke, Briefe, Tagebücher und Gespräche. Frankfurter Ausgabe* (Frankfurt/Main: Deutscher Klassiker Verlag, 1985), 1:857–58; hereafter cited in the text as *FA.*

13. *Prometheus* is quoted from *HA,* 1:44–64.

14. *An Schwager Kronos* is quoted from *HA,* 1:47–48.

15. Thus in the original version. The version revised for publication concludes more modestly.

16. Goethe to F. Jacobi, 11 September 1785.

17. Immanuel Kant, "Beantwortung der Frage: Was ist Aufklärung?" (1784), in *Was ist Aufklärung: Aufsätze zur Geschichte und Philosophie,* ed. Jürgen Zehbe (Göttingen: Vandenhoeck and Ruprecht, 1967), 55–61.

Chapter Three

1. Goethe's Shakespeare speech, *Zum Schäkespears Tag,* is quoted from *Works,* 3:163–65, here 165.

2. J. G. Herder, "Shakespeare," in *Sturm und Drang: Kritische Schriften* (Heidelberg: Lambert Schneider, 1963), 568.

3. Goethe to Salzmann, 28 November 1771.

4. References to the text of *Götz von Berlichingen* are to *Works,* 7:1–82, here 66.

5. References to the text of *Egmont* are to *Works,* 7:83–151, here 108.

6. Goethe to Boie, 23 December 1774.

7. Hans Wagener, ed., *Egmont* (Stuttgart: Reclam, 1974), 57; hereafter cited in the text.

8. Goethe to Charlotte von Stein, 20 March 1782.
9. Goethe to Charlotte von Stein, 29 January 1776.
10. Goethe to Charlotte von Stein, 14 May 1778.
11. Friedrich Schiller, *Sämtliche Werke,* vol. 4 (München: Hanser, 1960), 7, 20.

Chapter Four

1. Because many English editions of *Werther* are commonly in use, most references are by the date of a letter. Where necessary, page references are to *Works,* vol. 11.
2. See Kurt Rothmann, ed., *Die Leiden des jungen Werthers* (Stuttgart: Reclam, 1971), 91–99.

Chapter Five

1. See Irmgard Wagner, *Critical Approaches to Goethe's Classical Dramas* (Columbia, S.C.: Camden House, 1995), 77–85.
2. The text of *Iphigenie auf Tauris* is quoted from *Works,* 8:1–53, here 3.1.1081. Numbers in parentheses refer to act, scene, and line.
3. See Dieter Borchmeyer, *Die Weimarer Klassik,* 2 vols. (Königstein: Athenäum, 1980), 1:114.
4. Immanuel Kant, "Zum ewigen Frieden: Ein philosophischer Entwurf" (1795), in *Immanuel Kants Werke,* vol. 6, ed. Ernst Cassirer (Berlin: Bruno Cassirer, 1925), 425–74.
5. Goethe to Knebel, 15 March 1779.
6. More details in my "Goethe's 'Iphigenie': A Lacanian Reading," *Goethe Yearbook* 2 (1984): 51–67.
7. See his *Brief des Pastors zu *** an den neuen Pastor zu **** (1772), in *HA,* 12:228–39.
8. See the association with Saint Agatha in Italy, *Italian Journey,* 19 October 1786.
9. The translation in *Works,* "May you both fare well," brings out the plural form but includes only family, not the stranger Pylades.
10. "Zum Klassizismus von Goethes 'Iphigenie,' " *Die Neue Rundschau* 78 (1967): 586–99.
11. Christian Grawe, ed., *Torquato Tasso* (Stuttgart: Reclam, 1981), 91; hereafter cited in the text.
12. The text of *Torquato Tasso* is quoted from *Works,* 8:55–139, here 5.2.3070. Numbers in parentheses refer to act, scene, and line.
13. Joyce Carol Oates, herself an expert, discusses this problem in "The Madness of Art: Henry James's 'The Middle Years,' " *New Literary History* 27 (1996): 259–62.

14. Meredith Lee presents an informative interpretation of the *Römische Elegien* in *Studies in Goethe's Lyric Cycles* (Chapel Hill: University of North Carolina Press, 1978).

15. See, for example, Byron's *Lament of Tasso*.

16. Elizabeth M. Wilkinson, "Goethe's 'Tasso': The Tragedy of a Creative Artist," *PEGS* n.s. 15 (1946): 96–127.

Chapter Six

1. For the serious approach see Peter Morgan, *The Critical Idyll: Traditional Values and the French Revolution in Goethe's "Hermann und Dorothea"* (Columbia, S.C.: Camden House, 1990). For the ironic perspective, see Waltraud Wiethölter's comment in *FA*, 8:1150–69.

2. Diary entry, 11 September 1796.

3. Goethe to Schiller, 3 January 1798.

4. Schiller to Körner, 28 October 1796.

5. See especially the letters of 22 July, 1 August, and 17 September 1796.

6. Goethe to Schiller, 14 June 1796.

7. Goethe to Heinrich Meyer, 5 December 1796.

8. The text of *Hermann und Dorothea* is quoted from *Works,* 8: 247–307, here lines 637–40, 710–11. Numbers in parentheses refer to lines.

9. The translation in *Works* mitigates the absolute statement in the German: "Denn er ist Vater!"

10. At this time Goethe recommended publishing her latest work in *Die Horen.* See letter to Schiller, 5 December 1796.

11. The women included Caroline Böhmer Schlegel Schelling and Dorothea Mendelssohn Veit Schlegel.

12. See Schiller's report on Humboldt's critique of *Wilhelm Meister* in his letter to Goethe, 28 November 1796.

13. The *Works* translation changes the message: "And with masculine strength he bore her magnificent stature."

14. See, for example, the comment in *FA*, 8:973–1017, or J. Hillis Miller, "Interlude as Anastomosis in 'Die Wahlverwandtschaften,' " *Goethe Yearbook* 6 (1992): 115–22.

15. The text of *Die Wahlverwandtschaften* is quoted from *Works,* 11:93–262, here 116.

16. *Morgenblatt für gebildete Stände,* 4 September 1809. See *HA,* 6:621.

17. See his essay of 1792, "The Experiment as Mediator between Object and Subject," in *Works,* 12:11–17.

18. Thomas Mann got closer. His essay in *Die Neue Rundschau* of 1925 speaks of nature mystique and rational magic.

19. See his poem of friendly irony on the subject, *Weltseele* (*Universal Soul*), in *Works,* 1:166.

20. *Morgenblatt* announcement, see n. 16.
21. In a letter to K. F. v. Reinhard of 21 February 1810, Goethe made the connection explicit: his unconditional love makes Edward invaluable to the novelist.

Chapter Seven

1. Friederike Eigler, "Wer hat 'Wilhelm Schüler' zum 'Wilhelm Meister' gebildet? 'Wilhelm Meisters Lehrjahre' und die Aussparungen einer hermeneutischen Verstehens- und Bildungspraxis," *Goethe Yearbook* 3 (1986): 93–119, and the comments in *FA*, 9:1363–80, and *Sämtliche Werke nach Epochen seines Schaffens. Münchner Ausgabe*, vol. 5 (München: Hanser, 1985 –), 613–43, reflect the turn away from *Bildung* idealization.
2. Joseph R. Urgo, "An Obscure Destiny: This Business of Teaching English," *Profession* 1996, 137.
3. Schiller to Goethe, 8 July 1796. Goethe to Schiller, 19 November 1796: "daß sich der Leser produktiv verhalten muß."
4. Goethe to Schiller, 9 July 1796.
5. The text of *Wilhelm Meisters Lehrjahre* is quoted from *Works*, 9:1–379, here 271. The translation misses the equation between the two terms.
6. Also in *Works*, 1:132–33.

Chapter Eight

1. See also Ehrhard Bahr, *The Novel as Archive: The Genesis, Reception, and Criticism of Goethe's 'Wilhelm Meisters Wanderjahre'* (Columbia, S.C.: Camden House, 1998).
2. Not even the *MLA Bibliography* can make sense of the genre and lists the work and its parts separately under the categories of fiction and novel. Goethe published *Lehrjahre* with the subtitle *Ein Roman (A Novel)* and *Wanderjahre* without such information.
3. Goethe took up Chinese studies in earnest in 1813, at the time of Napoleon's fall.
4. Goethe to Rochlitz, 23 November 1829.
5. The two sets of aphorisms will be ignored. They were added as fillers and largely selected by Eckermann.
6. The text of *Wilhelm Meisters Wanderjahre* is quoted from *Works*, 10:97–435. References are to book and chapter, here 3.15.

Chapter Nine

1. *Works*, vol. 1, *Selected Poems*, translates the title somewhat obscurely as "The Parliament of West and East." References for this chapter's poetry are to this edition, with exceptions noted. Numbers in parentheses refer to lines.

2. References for *Noten und Abhandlungen* are to *HA,* 2:126–264, here 127.

3. In Hafis's poetry, Khizr is a green-clad old man, guardian of the source of life.

4. See, for the text of the model, Hans Albert Maier, *Goethe. West-östlicher Divan* (Tübingen: Niemeyer, 1965), 111.

5. Not in *Works,* vol. 1. See the poem *Derb und tüchtig (Coarse and Efficient)* in *HA,* 2:16.

6. *Hegira* is quoted from *Works,* 1:203, here line 5.

7. All in *Buch Suleika*: *Hochbeglückt in deiner Liebe (Supremely happy in your love), Was bedeutet die Bewegung? (What means the motion?), Ach, um deine feuchten Schwingen (Oh, for your moist wings),* and *Wie mit innigstem Behagen (With intensest well-feeling).*

8. The *Works* translation of the last line is inadequate. A better reading would be "Oops! he burned up on me."

9. *Über Kunst und Altertum,* 1820. See *HA,* 1:403–7.

10. For this long poem, first numbers refer to stanzas and numbers after a period to the lines within the respective stanza.

11. Roman numerals refer to the number of the poem within the cycle and arabic numerals to lines within a poem. The *Works* selection prints only one poem of this cycle (VIII). References are to *HA,* 1:387–90.

12. For Rilke's interest in this cycle see Lee, *Studies in Goethe's Lyric Cycles,* p. 176 and n. 17.

13. Shadow play was a Chinese entertainment much imitated in Europe at the time.

Chapter Ten

1. Recent books by Nicholas Boyle (*Goethe: Faust Part One* [Cambridge, England: Cambridge University Press, 1987]), Jane K. Brown (*Goethe's 'Faust': The German Tragedy* [Ithaca, N.Y.: Cornell University Press, 1986] and *Faust: Theater of the World* [New York: Twayne, 1992]), and John R. Williams (*Goethe's Faust* [London: Allen and Unwin, 1987]) and essay collections on interpreting and teaching *Faust* make this point and offer invaluable help in reading *Faust.* The discussion of *Faust* here can afford to be eclectic because we can refer the reader to Brown's inclusive reading of the work in the Twayne Masterwork series (1992).

2. Martin Esslin, "Goethe's 'Faust': Pre-Modern, Post-Modern, Proto-Postmodern," in *Interpreting Faust Today,* ed. Jane K. Brown, Meredith Lee, and Thomas P. Saine (Columbia, S.C.: Camden House, 1994), 219–27.

3. The text of *Faust* is quoted from *Works,* 2:1–305, here lines 12104–9. Numbers in parentheses refer to lines *(Faust Part I)* and acts and lines *(Faust Part II).*

4. See Oswald Spengler, *Der Untergang des Abendlandes,* 2 vols. (München: Beck, 1919).

5. See the essays in Douglas J. McMillan, ed., *Approaches to Teaching Goethe's "Faust"* (New York: Modern Language Association, 1987).

6. Boyle's (1987) introduction to *Goethe: Faust Part One* contains the most useful prehistory.

7. The version was preserved despite Goethe's intention. Luise von Göchhausen, lady-in-waiting at Weimar, had made a copy, which was discovered among her papers and published in 1887.

8. By this time, Goethe was familiar with Spanish *teatro del mundo.* He promoted Calderón and staged his plays at the Weimar theater.

9. My selection coincides largely, if not entirely, with that of the Kaufmann edition of *Faust* (*Goethe's "Faust": The Original German and a New Translation and Introduction: Part One and Sections from Part Two,* trans. Walter Kaufmann [Garden City, N.Y.: Anchor-Doubleday, 1961]), which according to McMillan in *Approaches to Teaching* (p. 4) is the most frequently used in undergraduate classes.

10. The *Works* translation misses the point: "I let time move while I stay here."

Bibliography

Primary Sources

Collected Works. 12 vols. Boston: Suhrkamp/Insel, 1983–1989. Paperback edition by Princeton University Press, 1994–.

Goethes Werke. Hamburger Ausgabe. 14 vols. Hamburg: Wegner, 1949–1960. The most recent edition (1981) offers new critical comments.

Sämtliche Werke, Briefe, Tagebücher und Gespräche. Frankfurter Ausgabe. 40 vols. Frankfurt/Main: Deutscher Klassiker Verlag, 1985 –.

Sämtliche Werke nach Epochen seines Schaffens. Münchner Ausgabe. 21 vols. in 32. München: Hanser, 1985 –1998.

The three German editions contain extensive analytical and interpretive comments.

Secondary Sources

Explanatory Notes

Erläuterungen und Dokumente is a useful series of explanatory notes and background documents published by Reclam (Stuttgart) for many Goethe texts.

Angst, Joachim, and Fritz Hackert, eds. *Iphigenie auf Tauris.* 1969.

Grawe, Christian, ed. *Torquato Tasso.* 1981.

Neuhaus, Volker, ed. *Götz von Berlichingen.* 1973.

Ritzenhoff, Ursula, ed. *Die Wahlverwandtschaften.* 1982.

Rothmann, Kurt, ed. *Die Leiden des jungen Werthers.* 1971.

Schmidt, Josef, ed. *Hermann und Dorothea.* 1970.

Wagener, Hans, ed. *Egmont.* 1974.

Goethe's Life and Work

Boyle, Nicholas. *Goethe: The Poet and the Age.* Vol. 1, *The Poetry of Desire (1749–1790).* Oxford, England: Oxford University Press, 1991. Interpretive biography with sensitive and innovative readings of the works through 1790 (poetry, *Götz von Berlichingen, Egmont, Iphigenie auf Tauris, Torquato Tasso,* and *Werther*). Volume 2 is promised for 1999.

Conrady, Karl Otto. *Goethe: Leben und Werk.* 2 vols. Königstein: Athenäum, 1982–1985. Informative biography with emphasis on social context. Useful interpretations of the works from a socioliterary perspective.

Friedenthal, Richard. *Goethe: His Life and Times.* Cleveland: World Publishing, 1963. Factual biography with critical but fair viewpoint. Much information in brief space.

Specific Works or Genres

FAUST

Boyle, Nicholas. *Goethe: "Faust Part One."* Landmarks of World Literature. Cambridge, England: Cambridge University Press, 1987. Introduction to *Faust Part I* only. Excellent for *Faust* prehistory.

Brown, Jane K. *Goethe's "Faust": The German Tragedy.* Ithaca, N.Y.: Cornell University Press, 1986. Extensive interpretation of *Faust Part I* and *Faust Part II* in the context of world literature. Attention on symbolism.

————. *"Faust": Theater of the World.* Twayne Masterwork Studies. New York: Twayne, 1992. Introduction from dialectical perspective.

Brown, Jane K., Meredith Lee, and Thomas P. Saine, eds. *Interpreting Goethe's "Faust" Today.* Columbia, S.C.: Camden House, 1994. Scholarly essays based on *Faust* symposium. Many aspects, approaches, and controversies are included.

McMillan, Douglas J., ed. *Approaches to Teaching Goethe's "Faust."* New York: Modern Language Association, 1987. Invaluable for instructors in a variety of settings and approaches. Extensive bibliographical aid.

Williams, John R. *Goethe's "Faust."* Unwin Critical Library. London: Allen and Unwin, 1987. Appreciative interpretation of both *Faust Part I* and *Faust Part II* in brief space.

OTHER WORKS

Bahr, Ehrhard. *The Novel as Archive: The Genesis, Reception, and Criticism of Goethe's "Wilhelm Meisters Wanderjahre."* Columbia, S.C.: Camden House, 1998. Excellent background of complex novel.

Blackall, Eric. *Goethe and the Novel.* London: Cornell University Press, 1976. Chapters on every novel. Still best for *Werther* and *Wilhelm Meisters Lehrjahre.*

Blair, John. *Tracing Subversive Currents in Goethe's "Wilhelm Meister's Apprenticeship."* Columbia, S.C.: Camden House, 1997. Detailed yet concise interpretation from culture-critical perspective.

Brown, Jane K. *Goethe's Cyclical Narratives: "Die Unterhaltungen deutscher Ausgewanderter" and "Wilhelm Meisters Wanderjahre."* Chapel Hill: University of North Carolina Press, 1975. For *Wanderjahre,* focus is on the inserted novellas.

Burckhardt, Sigurd. *The Drama of Language.* Baltimore: Johns Hopkins University Press, 1970. Close readings (of *Egmont, Iphigenie,* and *Tasso*) from an intellectual history perspective.

Lee, Meredith. *Studies in Goethe's Lyric Cycles.* Chapel Hill: University of North Carolina Press, 1978. Background and interpretation of *Römische Elegien* and *Chinesisch-deutsche Tages- und Jahreszeiten.*

Lillyman, William J., ed. *Goethe's Narrative Fiction: The Irvine Goethe Symposium.* Berlin: de Gruyter, 1983. Among others, the essays discuss *Werther, Wahlverwandtschaften* (2), *Lehrjahre* (3), and *Wanderjahre.*

Maier, Hans Albert. *Goethe: "West-östlicher Divan."* Kritische Ausgabe der Gedichte mit textgeschichtlichem Kommentar. Tübingen: Niemeyer, 1965. Informative and thought-provoking edition that includes the source poems of Goethe's *Divan.*

Morgan, Peter. *The Critical Idyll: Traditional Values and the French Revolution in Goethe's "Hermann und Dorothea."* Columbia, S.C.: Camden House, 1990. Serious analysis from cultural and intellectual history perspectives.

Peacock, Ronald. *Goethe's Major Plays.* Manchester, England: Manchester University Press, 1959. Still a sound and sensitive discussion of the most widely known dramas (*Götz, Egmont, Iphigenie, Tasso, Faust,* and others).

Wellbery, David E. *The Specular Moment: Goethe's Early Lyric and the Beginning of Romanticism.* Stanford, Calif.: Stanford University Press, 1996. In-depth analysis of Sturm und Drang poetry with a European perspective.

Wilkinson, Elizabeth M., and L. A. Willoughby. *Goethe: Poet and Thinker.* London: Arnold, 1962. Superb essays on imagery, symbolism, and basic concepts, specifically on poetry (*Wandrers Sturmlied, Egmont, Tasso,* and *Faust*).

Index

172   INDEX

The Author

Irmgard Wagner is professor of German at George Mason University. She studied German, English, French, Spanish, and comparative literature at Tübingen, Leicester (England), Tufts, and Harvard Universities. She received her Ph.D. from Harvard in 1970. She has published widely on Goethe, Hölderlin, Kleist, Kafka, and the theory of literature and history. She is the author of *Franz Fühmann: Nachdenken über Literatur* (1989) and *Critical Approaches to Goethe's Classical Dramas: "Iphigenie," "Torquato Tasso," and "Die natürliche Tochter"* (1995).

The Editor

David O'Connell is professor of French at Georgia State University. He received his Ph.D. in 1966 from Princeton University, where he was a National Woodrow Wilson Fellow, the Bergen Fellow in Romance Languages, and a National Woodrow Wilson Dissertation Fellow. He is the author of *The Teachings of Saint Louis: A Critical Text* (1972), *Les Propos de Saint Louis* (1974), *Louis-Ferdinand Céline* (1976), *The Instructions of Saint Louis: A Critical Text* (1979), and *Michel de Saint Pierre: A Catholic Novelist at the Crossroads* (1990). He has edited more than 60 books in the Twayne World Authors Series.